PS-AQV-910

D0122523

THE SINKING ARK

A new look at
the problem of disappearing species

Other Pergamon titles of related interest

Key Environments Series

BONNER & WALTON
Antarctica

CLOUDSLEY-THOMPSON
Sahara Desert

CRANBROOK
Malaysia

EDWARDS
Red Sea

JOLLY *et al*
Madagascar

MARGALEF
Western Mediterranean

PERRY
Galapagos

PRANCE
Amazonia

THE SINKING ARK

A new look at
the problem of disappearing species

NORMAN MYERS

PERGAMON PRESS

Member of Maxwell Macmillan Pergamon Publishing Corporation

OXFORD · NEW YORK · BEIJING · FRANKFURT
SÃO PAULO · SYDNEY · TOKYO · TORONTO

U.K.	Pergamon Press plc, Headington Hill Hall, Oxford OX3 0BW, England
U.S.A.	Pergamon Press, Inc., Maxwell House, Fairview Park, Elmsford, NY 10523, U.S.A.
PEOPLE'S REPUBLIC OF CHINA	Pergamon Press, Room 4037, Qianmen Hotel, Beijing, People's Republic of China
FEDERAL REPUBLIC OF GERMANY	Pergamon Press GmbH, Hammerweg 6, D-6242 Kronberg, Federal Republic of Germany
BRAZIL	Pergamon Editora Ltda, Rua Eça de Queiros, 346, CEP 04011, Paraiso, São Paulo, Brazil
AUSTRALIA	Pergamon Press Australia Pty Ltd., P.O. Box 544, Potts Point, N.S.W. 2011, Australia
JAPAN	Pergamon Press, 5th Floor, Matsuoka Central Building, 1-7-1 Nishishinjuku, Shinjuku-ku, Tokyo 160, Japan
CANADA	Pergamon Press Canada Ltd., Suite No. 271, 253 College Street, Toronto, Ontario, Canada M5T 1R5

First edition 1979
Reprinted (with minor corrections) 1980
Reprinted 1983, 1987, 1990

British Library Cataloguing in Publication Data

Myers, Norman
The sinking ark
1. Rare animals
I. Title
591'.042   QL82   79-40232
ISBN 0-08-024501-3

Printed in Great Britain by BPCC Wheatons Ltd, Exeter

To Mother

who taught me as much about nature
during my early years on a farm in
northern England as I learned during my
first ten years on safari in Africa.

"All that lives beneath Earth's fragile canopy is, in some elemental fashion, related. Is born, moves, feeds, reproduces, dies. Tiger and turtle dove; each tiny flower and homely frog; the running child, father to the man, and, in ways as yet unknown, brother to the salamander. If mankind continues to allow whole species to perish, when does their peril also become ours?"

World Wildlife Fund

Contents

Preface

This is not the first book on disappearing species. A good many have appeared in recent years. They have documented the dismal story of the tiger, the gorilla, the whooping crane, the whales, and scores of other creatures in trouble. They have warned that we are probably losing one species per year.

This book takes the theme further in two ways.

First, it looks at the prospect for all species on earth, 5-10 million of them. It proposes that we stand to lose at least 1 million by the end of the century, and several more million within just a few decades. Right now, we could be losing one species per day.

This means not only that our children will live in a world made poorer through the elimination of myriad life forms that have shared the common earth home with humankind. It also means that basic processes of evolution are being altered more drastically than since the sudden disappearance of the dinosaurs, 60 million years ago, and possibly more than since the emergence of life's diversity 3½ billion years ago. And it is all happening within the twinkling of an evolutionary eye.

A single species now dominates all others. Man's swelling numbers constitutes almost 200 million tons, a biomass that may be surpassed only by the krill of the southern oceans. This totally unique situation implies a total responsibility for man to consider what he is doing to his fellow creatures, and to himself. The position has been well described by U.S. Senator Patrick Leahy, during a mid-1978 debate on the question of whether a paperclip-long fish, the snail darter, should prevent the completion of the $116,000,000 Tellico Dam on the Little Tennessee River:

> "Ultimately, we are the endangered species. *Homo sapiens* is perceived to stand at the top of the pyramid of life, but the pinnacle is a precarious station. We need a large measure of self-

consciousness to constantly remind us of the commanding role
which we enjoy only at the favour of the web of life that sustains
us, that forms a foundation of our total environment .... We
share the planetary gene pool with that snail darter in the Little
Tennessee River.''

Under man's impact, natural environments on every side are undergoing ever more rapid disruption. We are well acquainted with the
more visible manifestations, notably pollution. If we become disen-
chanted with the way we foul our living space, we can generally
reverse the process. We can clean up our rivers and skies. But extinction of species is a whole different ballgame. When a species disappears,
it has gone for good. Often enough, that will be for bad. Every day,
people around the world consume more foods, take more medicines,
and utilize more industrial products that owe their origin to wild
species of animals and plants. We do not know just what new needs
will arise in the future. What we do know is that the future is likely to
be more different than we can fairly anticipate, so it makes sense to
safeguard as many raw materials as possible with which to encounter
new challenges. There can hardly be a more valuable stock of natural
resources on earth than the planetary spectrum of species with their
genetic reservoirs. Yet the earth's species are being depleted more
rapidly than the earth's mineral deposits.

Thus the problem of disappearing species: one of the great "sleeper
issues" of our time. It is difficult to imagine a problem more
profound in its implications, while less appreciated by the public at
large. During the past few years, increasingly alarmed noises have
been heard about a few charismatic creatures such as the chimpanzee,
the polar bear and the cheetah. Through exceptional efforts, several
of these endangered species have been brought back a step or two
from the brink of extinction. During the course of these same few
years, it is likely that several thousand species have disappeared,
unheard of and unregretted by the world's citizens and their leaders.

A second way in which this book takes a longer look at the species
problem is that it does not confine itself to biological and ecological
questions (for example, why the great cats are more susceptible than
rats, or cranes than starlings). It asks *why* species are allowed to
disappear: if species constitute an important part of humankind's

survival kit for the future, how is it that we casually watch them go under? The book suggests that we need to look at several further aspects of the problem — economic, political, legal, social and cultural factors.

It is simplistic to assert, as have certain commentators in the past, that species are driven extinct through the ignorance or stupidity or wanton destructiveness of modern man. Species disappear because of the way we prefer to live, all of us. For example, the expanding appetites of affluent nations for beef at "reasonable", i.e. non-inflationary prices, encourages the conversion of tropical moist forests into cattle ranches — and tropical moist forests harbour 40-50 percent of all species on earth, including plants that may offer drugs to combat a scourge of affluent nations, cancer. Hence an economic dimension that goes to the core of the problem straight off: which affluent-world conservationist does not enjoy the humble hamburger with its humble price?

Just as we are all involved in the extinction of species, and just as we shall all benefit from their preservation, so we should all contribute to the cost of a comprehensive strategy to save species. This strategy will not come cheap as compared with present efforts to safeguard the gorilla and the jaguar. But it will be a virtual give-away as compared with our other investments in the future.

This book has been written as part of a project conducted under the auspices of the Natural Resources Defence Council in Washington D.C. A committee was established for the project, consisting of a chairman, Mr. Thomas B. Stoel of NRDC, and two members, Dr. Kenton R. Miller of the School of Natural Resources, University of Michigan, and Dr. Thomas E. Lovejoy of the World Wildlife Fund in Washington D.C. I had known all these three persons for a good while before the project began, and I was more than glad to have them on board. Tom, as Chairman, proved to be far more conscientious in his duties than I could fairly have anticipated, and he repeatedly went through the manuscript with a fine toothcomb to check on every last detail. Ken and the other Tom allowed me to draw on their broad experience in economics and ecology, and it is only now, on looking back, that I appreciate how much I have benefited from their generous contributions. In addition to Tom Stoel at NRDC, I came to know several other members of the staff, notably Jacob Scherr, Faith Campbell, Sarah Compton and Cynthia Mackie. All these persons served to reinforce the strong impression I had formed of NRDC, before the project began, as an organization that is exceptionally skillful and energetic in furthering the conservation cause both within the United States and on the international scene.

The project received financial support from Rockefeller Brothers Fund in New York, to whom I wish to record my appreciation, particularly to one of the Fund's program officers, Mr. William S. Moody, for his constant interest and encouragement.

A book that adopts a wide-ranging approach to the problem of disappearing species has called on the advice of experts in many different fields. The total number of scientists, economists and other professionals who have willingly responded to my stream of enquiries runs to over 100 names, and I can do no more here than offer my very considerable thanks to all who have contributed. Without their help and guidance, I could not have undertaken an analysis of such a multi-faceted subject.

During the course of the project, however, a smaller group of colleagues has allowed me to turn to them repeatedly for detailed consultations, clarification of abstruse aspects, and many other forms of assistance, including checking of parts of the manuscript. I wish to record my special gratitude to Professor Homer G. Angelo, University of California at Davis; Mr. John A. Burton, Fauna Preservation Society, London, U.K.; Dr. Michael J. Clifton, National Museum of Kenya; Dr. Anthony Diamond, University of Nairobi; Dr. John D. Douros, U.S. National Cancer Research Institute; Dr. F. Raymond Fosberg, Smithsonian Institution, Washington D.C.; Professor D.J. Greenland, University of Reading, U.K.; Dr. Howard S. Irwin, New York Botanical Garden; Dr. Norman E. Johnson, Vice-President for Far Eastern Region, Weyerhaeuser Corporation; Mr. J.P. Lanly, Department of Forestry, FAO, Rome; Mr. Grenville L1. Lucas, Royal Botanic Garden, Kew, U.K.; Dr. T.J. Synnott, Department of Forestry, University of Oxford, U.K.; Professor Gordon H. Orians, University of Washington; Dr. Ghillean T. Prance, New York Botanical Garden; Dr. Reidar Persson, Royal College of Forestry, Stockholm; Dr. Robert W. Risebrough, Bodega Bay Institute for

Pollution Ecology, California; Dr. Nigel Smith, University of California at Berkeley; Dr. John Spinks, Endangered Species Office, Washington D.C.; Dr. Joseph A. Tosi, Tropical Science Center, San Jose, Costa Rica; Mr. R. Michael Wright, U.S. Nature Conservancy; and Dr. Peter Wyeth, Washington State University.

However, while these persons have contributed many amendments to the manuscript, they, like the members of my committee, are responsible for none of the book's deficiencies, which remain the province of the one who first perpetrated them.

During the course of several drafts, the manuscript grew to twice its present length. In fact, typists at one stage or another have worked their way through well over one million words. For exceptional application to the task, and for graciously cheerful spirit in "pressure-cooker" conditions, I wish to thank Sharmi Bhalla, Beverley Chester, Kate Gaffney, Sandy Lawson and Janice Young.

I write these final words at the family's beach bungalow on the Indian Ocean, during the course of our Christmas sojourn there. My wife, Dorothy, is down at the beach with the children, taking on still another of my "sandcastle stints" so that I can get through to the end of "that book". This is not the first occasion she has pitched in with her time, nor is it the hundredth; and in between she has contributed numerous ideas and a title for the book. More important still, she has offered patient understanding at the times when the book was turning into a Hydra-headed monster: as many a writer knows, support of this sort is particularly valuable during those difficult days before the monster is backed into a corner and beaten to its knees. For your help in more ways than you are aware of, my special thanks to you, Dorothy.

Dr. NORMAN MYERS
January 1979

Part I

THE PROBLEM OF DISAPPEARING SPECIES

1 Introduction

Ask a man in the street what he thinks of the problem of disappearing species, and he may well reply that it would be a pity if the tiger or the blue whale disappeared. But he may add that it would be no big deal, not as compared with crises of energy, population, food and pollution — the "real problems". In other words, he cares about disappearing species, but he cares about many other things more: he simply does not see it as a critical issue. If the tiger were to go extinct tonight, the sun would still come up tomorrow morning.

In point of fact, by tomorrow morning we shall almost certainly have one less species on Planet Earth than we had this morning. It will not be a charismatic creature like the tiger. It could well be an obscure insect in the depths of some remote rainforest. It may even be a creature that nobody has ever heard of. But it will have gone. A unique form of life will have been driven from the face of the earth for ever.

Equally likely is that by the end of the century we shall have lost 1 million species, possibly many more. Except for the barest handful, they will have been eliminated through the hand of man.

Extinction rates

Animal forms that have been documented and recognized as under threat of extinction now amount to over 1000. These are creatures we hear much about — the tiger and the blue whale, the giant panda and the whooping crane, the orangutan and the cheetah. Yet even though 1000 is a shockingly large number, this is only a fractionally small part of the problem. Far more important are those many species that have not even been identified by science, let alone classified as threatened.

3

Among the plant kingdom, these could number 25,000, while among animals, notably insects, the total could run to hundreds of thousands.

Extinction of species has been a fact of life virtually right from the start of life on earth 3½ billion years ago. At least 90 percent of all species that have existed have disappeared. But almost all of them have gone under by virtue of natural processes. Only in the recent past, perhaps from around 50,000 years ago, has man exerted much influence. As a primitive hunter, man probably proved himself capable of eliminating species, albeit as a relatively rare occurrence. From the year A.D. 1600, however, he became able, through advancing technology, to over-hunt animals to extinction in just a few years, and to disrupt extensive environments just as rapidly. Between the years 1600 and 1900, man eliminated around seventy-five known species, almost all of them mammals and birds — virtually nothing has been established about how many reptiles, amphibians, fishes, invertebrates and plants disappeared. Since 1900 man has eliminated around another seventy-five known species — again, almost all of them mammals and birds, with hardly anything known about how many other creatures have faded from the scene. The rate from the year 1600 to 1900, roughly one species every 4 years, and the rate during most of the present century, about one species per year, are to be compared with a rate of possibly one per 1000 years during the "great dying" of the dinosaurs.

Since 1960, however, when growth in human numbers and human aspirations began to exert greater impact on natural environments, vast territories in several major regions of the world have become so modified as to be cleared of much of their main wildlife. The result is that the extinction rate has certainly soared, though the details mostly remain undocumented. In 1974 a gathering of scientists concerned with the problem hazarded a guess that the overall extinction rate among all species, whether known to science or not, could now have reached 100 species per year.[1]

Yet even this figure seems low. A single ecological zone, the tropical moist forests, is believed to contain between 2 and 5 million species. If present patterns of exploitation persist in tropical moist forests, much virgin forest is likely to have disappeared by the end of the century, and much of the remainder will have been severely degraded. This will cause huge numbers of species to be wiped out. Similar processes of disruption and destruction apply in other natural environments, notably grasslands and wetlands. While not so ecologically diverse as tropical moist forests, these biomes feature their own rich arrays of species — and they are likewise undergoing fundamental modification at the hand of man. The United States once featured around 1 million km^2 of pristine prairie, but now the lot has disappeared under the plough or has been otherwise transformed, except for 16,000 km^2 in Kansas. Grasslands in many parts of the world are similarly giving way to cultivated crops, to feed a hungry planet. In advanced and developing regions alike, wetlands are being drained, dug up, paved over, so that they can be converted from their present "useless" state into something more profitable for man. The result: elimination of whole communities of species, virtually overnight.

Let us suppose that, as a consequence of this man-handling of natural environments, the final one-quarter of this century witnesses the elimination of 1 million species — a far from unlikely prospect. This would work out, during the course of 25 years, at an average extinction rate of 40,000 species per year, or rather over 100 species per day. The greatest exploitation pressures will not be directed at tropical forests and other species-rich biomes until towards the end of the period. That is to say, the 1990s could see many more species accounted for than the previous several decades. But already the disruptive processes are well underway, and it is not unrealistic to suppose that, right now, at least one species is disappearing each day. By the late 1980s we could be facing a situation where one species becomes extinct each hour. By the time human communities establish ecologically sound life-styles, the fallout of species could total several million. This would amount to a biological débâcle greater than all mass extinctions of the geological past put together.

Loss to society

We face, then, the imminent elimination of a good share of the planetary spectrum of species that have shared the common earth-home with man for millenia, but are now to be denied living space during a phase of a mere few decades. This extinction spasm would amount to an irreversible loss of unique resources. Earth is currently afflicted with other forms of environmental degradation, but, from the standpoint of permanent despoliation of the planet, no other form is anywhere so significant as the fallout of species. When water bodies are fouled and the atmosphere is treated as a garbage can, we can always clean up the pollution. Species extinction is final. Moreover, the impoverishment of life on earth falls not only on present society, but on all generations to come.

In scores of ways, the impoverishment affects everyday living right now. All around the world, people increasingly consume food, take medicines and employ industrial materials that owe their production to genetic resources and other startpoint materials of animals and plants. These pragmatic purposes served by species are numerous and growing. Given the needs of the future, species can be reckoned among society's most valuable raw materials. To consider the consequences of devastating a single biome, the tropical moist forests: elimination of these forests, with their exceptional concentrations of species, would undermine the prospects for modernized agriculture, with repercussions for the capacity of the world to feed itself. It could set back the campaign against cancer by years. Perhaps worst of all, it would eliminate one of our best bets for resolving the energy crisis: as technology develops ways to utilize the vast amounts of solar energy stored in tropical-forest plants each day, these forests could generate as much energy, in the form of methanol and other fuels, as almost half the world's energy consumption from all sources in 1970. Moreover, this energy source need never run dry like an oil well, since it can replenish itself in perpetuity.

Any reduction in the diversity of resources, including the earth's spectrum of species, narrows society's scope to respond to new problems and opportunities. To the extent that we cannot be certain what needs may arise in the future, it makes sense to keep our options open (provided that a strategy of that sort does not unduly conflict with other major purposes of society). This rationale for conservation applies to the planet's stock of species more than to virtually any other category of natural resources.

The situation has been well stated by Dr. Tom Lovejoy of the

World Wildlife Fund:

> "If we were preparing for a new Dark Age, and could take only a limited number of books into the monasteries for the duration, we might have to determine which single branch of knowledge would have the greatest survival value for us. The outstanding candidate would be biology, including its applied forms such as medicine, agriculture, forestry and fisheries. Yet we are doing just the contrary, by busily throwing out the biology books before they have been written."

Many other biologists —switched-on scientists, not "case-hardened eco-nuts" — believe that man is permanently altering the course of evolution, and altering it for the worse. The result will be a grossly impoverished version of life's diversity on earth, from which the process of evolution will be unlikely to recover for many millions of years. And it is not going too far to say that, by eliminating an appreciable portion of earth's stock of species, humanity might be destroying life that just might save its own.

Species conservation and economic advancement

There is another major dimension to the problem, the relationship between conservation of species and economic advancement for human communities.

As indicated, the prime threat to species lies with loss of habitat. Loss of habitat occurs mainly through economic exploitation of natural environments. Natural environments are exploited mainly to satisfy consumer demand for numerous products. The upshot is that species are now rarely driven extinct through the activities of a few persons with direct and deliberate intent to kill wild creatures. They are eliminated through the activities of many millions of people, who are unaware of the "spillover" consequences of their consumerist lifestyles.

This means that species depletion can occur through a diffuse and insidious process. An American is prohibited by law from shooting a snowy egret, but, by his consumerist lifestyle, he can stimulate others to drain a marsh (for croplands, industry, highways, housing) and thereby eliminate the food supply for a whole colony of egrets. A recent advertisement by a utility corporation in the United States asserted that "Something we do today will touch your life", implying that its activities were so far-reaching that, whether the citizen was aware or not, his daily routine would be somehow affected by the corporation's multifaceted enterprise. In similar fashion, something the citizen does each day is likely to bear on the survival prospects of species. He may have no wanton or destructive intent toward wildlife. On the contrary, he may send off a regular donation to a conservation organization. But what he contributes with his right hand he may take away with his half-dozen left hands. His desire to be consumer as well as conservationist leads him into a Jekyll-and-Hyde role. Unwitting and unmalicious as this role might be, it becomes more significant and pervasive every day.

Equally important, the impact of a consumerist lifestyle is not confined to the home country of the fat-cat citizen. Increasingly the consequences extend to lands around the back of the earth. Rich-world communities of the temperate zones, containing one-fifth of earth's population, account for four-fifths of raw materials traded through international markets. Many of these materials derive from the tropical zone, which harbours around three-quarters of all species on earth. The extraction of these materials causes disturbance of natural environments. Thus affluent sectors of the global village are responsible — unknowingly for sure, but effectively nonetheless — for disruption of myriad species' habitats in lands far distant from their own. The connoisseur who seeks out a speciality-import store in New York or Paris or Tokyo, with a view to purchasing some much-sought-after rosewood from Brazil, may be contributing to the destruction of the last forest habitat of an Amazon monkey. Few factors of the conservation scene are likely to grow so consequential in years ahead as this one of economic-ecologic linkages among the global community.

True, citizens of tropical developing countries play their part in disruption of natural environments. It is in these countries that most of the projected expansion of human numbers will take place, 85 percent of the extra 2 billion people that are likely to be added to the present world population of 4 billion by the end of the century. Of at least as much consequence as the outburst in human numbers is the outburst in human aspirations, supported by expanding technology. It is the combination of these two factors that will precipitate a transformation of most natural environments throughout the tropics. Equally to the point, impoverished citizens of developing nations tend to have more pressing concerns than conservation of species. All too often, it is as much as they can do to stay alive themselves, let alone to keep wild creatures in being.

Plainly, there is a lot of difference between the consumerdom of the world's poor majority and of the world's rich minority. For most citizens of developing countries, there is little doubt that more food available, through cultivation of virgin territories (including forests, grasslands, wetlands, etc.), would increase their levels of nutrition, just as more industrial products available would ease their struggle for existence in many ways. It is equally likely that the same cannot be said for citizens of the advanced world: additional food or material goods do not necessarily lead to any advance in their quality of life. The demand for products of every kind on the part of the 1 billion citizens of affluent nations — the most consummate consumers the world has ever known, many making Croesus and Louis XIV look like paupers by comparison — contributes a disproportionate share to the disruption of natural environments around the earth.

For example, the depletion of tropical moist forests stems in part from market demand on the part of affluent nations for hardwoods and other specialist timbers from Southeast Asia, Amazonia and West/Central Africa. In addition, the disruptive harvesting of tropical timber is often conducted by multinational corporations that supply the capital, technology and skills without which developing countries could not exploit their forest stocks at unsustainable rates. Such is the role of Georgia Pacific and Weyerhaeuser from the United States, Mitsubishi and Sumitomo from Japan and Bruynzeel and Borregaard from Europe. Similarly, the forests of Central America are being felled to make way for artificial pasturelands, in order to grow more beef. But the extra meat, instead of going into the stomachs of local citizens, makes it way to the United States, where it supplies the hamburger trade and other fast-food business. This foreign beef is cheaper than similar-grade beef from within the United States — and the American consumer, looking for a hamburger of best quality at cheapest price, is not aware of the spillover consequences of his actions. So whose hand is on the chainsaw?

A further source of destruction in tropical forests is the shifting cultivator. There are at least 140 million of these people, subsistence peasants who often have nowhere to sink a digging hoe except the virgin territories of primeval forests. Theirs is a form of agriculture that tends, by its very nature, to be inefficient: it is highly wasteful of forestlands. It could be made intensive rather than extensive, and thus relieve the pressure on virgin forests, through the perquisites of modern agriculture, notably fertilizer to make a crop patch productive year after year. But since the OPEC price hike in 1973, the cost of petroleum-based fertilizer has been driven sky-high — and has been kept sky-high through inflated demand on the part of affluent nations (Americans and Europeans use as much fertilizer on their gardens, golf courses and cemeteries as is used by all the shifting cultivators of tropical forestlands). As long as the price of fertilizer remains beyond the reach of subsistence peasants, there is less prospect that they will change their agricultural practices. Part of the responsibility for this situation lies with the OPEC cartel, part with the excessively consumerist communities of the advanced world.

An interdependent global community

Looked at this way, the problem of declining tropical forests can be seen to be intimately related to other major issues of an interdependent global community: food, population, energy, plus several other problems that confront society at large. It is difficult to make progress on one front without making progress on all the others at the same time. This aspect of the plight of tropical forests — the inter-relatedness of problems — applies to the problem of disappearing species in general.

Similarly, the advanced-nation citizen can hardly support conservation of species while resisting better trade-and-aid relationships with developing nations. The decline of tropical forests could be slowed through a trade cartel of Tropical Timber Exporting Countries. If the countries in question could jack up the price of their hardwood exports, they could earn more foreign exchange from export of less timber. For importer countries of the developed world, the effect of this move would be a jump in the price of fine furniture, specialist panelling and other components of better housing. Would an affluent-world citizen respond with a cry of protest about inflation, or with a sigh of relief at improved prospects for tropical forests? For a Third-World citizen, it is difficult to see how a conservationist can be concerned with the International Union for Conservation of Nature and Natural Resources, without being equally concerned with the New International Economic Order.

A second example concerns paperpulp. There could soon be a shortage of paperpulp to match present shortages of fuel and food. The deficit could be made good through more intensive exploitation of North American forests, or through more extensive exploitation of tropical forests — both of which alternatives might prompt outcries from environmental groups. A third alternative would be for developed-world citizens, who account for five-sixths of all paperpulp consumed world-wide, to make do with inadequate supplies, in which case the cost of newsprint would rise sharply. So perhaps a definition of a conservationist could be a person who applauds when he finds that his daily newspaper has once again gone up in price.

In accord with this view of the situation, this book emphasizes that problems of threatened species and disappearing forests can be realistically viewed only within a framework of relationships between the developed world and the developing world.

A prime conservation need everywhere, and especially in tropical regions, is for countries to set aside representative examples of their ecosystems in order to protect their stocks of species. In other words, to expand their present networks of parks, such as they are, by establishing extensive systems of protected areas. However, many developing countries are in no position to designate large tracts of their territory as "off limits" to development. (Through their present efforts to safeguard the bulk of the earth's species, they in effect subsidize the rest of the global community.) If emergent regions of the tropics are to help protect the global heritage of species for the community at large, the community should see to it that their development prospects are not thereby penalized. In short, ways must be devised to make conservation programs economically acceptable and politically palatable for developing nations.

How far should we go to save species?

Just as the whooping crane is not worth more than a mere fraction of the United States' GNP to save it, so the preservation of species in all parts of the planet, and especially in tropical regions, needs to be considered within a comprehensive context of human well-being. Anthropocentric as this approach may appear, it reflects the way the world works: few people would be willing to swap mankind, a single species, for fishkind with its thousands of species.

So the central issue is not "Let's save species, come what may". Rather we should ask whose needs are served by conservation of species, and at what cost to whose opportunities for a better life in other ways. Instead of seeking to conserve species as an over-riding objective, we should do as much as we can within a framework of trying to enhance long-term human welfare in all manner of directions.

As we have seen, people already make "choices" concerning species. Regrettably they do not make deliberate choices after careful consideration of the alternatives. Rich and poor alike, they unconsciously contribute to the decline of the species, in dozens of ways each day. Not that they have malign intentions toward wild creatures. According to a 1976 Gallup Poll, most people would like to see more done to conserve wildlife and threatened species — 87 percent in the United States, 89 percent in Western Europe, 85 percent in Japan, 75 percent in Africa, and 94 percent in Latin America (though only 46 percent in crowded India). Subsistence communities of the developing world have limited scope to change the choice they implicitly make through their ways of making a living. Rich-world people, by contrast, have more room to manoeuvre, and could switch toward a stronger expression of their commitment in favor of species. Meantime, through their commitment to extreme consumerism, they in effect express the view that they can do without the orangutan and the cheetah and many other species — and their descendants, for all ages to come, can likewise do without them. In theory, they would like the orangutan and the cheetah to survive in the wild, but in practice they like many other things more. However unwittingly, that is the way they are making their choice right now.

Fortunately, affluent-world citizens still have plenty of scope to make a fresh choice. They may find it turns out to be no easy choice. If they truly wish to allow living space for millions of species that existed on the planet before man got on to his hind legs, they will find that entails not only a soft-hearted feeling in support of wildlife, but a hard-nosed commitment to attempt new lifestyles. While they shed a tear over the demise of tropical moist forests with their array of species, they might go easy on the Kleenex.

2 How Many Species?

There are anywhere from 5 to 10 million species on earth. This represents a culmination of around 3½ billion years of evolution of life forms, and 700 million years of diversification among most modern categories of life — plants, insects, mammals, birds and the rest.

What is a species?

Species come in all shapes and sizes. The largest organism now alive is a giant sequoia, estimated at 6265 metric tons. The oldest is probably a Japanese cedar, believed to date from roughly 7200 years ago. The shortest lifespan is probably that of the colon bacterium, which divides under favourable conditions after 20 minutes. This also places the bacterium among the most fecund of species: within 3 hours it can increase its numbers 1000-fold, and within 1 day throw off billions of progeny. The human body contains more bacteria than there are humans on earth. A bacterium is also small: the virus that causes hoof-and-mouth disease, roughly spherical in shape, is about one-millionth of a millimeter in diameter. If the period at the end of this sentence represents an average-sized virus, then a German shepherd dog magnified by the same factor, times 5000, would be about 5½ km long. By contrast, the largest animal is the blue whale, weighing 150 tons. It is not only the largest animal now alive, but the largest animal ever, 3 times heavier than the largest land animal, the brontosaurus.

Organisms exist in clusters, apparently in accord with their biological characteristics. At a level where these differentiating characteristics become significant, clusters of organisms can be classified as species. To put it more precisely, a species is a natural biological group united by the sharing of a common pool of genes (the basic units of heredity). All members of the group can interbreed, and they cannot generally breed with other species in the wild to produce fertile offspring. This, of course, limits the definition to bisexual organisms, so does not apply to those "lower" species that reproduce by asexual or vegetative means.

How many species?

Until the mid-1960s the number of species on earth was estimated at around 3 million. Of this total, about half had been identified. That is, they had been found to exist, they had been given scientific names, and they had been described, even though 99 percent of them were known only in terms of an occasional locality and a few physical characteristics. The earth was considered to support about 4100 known species of mammals, 8700 birds, 6300 reptiles, 3000 amphibians, 23,000 fishes, roughly 800,000 insects, and over 300,000 green plants and fungi, plus several thousand micro-organisms such as bacteria and viruses. Of these identified species, around 1 million were known to exist in temperate zones and half a million in tropical zones. As for the other 1½ million species, they were believed to exist somewhere on the planet, mostly in the tropics, though no field researcher had actually come across them.

To arrive at the overall figure, scientists would examine, for example, a patch of forest. They would document the number of species in it, and then make heroic generalizations about species totals in other areas of similar forests. This process enabled them to come up with informed estimates for numbers of species in all forests of that type. They did the same for all categories of global environments, or "biomes", and thereby arrived at a figure of 3 million.

Since the mid-1960s, the estimate has been pushed steadily upwards. Scientists have learned more about life's diversity on earth, and they have refined their methods of taxonomic classification. At the same time, they have developed more accurate ways to extrapolate their statistical curves for species abundance. In particular, three factors have emerged to increase the earlier estimate. First, habitats that had been thought to be barren or to support only low numbers of species have been found to contain a rich variety of organisms. For example, the deep-sea floor features many more creatures than had been expected.[1] An entire phylum, or "super-category", of invertebrates, out of twenty phyla known in the seas, has been discovered only in the past 25 years, while groups such as marine annelids (segmented worms) are proving exceptionally rich in numbers and diversity. Secondly, whole faunas, not only those of the deep oceans but of many insect groups, have scarcely been investigated — and insects probably comprise well over two-thirds of all animal species. Among several major categories of insects — beetles, wasps, leaf miners and micro-lepidoptera — entomologists consider they have probably tracked down only one in ten of tropical species. Thirdly, scientists have discovered that a great many living species are difficult to distinguish from one another, and large complexes of very similar but geographically separate populations of the "same species" turn out on investigation to be made up of many different species. For instance, one species of the salamander genus in western North America has recently been found to comprise ten species. Sometimes, of course, the reverse applies. The fig tree genus, once believed to comprise over 2000 species world-wide, is now reckoned to total well under half as many. In the main, however, the trend is toward a steadily larger number of species.

By the early 1970s a new figure was being proposed for the total number of species on earth: 10 million.[2] True, this was no more than an order-of-magnitude conjecture. But it helped scientists to recognize the scale of the challenge they were facing: how to preserve the panoply of earth's life forms, which is proving far more varied and complex than anyone has supposed? Since the mid-1960s science has identified only another 100,000 or so species, which means that if a total figure of 10 million is accepted, almost 8½ million species, or roughly six out of seven, do not yet have a name.

Of course the figure of 10 million is no more than an informed "guesstimate". Some observers say it is inspired as much as informed. Certainly, it could turn out to be a good way off target, either too high or too low. Given what we know of the 1.6 million species hitherto identified, it is reasonable to assume that certain groups will turn out to be very numerous. For instance, it would be surprising if there were not at least 1 million mites. Moreover, new species are readily discovered. In 1976 Dr. David Hollis, an entomologist from the British Museum, visited Kenya and Tanzania for 5 weeks, during which time he increased East Africa's tally of known species of a family of bugs, the Psyllidae, from nine to eighty-four. Similarly, Dr. Oliver Flint of the Smithsonian Institution in Washington D.C. recently collected fifty-five Caddis flies of the family Hydroptilidae in Amazonia and found that fifty-three of them were new species. New species are still being found even in the United States and Europe, where the fauna has been extensively researched for decades. In late 1977 Dr. C.W. Sabrosky of the U.S. National Museum sorted through a large collection of Chloropidae grassflies from California, an area more closely investigated by entomologists than any other place on earth, and found thirty-five to forty new species.

Conversely, some categories of species are turning out to be less numerous than had been anticipated. Only a few years ago scientists had thought that there could be up to 1 million ichneumonid wasps, mostly in the tropics. But it is now being discovered, surprisingly, that the Hymenoptera, of which the wasps form a large segment, are less numerous in the tropics than in temperate zones.[3] This finding and similar investigations are persuading some scientists to revise their earlier estimates of 10 million species, even to reduce the figure as low as 5 million.[4]

The reader may wonder why it is appropriate to come up with any figure at all when the evidence is so inconclusive one way or the other. For practical purposes of saving species, however, it is important to establish a "ballpark estimate". Conservationists need to have an idea, in whatever crude terms, of how many species share the planet with man. This allows them to "get a handle" on the problem of how many species may go extinct within the foreseeable future. If, as is entirely possible, we lose one-quarter of all species by the year 2000, and if conservationists were to stick with a "safe" minimum estimate of 3 million species, that would imply a loss of 750,000 species. But if an estimate of 10 million is on the cards, then we would lose 2½ million — a problem of altogether different size. It is through considerations such as these that conservationists can decide questions of, for example, protected areas — how many we need, where they should be located, whether large or small, etc. — in order to safeguard the earth's stock of species.

Ironically, the question of how many species actually exist on earth will probably never be resolved. The past 10 years have seen only another 100,000 species identified, bringing the total to 1.6 million. If an overall figure as low as 5 million is accepted, then another 3.4 million remain to be discovered — more than twice as many as have already been listed, and if the actual total is 10 million, then roughly five out of six species remain completely unknown to us. Even were the number of specialist scientists to be increased tenfold, it is doubtful if they could do more than take a solid poke at the problem before the end of the century. By that time, it is virtually certain that, unless there are massive changes in conservation attitudes and activities, a sizable proportion of all present species will have disappeared, forever.

A highly numerous category of species: insects

Some categories of species are more numerous than others. The phylum of Arthropods ("jointed feet"), comprising insects, arachnids such as spiders and ticks, millipedes and centipedes, mites and others, plus their sea-living counterparts, the lobsters, crabs and other crustaceans, accounts for four out of five of all known animal species. Among the Arthropods, around 90 percent are currently considered to be insects, while among the recognized insects, around 40 percent are beetles, and another 40 percent are made up of moths and butterflies, ants, bees, wasps and true flies. The number of known insect species is 20 times greater than of all the classes of higher animals, viz. the vertebrates with 41,000 species, while the total of insect species in existence is probably 100 times greater, possibly twice as large again.

Some insect species are very numerous.[5] Less than one-half hectare of forest soil has been estimated to contain 425 million insects of various sorts.[6] A few of the more abundant species could reach between 3×10^{16} and 5×10^{16} individuals.[7] Total populations for all insects may be of the order of 10^{18} (10 billion billion) individuals. If the average weight of an individual insect is 2.5 milligrams, or less than one-thousandth of an ounce, the weight of all insects on earth exceeds that of the human population by a factor of 12.[8]

Despite their overall abundance, however, a good number of insect species are limited in range to localized habitats. Many entomologists believe that 10 percent of all insect species could be confined to areas of less than 100 km². In addition, many insect species that feed off only a few plant species or other food sources tend to exist at un- usually low densities. Both these traits apply notably to insect species in the ecological zone that contains more insect species than the rest of the world put together, the tropical moist forest.[9] Specialized lifestyles and low densities also go far to explain the extraordinary diversity of insects to be found in small areas of tropical forest; a 300-meter quadrant in Singapore has recorded sixty-eight genera of ants alone.[10] So limited is the range of some insect species that certain ones occupy isolated patches of forest, sometimes as little as a single valley; some live only in the uppermost storeys of the forest canopy; many exist in such low numbers that many thousands of these species could not produce a total number of individuals to match an "average abundance" insect species of temperate zones.

Curious as these traits are for species biology, they are critical for conservation. Creatures with such particularized lifestyles are vulnerable to sudden extinction when their forest habitat is grossly disrupted, let alone destroyed, in the manner that modern man can inflict with his chainsaws and bulldozers. A butterfly species in Kenya, whose undisturbed range originally extended to less than 10 km² of Taita Hills forest, is now reduced to a mere 15 hectares of habitat, and its last patch of forest is little likely to withstand the demands of local people for fuelwood. Many of the seventy-five new bug species that Dr. David Hollis recently discovered in Kenya and Tanzania are closely linked with a few plant species that they use as hosts, a factor that means a number of them will come under rapid and severe threat as their natural-forest habitats are replaced by conifer plantations and other man-made forests.

In fact, it is not going too far to say that of the millions of insect species that certainly exist in tropical moist forests, a good proportion could be eliminated by the end of the century. The same fate could overtake whole communities of insect species in other biomes. In the view of Dr. Donald R. Davis, Chairman of the Department of

Entomology of the Smithsonian Institution in Washington D.C., "Within the next 25 years we may witness the extinction of more than one-half of the world's insect species, i.e. about 3 million, even before they have been collected (and made known to science). . . . The vast majority represent essential keys to future pest management programs, crop pollination, soil productivity, and, in brief, healthy ecosystems ...".[11] It would be surprising if many thousands of these insect species are not disappearing right now, unrecorded and largely unregretted.

The best-known category of species: vertebrates

Much better recorded, and much more regretted when they disappear, are the higher creatures, the vertebrates. Yet even the mammals and birds are not all known to science. As recently as 1967, a new honeycreeper, the po'o-uli, was discovered in Maui, Hawaii, occupying a range of a few square kilometers of montane forest, in a canyon that is inaccessible to man except by helicopter.[12] This bird has been allocated to a whole new genus. In northern Japan the Irimote cat has come to light on an island of that name, together with a dwarf pig. In South Australia a mountain possum has recently been found. In Paraguay a peccary has re-emerged,[13] though its habitat is soon to be bisected by an all-weather road, which will leave the peccary, a pig-like creature, accessible to hordes of human hunters. Similarly, one of Madagascar's lemurs, the ayeaye, was thought to have held out no longer than 1930 or so, until it was rediscovered in 1957. Quite a few other species have survived their obituaries, especially small obscure species that live in remote inhospitable habitats.

In normal respects, of course, a wildlife species can never be "recalled from the dead". A curious exception arises, however, when a species' unique genetic information has been maintained in domesticated forms. Two German zoologists have independently pursued the theory that if breeds of domestic cattle have been originally selected from the aurochs a wild ox of Europe that went extinct 350 years ago, the aurochs' genes would still be scattered through modern breeds. After assembling primitive strains of cattle from all over Europe and breeding for characteristics that resembled those associated with the aurochs, the scientists produced "aurochs facsimiles", one of each sex. When these animals were paired, they bred true without throwbacks appearing from their many offspring over several generations. The same process has proved successful for the tarpan or wild horse, extinct since 1876.

In the main, of course, most living species of mammals have been tracked down by now (except for bats, of which several hundred probably await discovery — a whole new family has recently been discovered in Thailand, each individual weighing a mere 1.8 grams). Much the same applies for birds. At least 90 percent of reptiles are thought to have been listed. By contrast, new species of fish are constantly being discovered; near Hawaii a 5-meter, 750-kg shark has been discovered, a creature so exceptional that it has been assigned to a whole new family of sharks.

As for other categories, we have already noted how easy it is to find new insect species. An average of twenty new insects are made known to science each day. Something the same applies to plants, though the average works out to less than fifteen per day, again almost all in the tropics. A recent expedition to the Panama-Colombia border found almost fifty new plant species on a single mountain.[14] If a wildlife enthusiast wishes to have a new species named after him, he need take no more than a day or two in many parts of the tropics to locate a candidate.

Distribution of species

By far the richest biological region on earth is the tropics. Comprising only 42 percent of the earth's land area, and 12 percent of the planet's surface, the zone features a broader range of ecological regions and of species communities than all others put together. This tropical diversity is due to a number of factors, notably exceptional amounts of light, warmth and moisture, that foster favorable conditions for speciation, such as the large number of micro-habitats leading to a strong probability of adaptive radiation of species' populations.[15]

Not surprisingly, the tropics are believed to contain the great bulk
of all species on earth. In terms of flowering plants, tropical America
is estimated to contain roughly 90,000 species, tropical Asia plus
tropical Australia and the Pacific at least 35,000, and Africa
south of the Sahara 30,000. By contrast, the northern temperate zone
(North America as far south as the Tropic of Cancer, North Africa,
and Asia as far south as the Himalayas) contains perhaps 50,000
species, temperate-to-arid Australia and New Zealand around 15,000,
the Cape Region of South Africa and bordering arid zones some
10,000, and temperate South America 10,000.[16] This makes a total of
240,000 flowering plants, to which should be added a further 60,000
that are believed to exist somewhere on earth, mostly in the tropics as
the richest and least explored region. This means that the tropics
contain at least two-thirds, and probably three-quarters, of all higher
plants on earth. In addition, there is a good number of "lower" plant
species, i.e. mosses, lichens, liverworts, algae and fungi, of which the
tropics almost certainly feature 110,000, with the rest of the world
containing about 35,000.

Similarly, the tropics feature a rich array of animal species.
Roughly speaking, and as demonstrated by the evidence of well-
studied groups such as mammals, birds, amphibians, reptiles and
butterflies, it is reckoned that for every one higher plant species there
are between ten and thirty animal species. This means a planetary total
of between 3 and 9 million animal species, with at least 2 million and
possibly as many as 6¾ million of them in the tropics (because of
greater ecological diversity in tropical environments, both the average
and the mean number of animal species per tropical plant is likely to
be nearer thirty than ten).

The general situation can be illustrated by looking at regional totals
for two of the best-known categories of species, plants and birds.
Barro Colorado Island in the Panama Canal, measuring less than 15
km², contains at least 1360 higher plant species, whereas West
Germany's 239,932 km² contain only 2352. In North America,
meaning the region roughly north of the Tropic of Cancer, there exist
around 750 bird species, while the rest of the Americas contain 2780
species.[17] When we look at individual areas, the contrast is still more
striking. Whereas Alaska's 1,467,059 km² contain 227 bird species,

and California's 464,975 km² 286 species, Panama's 75,643 km² contain 1100 species. A mere 2.6 km² of lowland forest in Costa Rica have been found to contain 269 bird species,[18] about twice as many as in all the broad-leaved forests of eastern North America.

Much the same applies to other major groups of animals. Canada features 22 species of snakes, the United States 126, and Mexico 293. The Great Lakes of North America, with an area of 197,000 km², contain 172 species of fish, while Lake Tanganyika, with 34,000 km², contains 214 species.[19] In a single square kilometer of Freetown, Liberia, around 300 species of butterfly have been recorded, more than twice as many as in Michigan's 147,156 km², and possibly more than in the whole of the eastern United States.[20]

Especially rich are the moist forests that cover almost half of the tropics. This one biome, amounting to little more than 9 million km² (the same as the United States), could well contain two-fifths of the planet's entire stock of species, conceivably as many as half. Malaysia's lowland forests, covering only 132,000 km², are believed to contain at least 7900 flowering plants.[21] A small forested volcano, Mount Makiliang in the Philippines, contains more woody plant species than the whole of the United States. Amazonia's rainforests contain at least 50,000 vascular plants, 2½ times as many as in the 3-times larger area of the United States and Canada.[22] (For further details on tropical moist forests, see Chapter 8.)

In terms of plant and animal species together, the richest area anywhere is probably Amazonia, with possibly 1 million altogether. Southeast Asia must be reckoned a close rival, whereas tropical moist Africa is a good way behind.[23] Apart from Amazonia's 50,000 higher plants already mentioned, the basin features over 1800 species of birds, or more than one in five of all birds on earth. It also contains almost 2000 known species of fish — 4 times as many as in the Zaire River basin, 8 times as many as in the Mississippi system, and 10 times as many as in the whole of Europe.

But of Amazonia's 6 million km² of forest, as much as 100,000 are cleared each year to open up virgin land for livestock and crops as well as to exploit timber and other forest products (Food and Agriculture Organization, 1976). Venezuela has lost one-third of its northern rain-forests during the brief period 1950-75.[24] Even were the present rate of clearing not to increase (as it almost certainly will, due to expansion of human numbers and human aspirations), it means that all Amazonia's forests could disappear in another 60 years. A similar story of depletion applies to tropical moist forests elsewhere, with a far worse situation in Central America, Southeast Asia and West Africa.

Endemism

Apart from tropical forests, certain other ecological zones support exceptional numbers of species. Notable examples are tropical swamplands and coral reefs. These areas also feature many species that are found nowhere else, i.e. endemic species. These twin characteristics of certain ecological zones are important for conservation strategies, since these areas deserve priority protection.

One such ecological zone lies outside the tropics; namely, the "Mediterranean-type" environments. The zone comprises not only the Mediterranean basin itself, but parts of California, central Chile, southwestern and southern Australia, and the Cape sector of South Africa. Of the region's 25,000 species of flowering plants, around half are endemic, and many are extremely localized in range.[25]

For example, a hillside overlooking the Pacific Ocean near San Francisco features the Presidio Manzanita, a plant known to science only since 1972, with possibly only one individual left — a condition that probably several other California plant species could match. The southwestern coastal zone of South Africa features an exceptional concentration of plant species. The original zone of 46,000 km² amounted to only 0.04 percent of the earth, yet it contained 6000 species of higher plants, at least 3500 of them endemic. A good number are already extinct, and around 1500 of the remainder must be considered rare or endangered.[26] The principal source of trouble has been loss of habitat — the original zone has been reduced by 61 percent through various human activities. One exceptionally attractive plant, discovered by botanists only in 1973, seems to be limited to a single granite outcrop, a last habitat that is now being quarried for building stone.

Islands

In particular, islands feature large numbers of endemics. This is because small isolated communities present first-rate circumstances for adaptive radiation and rapid evolutionary change. An island effectively seals off a segment of a gene pool that, in the context of a continent, could spread across a much larger territory. Since isolation fosters local specialization, evolutionary processes find outstanding opportunities for speciation on islands.[27] Of Cuba's 6000 plant species in the island's 110,545 km², over half of them are probably endemic.

The classic instance of island endemism is the Galapagos Islands. As Darwin concluded, a parent stock of finches threw off a series of new species in accord with slight environmental differences between the islands. A still more striking example occurs among the Hawaiian islands, where one or perhaps two ancestral species of drosophilid flies probably provided the origins from which Hawaii's 500 known species have evolved, an array that represents roughly one-third of all drosophilids listed in the world — though it is a measure of how little we know about insects, even in Hawaii which is part of a scientifically developed nation, that there may be another 200 drosophilids on the islands awaiting discovery.[28]

Hawaii also represents a prime instance of extinction patterns for island endemic species. The islands' plants did not develop botanical defenses such as prickles, stinging hairs, acrid or poisonous chemicals, and tough root systems that plants feature in areas where large herbivores abound. They did not need such protection. Because of the localized conditions that fostered speciation, 97 percent of Hawaii's 2400-plus species and varieties of flowering plants are endemic. Then came Captain Cook in 1778 with his pigs and goats, followed in 1793 by Captain Vancouver with his sheep and cattle. These two catastrophic events wreaked more havoc than the volcanic upheavals that have marked Hawaii's millions of years of history. By the present day, many of Hawaii's highlands have been converted to pasture for domestic livestock, and the lush lowlands have been mainly given over to crops, industry, military bases, housing and other forms of economic development. On top of this, more than 3000 species of exotic plants have been introduced. The upshot is that 273 native plants have gone extinct, and 800 of the remainder are endangered, together with another 99 that are rare and 34 that are highly localized.[29] Of the islands' roughly 250 tree species, 225 are endemic — and about one-half of these are restricted to only one of the eight islands, many of them having a range of only a few square kilometers, some being known from no more than a single locality such as a mountain or a valley. Hawaii now has more endemic trees on the U.S. Endangered Species List than all the other forty-nine states combined. Moreover, probably at least one-third of Hawaii's insects have become extinct since modern man's arrival, including nearly all of the lowland entomofauna.

As well as geographical islands, there are ecological islands. In Africa, Lake Malawi has more known species of fish than any other lake in the world, while Lake Victoria ranks second and Lake Tanganyika third.[30] These lakes also feature endemic species on a scale unknown elsewhere, the main family being the cichlid fishes. Of more than 200 cichlid species in Lake Malawi, all except four are endemic, while all 134 in Lake Tanganyika are endemic. Although the two lakes are only 320 km apart, they have not a single cichlid in common. In Lake Nabugabo, a small lake separated only 4000 years ago from Lake Victoria by a sandstrip that now measures 3 km wide, live six species of Haplochromis, five of them endemic (these rank among the "youngest" species known, and their evolution shows how isolating mechanisms can promote super-swift speciation). In Central Asia, Lake Baikal is the oldest, deepest and most remote large lake on earth, having been geologically isolated for 30 million years. Of its 2000 species, 1500 are found nowhere else. Were Lake Baikal to become unduly polluted through the fifty factories recently established in its environs, through erosion due to clear-felling of forests on local hillsides, and through paperpulp industries spreading along its shores, the species fallout could be high indeed.

Many other sorts of ecological islands exist, not all in such obvious form as lakes. In tropical lowland forests, certain localities show marked biological difference from surrounding areas. During the Pleistocene with its Ice Ages, the amount of rainfall in the tropics varied sharply. This caused forests to expand during wet periods and to contract during dry phases. By consequence, many distinctive, localized ecosystems have arisen within tropical lowland forests — in effect, islands. Amazonia's forests, for example, are far from being one large unvarying tract. Rather it is a remarkably diversified zone, with much local differentiation in ecological conditions.[31] This, together with other factors of tropical evolution, has led to a good deal of speciation in certain localities, leaving some species restricted to only a few hundred, or even a few dozen square kilometers. In turn, this means that broadscale development projects, extending across thousands of square kilometers, can eliminate whole concentrations of species. Conversely, of course, if conservation can "lock away" an area of high variety and endemism, the move can achieve far more per dollar than through protecting a similar-sized area elsewhere.

How species arrive and disappear

The evolutionary process that throws off new species, speciation, has been underway virtually since life first appeared. As a species encounters fresh environments, brought about by factors such as climatic change, it adapts, and so alters in different ways in different parts of its range. Eventually a new form becomes differentiated enough to rank as a new species. The parent form, if unable to fit in with changed circumstances, disappears, while the genetic material persists, diversified and enriched.

By contrast, some species are not so capable at the process of adaptation and differentiation. This applies especially to those that have become so specialized in their lifestyles that they cannot cope with transformed environments. They fade away, and their distinctive genetic material is lost forever.

Since life began about 3½ billion years ago, vast amounts of unique genetic formations have been eliminated. The total number of species that is believed to have existed is put at somewhere between 100 and 250 million,[32] which means that the present stock of species, estimated at 5-10 million, represents between 2 and 10 percent of all species that have ever lived on earth. It also means that extinction is not only a biological reality, but it is a frequent phenomenon under natural circumstances. Moreover, whereas the process of speciation is limited by the rate of genetic divergence, and so generally throws up a new species only over periods of thousands or millions of years, the process of extinction is not limited by any such constraint, and can occur, through man's agency, within just a year or two, even less.

How many species have existed at each stage of evolutionary history is only roughly known. The fossil record is so limited that it is a pitiful reflection of past life. But it now appears likely that, after a gas cloud solidified into the present planet approximately 6 billion years ago, earth remained lifeless for another 2½ billion years. When life eventually appeared, it left virtually no trace of its existence for a long time, except for micro-fossils of early algae such as have been found in Swaziland. Not until about 1500 million years ago did nuclear-celled organisms appear, and not until about 700 million years ago, following an outburst of evolutionary activity during the Cambrian period, did most modern phyla become recognizable. This array of species diversified only gradually, or even remained pretty constant, for the best part of 400 million years, until it crashed spectacularly with the extinction of many marine organisms towards the end of the Permian period. Thereafter the abundance and variety of species steadily increased, until a further mass extinction during the late Cretaceous period, 70 million years ago, put an end to around one-quarter of all families, including the dinosaurs and their kin. Since that time the trend has been generally towards ever-greater diversity of species. In short, the evolutionary record does not show a steady upward climb in earth's total of species, rather a series of step-wise increases. The current stock of species is reckoned to be 10 or even 20 times larger than the stock of species inhabiting the Paleozic seas before the Permian crash.[33]

During the past few million years, however, extinction rates seem to have speeded up. At the time of the late Pliocene, some 5 million years ago, there may have been one-third more bird species than today.[34] During the early Pleistocene, around 3 million years ago, a bird species probably had an average life expectancy of 1½ million years. This span progressively contracted until, by the end of the Pleistocene, it could have amounted to only 40,000 years.[35] Equally likely is that the pace of speciation has probably speeded up, and full speciation among certain classes of birds could now be far more rapid than the quarter of a million years once believed necessary. Indeed, it conceivably takes place in as little as 15,000 or even 10,000 years.

The house sparrow, introduced into North America in the 1850s, has thrown off a number of clear subspecies during the course of only 110-130 generations.[36] In certain circumstances, for instance when new variations are radiating from an unspecialized ancestor, a new plant species can evolve, it is estimated, in only 50-100 generations.[37] (Experiments with fruit flies, under special laboratory conditions that serve to "force the pace", show that speciation can occur in less than a dozen generations.) Among mammals, with generally slower breeding rates than birds, the average life expectancy for a species could now be, under natural circumstances, around half a million years.

Man's impact on extinction rates

More recently, extinction has stemmed increasingly from the hand of man. For much of his last 50,000 years as a hunter-gatherer, primitive man, perhaps in conjunction with climatic upheavals, proved himself capable of eliminating species through over-hunting and through habitat modification by means of fire.[38] In the main, the process was relatively rare and gradual. By around the year A.D. 1600, however, man became able, through advancing technology, to disrupt extensive environments ever more rapidly, and to employ modern weapons to over-hunt animals to extinction in just a few years. It is from this recent watershed stage that man's impact can no longer be considered on a par with "natural processes" that lead to extinction. Of course, this is not to say that natural extinction is not still taking place. The Labrador duck appears to have disappeared through no discernible fault of man, while the white-nosed saki of Brazil has been losing more of its range to other Amazon monkeys than to man.

To reduce the history of species on earth to manageable proportions, suppose the whole existence of the planet is compressed into a single year. Conditions suitable for life do not develop for certain until May, and plants and animals do not become abundant (mostly in the seas) until the end of October. In mid-December, dinosaurs and other reptiles dominate the scene. Mammals, with hairy covering and suckling their young, appear in large numbers only a little before Christmas. On New Year's Eve, at about five minutes to midnight, man emerges. Of these few moments of man's existence, recorded history represents about the time the clock takes to strike twelve. The period since A.D. 1600, when man-induced extinctions have rapidly increased, amounts to 3 seconds, and the quarter-century just begun, when the fallout of species looks likely to be far greater than all mass extinctions of the past put together, takes one-eighth of a second — a twinkling of an eye in evolutionary times.

It is sometimes suggested that, as some sort of compensation for the outburst of extinctions now underway, two evolutionary processes may gather pace, one a natural process and the other contrived by man. The argument in support of the first process is that as species disappear, niches, or "ecological living-space", will open up for newly emerging species to occupy. In fact so many vacant niches could appear that they might well stimulate a spurt of speciation. Sound as this argument is in principle, it is a non-starter in practice. The present process of extinction, vastly speeded up, will not lead to anything near a similarly speeded up process of speciation. As natural environments become degraded under man's influence, there will be few areas with enough ecological diversity to encourage many new species to emerge. Furthermore, as natural environments become homogenized, there will be little geographical isolation of populations, and hence little reproductive isolation of genetic reservoirs, to enable speciation to continue as it would under less disturbed conditions.

The second argument deals with man-contrived speciation. Opportunities are now emerging to synthesize genes in the laboratory by combining segments of the master molecule of life, DNA, from different species. This opens the way to creation of forms of life distinct from any that now exist. Regrettably this argument too is not valid. Producing a new species will be costly in the extreme, far more so than conserving the gene pool of virtually any species in its natural habitats. Moreover, a synthetic species may not be adapted to conditions outside the laboratory, in which case it may either quickly be eliminated or may encounter no natural controls to restrict its increase.

Meantime, man's activities, especially his mis-use and over-use of natural environments, continue to drive species extinct at an increasing rate. From A.D. 1600 to 1900, man was certainly accounting for one species every 4 years. From the year 1900 onwards, the rate increased to an average of around one per year. These figures refer, however, almost entirely to mammals and birds; and they are limited to species which man knows have existed and which man knows have disappeared. When we consider the other 99 percent of earth's stock of species, the picture appears far different from a "mere" one species per year.

As this book has already made clear, it is likely that during the last quarter of this century we shall witness an extinction spasm accounting for 1 million species. The total fallout could turn out to be lower; it could also, and more probably, turn out to be higher. Taking 1 million as a "reasonable working figure", this means an average of over 100 extinctions per day. The rate of fallout will increase as habitat disruption grows worse, i.e. toward the end of the period. Already, however, the process is well underway. In the region where rainforest destruction is most advanced, Southeast Asia, we can expect a wave of extinctions by the mid-1980s. Thus it is not unrealistic — in fact, probably optimistic — to say that we are losing one species per day right now. Within another decade, we could be losing one every hour.

3 Species Under Threat

Species come under threat for various reasons. Some forms of threat are more easily dealt with than others. In terms of practical conservation, certain species are far more costly in money to protect than others. In order to formulate conservation strategies, we need to know where our best options lie. This chapter looks at several groups of species that, due to attributes of their ecology and behaviour, are especially susceptible to threat.[1]

1. Rare species

Many species have low numbers at best. Insofar as rarity is to be measured in terms of a species' numbers as compared with other species in the same habitat, most species are rare. In an ecological zone with, say, 100 species, one dozen or so may well be common and widespread, while the rest will feature only small numbers. This is especially the case for diverse and complex communities of species, notably those of tropical moist forests. Under natural conditions, the myriad rare species of these forests stand a fair chance of extinction purely through random or stochastic processes. As soon as man intervenes with his disruptive activities, this chance is increased many times over.

In its attempts to survive and evolve, a species can follow one of two adaptive strategies.[2] The first is to develop into a good competitor, and thereby become predominant in environments that favor it — even if that means it is little able to survive in habitats that are colder or drier or otherwise less suitable. This strategy tends to make a species widespread and numerous. The second strategy, which tends to leave a species with low numbers and widely scattered populations, lies in developing physiological attributes and behavioral characteristics that allow the species to exploit extreme or specialist habitats, even though this generally means it cannot compete in favorable or common environments.

In the main, a rare species is likely to be either highly localized, or highly specialized, or both. For example, the bighorn sheep of North America, which probably numbered 1½-2 million before the white man appeared, now totals only 5000 or so, in small, widely scattered populations. Due to its specialist lifestyle, which induces each herd to sense a strong attachment to its traditional range, the species is not inclined to colonize new territory, not even former habitat. Because the bighorn sheep is a highly conservative creature, it seems almost pre-adapted to rarity.[3] The giant sequoia of California was rare long before man arrived on the scene. The tree has a very restricted range due to the fact that it is a "relict" species, left over after geoecological change eliminated related species.

Lists of threatened species contain a high proportion of what biologists term "K-selected" species. These unfortunates include the whales, the rhinos, several large birds such as seven out of fifteen crane species in the world, and many other creatures that seem predisposed to survival problems. If, through whatever cause, a K-selected species loses a large proportion of its numbers, it may prove critically unable to build up its stocks again, no matter what protection measures are provided. Thus special steps need to be taken to safeguard K-selected species while their numbers are still well above what would be acceptable levels in other species.

K-selected species make unusually efficient use of particular environments. Becoming adapted to an apparently stable situation, they direct less energy to producing many offspring, more to caring for their young. In addition, they live for a long time, with lengthy gaps between generations. In other words, they balance off a high rate of increase (and thus an ability to exploit transient good times) against a low rate of increase, a correspondingly low rate of mortality, and a tendency to maintain stable numbers. All this means they are closely adjusted to the long-term capacity of their habitats to support them. This is a sound strategy for predictable environments, but a high-risk strategy for a man-disturbed world.

By contrast, "r-selected" species, for example rats, rabbits, sparrows and starlings, are usually short-lived, have brief gaps between generations, and feature high rates of increase. This enables them to disperse quickly into new environments and to make excellent use of "boom seasons". Because of their opportunistic attributes and their built-in capacity to expand their numbers rapidly, they are successful in a man-disrupted world, to the extent that they often become pests.

A notable example of a K-selected species is the California condor. The condor does not breed until at least 6 years of age, it generally does not nest every year, and it lays only one egg. By contrast, the quail, an r-selected species, often nests during its second year, and lays fifteen or more eggs per clutch. Thus a pair of condors must take 10 or 15 years to replace themselves with two offspring, whereas the quail can do as much in its first year of breeding.

A further special category of rare species comprises the carnivores. By reason of their position toward the end of food chains, they are unusually vulnerable to disruption in their ecosystems. Especially disadvantaged are the larger predators, that must roam widely to find their prey. Well-known examples include the mountain lion, timber wolf, golden eagle, cheetah and the African hunting dog. Likewise, birds of prey are highly susceptible to disturbance. In Europe, they are reputed to have lost as much as 99 percent of their numbers since 1800.[4]

Finally, a number of species are confined to very small localities. An Arizona cactus, with diameter no larger than that of a quarter-dollar coin, exists in a valley less than 10 km long. The El Segundo butterfly lives in only a few hectares at the end of a runway at Los Angeles Airport, and would be subject to summary elimination if the airport were to be extended across its sole habitat. In northern California, a critically imperilled butterfly, Lange's Metalmark, is confined to an 8-hectare patch of sand dunes, yet due to demand on the part of land developers, this last scrap of living-space is valued at more than $1 million.[5] The laysant teal inhabits the marshy shores of a 5 km² lagoon on a Hawaiian island. The Abbott's booby, totalling 4000 individuals, exists in a 130 km² habitat on Christmas Island; its refuge consists almost entirely of phosphate of lime, and the fertiliser is being scooped out at a rate of 2 million tons per year, threatening to destroy three-quarters of the booby's habitat within 25 years or so. In Colombia and Ecuador, around 160 endemic bird species have ranges that average only little more than 300 km².[6] The snail darter, a paperclip-long fish numbering 10,000-15,000, lives in 61 kms of shallow, fast-flowing water of the Little Tennessee River, where its presence has blocked the final closing of the $116 million Tellico Dam (in Tennessee alone, there are eighty to ninety species of darter, with new ones being discovered at a rate of about one per year). The furbish lousewort, a member of the snapdragon family, comprises 880 individuals, 40 percent of them within the impoundment area of the $700 million Lincoln-Dickey hydroelectric project (larger than Egypt's Aswan Dam) on the St. John River in northern Maine.

2. Island species

As already indicated in Chapter 2, island species, which are often endemic, are especially liable to threat. Only 20 percent of all bird species are island birds, but 90 percent of birds driven extinct in historic times have been island dwellers.

The vulnerability of island species is due largely to their tendency to evolve with specializations that suit them for survival in a confined locality where there are few competitors and usually no predators. This evolutionary equipment leaves them grossly unable to cope with incursions by creatures brought in from outside by man, notably goats, pigs, rats, dogs and cats. What were formerly enclaves of security turn into "killing grounds" from which there is no escape. Island species are also ill-adapted to forest felling, grass burning, erosion, competition from alien weeds, and other disruptions on the part of man. Perhaps worst of all, many island creatures have lost the capacity to escape from dangers. Within the restricted security of Mauritius, the dodo did not need to fly. When the white man arrived with guns and clubs, he found the bird unbelievably easy to despatch. In the entire Mascarene group of islands, not just Mauritius but several others, an original stock of more than seventy endemic vertebrate species has now been reduced to only twenty-four, fifteen of which are endangered. All the rest have been accounted for by the concerted impact of rats and pigs, axe and plough. Fifty years after St. Helena was discovered by the white man in 1502, the island featured huge herds of goats, whereupon its plant life declined steadily. When a botanical inventory was made in 1810, thirty-three endemic plant species were recorded, of which twenty-two have since gone extinct, on top of the scores that disappeared before 1810.

3.   Wetland-living species

Several categories of species like a lot of water in their environment. Amphibians, for example, are highly dependent on water. Their young must live in this element entirely during their first stages of life, while an adult cannot be separated from moisture for long. This means that amphibians are unable to move beyond a limited range of habitat. In turn, it also means that, like other wetland-dwellers, amphibians cannot survive man's interference with their life-support systems to the extent that birds, insects and many other animal groups can. Moreover, frogs, toads, salamanders and others do not like to spawn in rivers or large lakes, but prefer the still, slack waters of ponds and marshes — precisely the areas that man most readily modifies or eliminates.

By consequence, wetland-dwellers — including not only amphibians, but molluscs and several other categories of species — are very vulnerable to drainage projects, water impoundments and other manipulations of hydrological systems. In many parts of the world, notably developed regions, wetlands are disappearing faster than any other type of environment. Man exploits "unproductive" zones such as marshes and tidal flats by draining them to make them arable, or by covering them with industrial plants, housing estates, highways and the like. In the United States, Wisconsin once had over 30,000 km² of wetlands, now only around 6000.

Moreover, because 70 percent of the world's population lives fairly close to coasts, or along the lower reaches of rivers flowing into coastal waters, the earth's coastal zones are among the areas most heavily disrupted by human activities. Of U.S. coastal wetlands, 20,000 km² have been lost during the past 20 years to dredging and filling operations. As long ago as 1970, the U.S. Fish and Wildlife

Service estimated that 23 percent of the country's estuaries, with their rich concentrations of species, were severely degraded, plus another 50 percent moderately degraded, through pollution from oil refineries and other industrial complexes. Along the Gulf of Mexico and the Atlantic coasts of the United States, destruction of marine habitats has been so extensive that commercial fisheries are suffering losses worth over $55 million each year — a measure of the damage that is being caused to marine organisms of every sort. In 1977 the U.S. Congress approved $10.3 billion worth of wetland-destroying water projects.

In the wake of this broad-scale disruption of U.S. wetlands, amphibians could well rank as the most threatened of the country's vertebrate groups. As many as 40-50 percent of molluscs are either endangered or extinct. Of 2000 inland snails, 400 may be threatened. (One snail used to range from Iowa to southern Ontario, but now survives only under the spray of the Chittenango Falls in Madison County, New York.)

A yet more dismal record is to be found in countries with denser human populations. According to the Council of Europe, one-third of Europe's amphibians are endangered, and a further number are threatened. In Great Britain, almost all amphibians are threatened, including even the common frog in many areas.

Despite their bleak outlook, however, wetland-dwellers do not receive a fraction of the publicity accorded to mammals and birds. For every 100 people who are concerned about the tiger and the peregrine falcon, only one is likely to have heard of the Houston toad.

4.   Tropical forest birds

Another vulnerable category comprises tropical forest birds. They are all the more significant in view of the threats to which tropical forests themselves are subject.

Having evolved within relatively stable environments, tropical forest birds are highly sensitive to disturbance of any kind.[7] They tend to have low reproduction rates, laying two to three eggs at a time, instead of the four to six of temperate forest birds. Because of more intensive predation in tropical forests, their ratio of young fledged to eggs laid is low compared with temperate forest birds. Overall, they maintain low population densities. These factors mean that tropical-forest birds are slow to recover from disturbance, by contrast with temperate-forest birds whose numbers "bounce back" from population crashes within a few seasons.

Partly because they are adapted to the darkness of their environments, many tropical forest birds cannot tolerate bright areas. They even avoid forest streams and game tracks, while small man-made intrusions such as park roads can represent insurmountable barriers. This means that tropical forest birds are little inclined to disperse away from man's disruptive activities in their forest habitats. By contrast, two out of three forest bird species in eastern North America are partially or wholly migratory, which makes them well adapted for dispersal. In addition, having lived in a primary forest environment for millions of years, tropical-forest birds have had no need to cope with secondary growth such as springs up when primary forest is cleared, whereas temperate-forest birds mostly find secondary vegetation acceptable.

These various attributes make tropical forest birds exceptionally sensitive to disturbance. (Of 401 bird species and sub-species listed as threatened in the Red Data Books, 291 occur in tropical moist forests.) As large tracts of tropical forests become degraded or are eliminated, the fallout of bird species is likely to be high. By contrast, temperate-forest birds are better able to live with man's activities. During the period when the forests of the eastern United States were severely reduced, only two bird species at most disappeared.

The main form of threat: habitat disruption

There is no doubt what now constitutes the main form of threat: habitat disruption. Until a few decades back, the principal threats were of a more direct and deliberate kind, notably over-hunting. But now, as man's activities encroach on natural environments in virtually every last corner of the earth, habitat disruption accounts for an overwhelming share of the troubles that beset wild creatures.

In the main, habitat disruption is difficult if not impossible to rectify. When it is allied to another source of threat, such as island endemism, the one reinforces the other making the overall impact exceptionally severe. Far worse than in the case of earlier forms of threat such as over-hunting, habitat disruption accounts for not only individual species but entire communities of animals and plants.

"Habitat disruption" includes any significant modification of natural environments and life-support systems. It extends from agriculture and forestry to settlement schemes, highway construction, pollution and a long list of man's activities. Even before the arrival of advanced technology, habitat disruption caused massive loss of living space for wild creatures. Super-sophisticated technology can now inflict as much damage on wildlife habitat in a single year as would have taken a decade in earlier times.

World-wide, the most widespread type of disruption is cultivation. Since this entails the replacement of natural vegetation with domestic crops, it amounts to a fundamental transformation of habitat. The process and its impact are so apparent that they are not dealt with further here. Not so obvious in its effects is another form of agriculture, livestock husbandry. The world now contains 2.7 billion cattle, sheep, goats, camels and the like, a total that is increasing much more rapidly than that of the human population at 4.2 billion. As domestic animals take ever larger amounts of vegetation and water, little is left for wild herbivores. And as wild herbivores fade from the scene, wild predators turn for prey to man's domestic herds, which in turn brings retribution on their heads.

Of continental mammals eliminated in various parts of the world, around 40 percent have been large herbivores that have been overwhelmed by competition with man's domestic stock. In the Mongolian People's Republic, whose 150,000 km^2 supported 640,000 people and 9.6 million head of livestock in 1920, and now contain twice as many people and 2½ times as many domestic stock, only remnant numbers remain of the wild Bactrian camel and the Mongolian wild ass, while the tiger and other large predators have been wiped out.

Even more serious is the trend for grasslands to become over-grazed and then turn into deserts, perhaps as much as 100,000 km^2 per year. This places more pressure on remaining grasslands and leads to a still greater squeeze for wildlife.

A form of habitat disruption that becomes even more prominent is pollution. The peregrine falcon and the brown pelican have told a dismal story that now applies to untold numbers of species. The most salient aspect of the pollution threat is that we know little about how large the threat is, except that hundreds of thousands of kinds of new synthetic molecules are now being dumped into inland waters and the seas, with potential impact unknown in almost every case.

In recent years, a new and exceptionally powerful source of habitat disruption has emerged: mega-scale technology. When the Great Lakes of North America were joined by the Erie and Welland Canals, the sea lamprey entered and decimated the lake trout and other fish. A similar careless mixing of aquatic biotas, though on a far larger scale, could occur if a new sea-level canal were constructed across the Isthmus of Panama. The Isthmus emerged 3-5 million years ago, leading on the Atlantic side to a coastal environment with moderate tides, mangrove swamps, sandy beaches, and rich coral reefs, and on the Pacific side to strong tides, silt-laden water, rocky shores created by extensive lava flows, limited and depauperate reefs, and periodic upwellings of cold nutrient-rich water. The two environments feature roughly 20,000 species of animals and plants, yet perhaps only 10 percent are found in both regions, less than 1 percent in the case of fishes and molluscs.[8] The present canal features a series of freshwater locks that prevent migration of marine organisms from the Atlantic to the Pacific Oceans and vice versa. The new canal would be blasted straight through the mountains, and could allow creatures to wander freely from one ocean to the other. The Pacific communities, having evolved in an in-shore environment with marked fluctuations, and having thus developed a higher proportion of opportunistic species capable of wedging their way into existing biotas, might grossly disrupt the Atlantic communities. At the same time, if the Atlantic biota, with its diversity of species and hence its greater competitive capacity, were to invade the Pacific biota, as many as 5000 species could become extinct. If the yellow-bellied sea snake alone were to make its way from the Pacific into the Caribbean, it could inflict so much economic as well as ecological damage that it would be worthwhile to try to prevent any migration at all, through engineering measures such as bubble curtains, ultrasonic screens and intrusions of heated or fresh water.

A further example of mega-scale technology lies with the Jonglei project to drain part of the Massachusetts-sized Sudd Swamp in southern Sudan. The White Nile flows in a huge semicircle through the swamp, and the project's aim is to bypass the swamp with a 350 km canal (twice as long as the Suez Canal). Since half the White Nile's flow evaporates while it makes its sluggish way through the swamp, the canal should ensure an appreciable saving of water. Both Sudan and Egypt need lots of extra water. Sudan plans to irrigate 12,000 km² of land, requiring another 8 billion m³ of water per year. Egypt, that used to enjoy 25 m³ of daily water from the Nile per head of its populace in 1900, now tries to manage with less than 4 m³, and faces the prospect of only 2½ m³ by the end of the century if its river supplies are not increased. The new canal will drain off 20 million m³ of water per day, or one-quarter of average annual flow, possibly extending to another 23 million m³ later. The project will reduce evaporation losses by 4.7 billion m³ per year, or one-sixth of the White Nile's flow — a considerable saving.

As a result of this diversion of water, part of the swamp will become grassland, which will assist stock-raising. However, a number of estimates suggest that extensive areas of surrounding savannah could become arid, and one-tenth of the richest pastures seem likely to disappear. No clear indication of the overall environmental consequences is yet available, since the $350 million budget has made only limited provision for pre-project assessment of environmental impact, nor is any significant investigation envisaged except such as can be undertaken in the course of engineering operations between 1978 and 1985 — almost certainly too late for radical revision of construction plans, should ecological considerations make this advisable. Partly for economic advancement and partly for political security, both Sudan and Egypt seem determined to press ahead with the project, which is financed with Arab oil money and executed by a consortium of French and Dutch engineers.

A further purpose of the Jonglei project could lie with converting 16,000 km² of the zone into a major grain-producing area. As is usual with tropical agriculture, this potential "bread basket" would attract many new insect pests. The best way to tackle these pests would be to utilize closely associated predators and parasites from the insect communities of the present swamps — and it is highly likely that the Sudd, being a long-established island of moisture amid a semi-arid zone, features an exceptionally rich array of species, many of them endemic. If it turns out that the Sudd's ecosystem is to be fundamentally modified by the Jonglei Canal, whole assemblies of species could go extinct in just a few years.

These various examples serve to illustrate the scale of habitat disruption that can occur across extensive territories. Sometimes, however, the conflict can be exceptionally acute while much more localized. Mount Nimba in West Africa, at the junction of Liberia, Ivory Coast and Guinea, contains over 200 endemic animal species, making it one of the most remarkable wildlife communities in the whole of Africa. It also contains rich deposits of high-grade ore, which makes it highly attractive to mineral exploiters. Similarly, Brazil features a number of limestone outcrops that harbour veritable treasures of botanical rarities and endemic plants, yet these areas are being intensively exploited to meet Brazil's growing demand for cement. On Palau, a small group of Micronesia islands administered by the United States under U.N. Trusteeship, a Japanese-Iranian-American business consortium has planned to build a $500 million oil-storage facility with petro-chemical industries. The island group, 880 kms east of the Philippines, is surrounded by unique coral and marine life, and many scientists consider the area to be an ecological treasure trove unrivalled in Oceania. The project would entail much engineering modification of the islands and could lead to heavy pollution of off-shore waters.

Thus the main category of threat now derives from modification or outright loss of habitat. This means that the main problem for declining wildlife is not the person with conscious intent to exploit or kill: it is the citizen who, by virtue of his consumerist lifestyle, stimulates economic processes that lead to disruption of natural environments.

As a measure of how unwittingly destructive these trends can be, let us look briefly at that citadel of advanced technology, the United States. Scientists believe that the nation's official Endangered Species List, which is constantly being expanded, should include 250 mammals, 209 birds, 54 reptiles, 40 fish, 30 amphibians, 24 clams, 6 insects and 1 snail and well over 2000 out of 22,200 plant species. Of course, the List includes only species known to be in trouble. In many instances, nothing is known about a species' survival prospects, though "informed guesses" suggest that a comprehensive list would be much longer (for example, the number of inland snails thought to be threatened is unofficially put at 400 out of 2000). The great majority of these endangered species owe their plight to that amorphous and unwittingly destructive process known as "development".

A triage strategy for species?

Even with a several-times increase in funding to assist threatened species, we could not save all those that appear doomed to disappear. The processes of habitat disruption are too solidly underway to be halted completely. Since man is intervening in the evolutionary process with all the impact of a major glaciation, he should do it with as much conscious awareness of what he is about as he can muster. That is to say, now that he is committed to playing God and determining the extinction of large numbers of species, he might as well do it as selectively as possible. But how to accomplish this? If we cannot be sure of the details, can we at least establish the right direction to move in?

These are large questions to ask. How are we to decide which species shall be allowed to go extinct through our deliberate decision, and thereby concentrate our conservation efforts — limited as they are bound to be — on "more deserving" species? This would mean that certain species would simply disappear because we pulled the carpet out from under them. We might abandon the Mauritius kestrel to its all-but-inevitable fate, and utilize the funds to proffer stronger support for any of the hundreds of threatened bird species that are more likely to survive. In short, a proportion of species would disappear through human design. Agonizing prospect though this might be, it is better than allowing species to disappear merely through human default.

An approach along these lines would amount to a "triage strategy" for species. The term derives from French medical practice in World

War I, when battlefield doctors found there were more wounded than they could handle. So they assigned each soldier to one of three categories: first, those who could certainly be helped by medical attention; second, those who could probably survive without attention; and third, those who were likely to die no matter how much attention they received. The first category absorbed pretty well all the medical services available, so the other two categories were ignored. If a strategy along similar lines were applied to threatened species, it would amount to a more rational approach than that practised hitherto. It would be systematic rather than haphazard, and it would enable conservationists to make best use of their finances and skills.

How would choices be made? How could we decide between the Bengal tiger and a crab in the Caribbean? Should we focus on remnant patches of rainforest in countries that have experienced decades of destruction, or should we try to "lock away" vast tracts of forest in regions that have been little touched? These will be difficult decisions. A start could be made through systematic analysis of factors that make some species more susceptible to extinction than others; for example, sensitivity to habitat disruption, reproductive capacity, and "K-selection" traits. In addition to these bio-ecological factors, there is need to consider economic, political, legal and sociocultural aspects of the problem: the Bengal tiger requires large amounts of living space in a part of the world that is crowded with human beings, but it could stimulate more public support for conservation of its ecosystem (and thereby help save many other species) than could a less-than-charismatic creature such as a crab. When we integrate all the various factors that tell for and against a species, we shall have a clearer idea of where best we can apply our conservation muscle.

Many tough decisions will have to be made. Nobody will like the challenge of deliberately consigning certain species to oblivion. However, insofar as man is certainly consigning huge numbers to oblivion, he might as well do it with some selective discretion. It is with these considerations in mind that the next chapter asks just what purposes are served by species survival, and whether some species are more "useful" than others.

4 What are Species Good For?

Species deserve to be preserved for several reasons. These are considered briefly here, with a view to picking out the arguments that offer strongest support for conservation measures.

1. Aesthetic argument

Aesthetically, species add to the diversity and texture of life's fabric on earth. All are complex and interesting, even the smallest microorganism. Look at a diatom under a microscope, and you will see that in form it is as beautiful as any antelope or butterfly.

In fact, many people in affluent nations spend appreciable sums on enjoying the spectacle of wild creatures. Bird watchers in the United States alone spend over $500 million each year. A growing number of people from North America, Europe and Japan annually roam the earth in search of wildlife, spending billions of dollars to catch a glimpse of a rhino in Africa, a tiger in Asia, or a tapir in South America.

True, no individual person can hope to enjoy the sight of more than the most trifling fraction of all species on earth. Generally speaking, however, he appears to get a kick out of the mere idea that he shares the earth with the orangutan, the cheetah and creatures so obscure in the depths of Amazonia that nobody has discovered them. At least, such is the case in advanced societies, where people spend much time and money on television, films and books about wildlife.

In the case of certain species, of course, people cannot express their interest by going to see the creatures, even if they have the funds available. They would find it hard to take a look at, for instance, a blue whale, not only because the creature is now very rare, but because

45

it lives in the high seas. So if the blue whale were to disappear, would people actually feel as impoverished as at the thought that they will never see a dodo? In point of fact, it is unlikely that even the keenest conservationist loses much sleep over the dodo — just as the most ardent Greek scholar does not overly concern himself that he must make do with the seven Sophocles plays that have survived out of the dozens written. Yet many people might genuinely feel that their quality of life would lose something if the blue whale were denied life at all. In that case, they should be enabled to continue to enjoy their "option satisfaction" in the whale's survival.

Still more to the point, many people would almost certainly feel impoverished if they woke one morning in the year 2000 to find that they could no longer derive satisfaction from, say, 1 million species that had been eliminated within the previous 25 years.

2.   Ethical argument

As implied, the aesthetic argument quickly shades off into an ethical one. Briefly stated, this argument urges that all forms of life on earth have a right to exist. Conversely, humanity has no right to exterminate a species. To push the point a stage further, one could well ask whether humanity has the right to precipitate, through the elimination of large numbers of species, a fundamental and permanent shift in the course of evolution. While the aesthetic argument is virtually a prerogative of affluent people with leisure to think about such questions, the ethical concept of man's "steward-ship" for earth's other creatures is inherent in many religious and cultural traditions around the world.[1]

Yet even this argument needs to be looked at carefully. Are we so sure that we wish to preserve all forms of life for their own intrinsic worth? Would many people not be glad to see the end of the virus that causes the common cold? And would the same not apply to whatever organisms contribute to cancer? These are unique forms of life with just as much "right" to existence as the giraffe or the whooping crane. We have now reached a stage when the smallpox virus has been backed into a corner, to the extent that no human being suffers from the disease and the organism exists only in the laboratory. Should man, by conscious and rational decision, obliterate this manifestation of life's diversity?

Similarly, it is unrealistic to postulate that a species represents an absolute value, and cannot be traded off against other value(s) on the grounds that a unique irreplaceable entity is beyond measurement of "worth". In point of fact, virtually no value is considered by society to be absolute. Not even human life qualifies. To be sure, an individual person views his own life as an untradeable asset. But as a member of the community, he does not view human life in general as anywhere near an absolute. The rate of road-accident deaths each year — 55,000 in the United States, 110,000 in Europe, and over one quarter of a million worldwide — amounts to an appalling loss of life, yet it is apparently considered by society as an "acceptable" price for rapid transportation. One simple way to reduce road accidents would be to enforce the use of seatbelts, airbags and lower speed limits. But the cost of these safeguards is apparently reckoned too high to match the amount of human life saved.

Presumably there is only one value which represents an absolute, and that is the survival of life on earth. To this absolute value, species makes an absolute contribution: when there are no more species left there will be no more life. But not all species make the same amount of contribution, since some are considered by ecologists to be more important for the workings of their ecosystems, by virtue of their numbers, biomass and energy flow. So the value of a species, far from being absolute, is very much a relative affair.

Especially difficult is the question of relative value between human life and other species. Already the conflict is plain to see in many localities, where people compete with wildlife for living space. This conflict is going to get worse, fast. True, in a few instances there is no clash; the blue whale enroaches on no human environment for its survival needs, and thus its demise would be all the more regrettable. For most species, however, the problem is basic: sufficient habitat for them means less habitat available for human communities with their growing numbers.

How is this conflict to be resolved? The problem raises complex ethical issues that deserve in-depth treatment elsewhere. Suffice it to say here that many conservationists could probably accept the elimination of a species if it could be finally demonstrated that the creature's habitat would produce crops to keep huge communities of people alive (and provided that the food could not be grown elsewhere, that the people could not find any other means to sustain themselves, that the species could not be translocated to an alternative location, etc.). If the situation were reduced to bald terms of one species against one million people, it might well be viewed as a tolerable if regrettable tradeoff.

But the prospect facing humankind in the next few decades is a whole different ballgame. In order to allow expanding numbers of people the amount of living space they seem to think they need, at least one-fifth, possibly one-third, conceivably one-half, of all species on earth may well be driven extinct. Would this be in the best interests of human communities within the short-run future, let alone generations of the longer-run future? In view of the utilitarian benefits for agriculture, medicine, industrial materials (see next chapter) that stem from species' genetic resources, it is virtually certain that humankind would suffer greatly through the disappearance of, say, one million species.

Such, then, is the nature and scale of the ethical conflict we now confront. It is a challenge that merits much more attention than it has hitherto received from conservationists, technologists, political leaders, economist planners and whoever else determines the future course of our earth home.

3. Ecological diversity and stability

It is often argued that the more numerous an ecosystem's species, the greater is the ecosystem's stability. There is much evidence for an association between these two characteristics.[2] For one thing, more species can use the sun's energy more efficiently than can a few. For another thing, an ecosystem can probably withstand perturbations better if each species can depend on many rather than few food sources, and be regulated by many rather than few predators — whereupon the eggs-in-one-basket effect is reduced.

Not that the idea is to be taken in the simple sense that variety is the essence of life. The relationship is far more complex. Diversity in this context refers to quality as well as quantity of differences among species, while stability can refer to numbers and relative abundance of species, or to dominance by a few species. So to assert that diversity equals stability is to over-state the case.[3] A more concise way to express the situation might be to say that diversity and stability have had evolutionary relationships that run parallel without being causal. Alternatively, one can say that high environmental stability leads to higher community stability, which in turn permits, though is not determined by, high diversity of species.

This line of analysis goes part way to explain the fact that natural monocultures, for example the United States' east-coast saltmarsh grass, are often highly stable. When man's agricultural monocultures, notably crops, show poor stability, the fault may lie not so much with their simplicity in itself as with their "unnaturalness" or "lack of evolutionary pedigree".[3] Similarly, the most complex ecosystems, while stable enough under natural conditions, tend to show unexpectedly little resilience when they encounter types of disruption outside their normal experience, notably man-made disturbances. In other words, their communities of species appear to have become so closely attuned to stability of environment that they have sacrificed the ability to recover from disruption. The most complex ecosystem on earth, the tropical moist forest, is exceptionally sensitive to disruption by man, especially when it loses an appreciable part of its diversity through the activities of, for example, the timber harvester — whereupon the delicate equilibrium of its ecological processes may be unable to recover their former richness and intricacy of relationships.[4]

As with many aspects of the challenge of conserving species, the problem of "how much diversity fosters how much stability?" boils down to a question of difference between marginal and absolute losses. If an ecological community with fifty species loses one, that may be considered, in certain circumstances, akin to a human being having a toe amputated — a bother, but no great setback. If three or five species disappear, that is like losing a foot — serious, but not necessarily critical to the foot owner's survival. If twenty are eliminated, that is a basically different situation, akin to a human losing much of his digestive system through surgery. Leaving aside for a moment the fact that the loss of any species amounts to an irretrievable loss of a unique resource, and considering only the contribution of species to ecological stability, the loss of an individual species here or there, while regrettable, is hardly so catastrophic as it is sometimes represented. By contrast, if a significant segment of the species spectrum disappears, that is an altogether different order of loss, since it may strike at the adequate functioning of all life in the community at issue. So a key question arises: where do losses shift from "regrettable but marginal" to "critical or worse"?

To tackle this issue at global level, one can surely say, at one extreme, that the loss of one species out of a total of (say) 5 million is a pretty minor matter, while at the other extreme, the loss of 5 million species out of 5 million would amount to total catastrophe. Backing off one step from the latter situation, it is difficult to imagine a species that could exist entirely on its own on earth; and a community of a bare ten species, or even 100, or possibly 1000, might find themselves in a very precarious position. To revert to the other end of the gradient of possibilities, how many species can be lost before the impoverishment is no longer marginal in terms of stability for the planetary ecosystem? Or, to break the question down one stage further, how many species can be lost from regional ecosystems with scant consequence for the planetary ecosystem?

One answer is to say that a good deal depends on which species, since some contribute more than others to ecosystem workings by virtue of their numbers, biomass, capacity to exploit the sun's energy, and status in the food pyramid. Another answer is to say that certain species may have value as "indicator species", particularly if they are threatened. A species in trouble often signals general ill health in an ecosystem that may thereby contain other threatened species. For example, the cheetah, a highly specialized predator, plays an important role in regulating savannah ecosystems. By virtue of its susceptibility to more threats than seem to afflict the lion, leopard, and other predators (threats such as changes in prey communities and vegetation patterns), the cheetah can give warning of environmental stress when its numbers decline markedly.[5] Similarly, we have to thank the peregrine falcon, the brown pelican and other birds of prey for drawing attention to DDT and other toxic pollutants that, when they reach excessive levels in the environment, prove poisonous to carnivores, including man. It is this role of "indicator species" that makes them especially useful to human society, in ways we do not anticipate until they flash a red light concerning new threats to our welfare. The most sensitive indicator species are often those at the end of food chains, i.e. those that concentrate contaminant materials in their tissues; at the same time, their position at the end of food chains usually means that they occur in small numbers as compared with, say, herbivores, which makes them more susceptible to extinction.

In this sense, the serendipity value of species is exceptional — even though the value is exceptionally difficult to pin down. A world with fewer species would be a world in which we would find it much more difficult to keep up with baseline monitoring of what is happening to our natural environments, precisely at a time when the need for monitoring is becoming all the more critical. But if indicator species can offer us answers to questions we scarcely know how to ask, how are we to pick out the species that serve this valuable function?

These are all problems of fundamental ecology that deserve urgent attention. Since we are clearly going to lose many hundreds of thousands of species before the end of the century, we need to know which ones we can "best afford" to lose, which ones would certainly leave major ecosystems with critical injury if they disappeared, which ones should be saved because their loss could precipitate ecological breakdown whose dimensions we can hardly start to envisage, and which ones should be preserved virtually at any cost. While conservation efforts need to be greatly expanded, they need also to become more selective: the time is past when we can achieve much by running hither and yon with buckets of water.

Of course, sufficient funds are not allocated for research of that order. Perhaps more could be achieved, however, if the funds which are currently put into "last-ditch" conservation efforts were applied instead to a systematic attempt to advance our understanding of the structure and function of major ecosystems, especially in relation to species survival. Each year around $15,000 are spent in assisting what is believed to be the most endangered bird on earth, the Mauritius kestrel with only nine individuals left in the wild and around one dozen in captivity. Apart from the doubtful prospects of a creature recovering from such a grossly reduced gene pool, there is a closely related kestrel on the African mainland that flourishes in its many thousands. On the same African mainland, there are ecologists who are stalled in their field investigations of complex ecosystems due to lack of funds to put gasoline in their research vehicles. Not that there need be an agonizing choice between the Mauritius kestrel and tropical research. We now know more about sectors of the moon's surface than we know about the depths of tropical rainforests; a switch of 10 percent of funding from space exploration into ecological understanding of our earth home would increase research budgets many times over, and would greatly advance our skills in planetary management. Meantime, while insect species are almost certainly going under at a rate of hundreds if not thousands per year, the annual budget of what is perhaps the world's leading research agency in this field, the Division of Entomology, the Smithsonian Institution in Washington D.C., is a mere $775,000.

4.   Genetic resources

A major argument in support of species conservation is that it maintains the earth's stock of genetic material in all its variety.

The extraordinary range of genetic forms is apparent in two ways. First, there is the spectrum of species themselves, with their differentiated forms, genetically separate from one another. Secondly, there is a great deal of "genetic spread" within each species, manifested through different races (sub-species), distinct in themselves while genetically related to each other. The breadth of genetic variability inherent in a species is demonstrated by the many types of dogs which man has developed, until we now have the St. Bernard and the Pekinese, the waddling Basset and the greyhound. These dog races, however differentiated they may appear, are much closer to one another than is the sparrow to the robin.

It is difficult to say which is the more significant, diversity between species or diversity within species. The disruption of North America's forests led to the proliferation of the white-tailed deer, a successional species that thrives on disturbed vegetation. As a consequence, the deer has increased in numbers from perhaps half a million to 12½ million. The disruption of the forests also led to the extinction of the passenger pigeon, a species that could not adapt when its particular form of forest habitat disappeared. Which is the more significant for the earth's genetic wealth, the enlargement of the deer's gene pool or the loss of the pigeon's gene pool? Probably the second — but by how much? How can we measure the comparative change, so that conservationists can make informed decisions when they encounter similar tradeoffs in future?

Hitherto there has been no tolerably accurate way to assess genetic variability. That may be changing. A new technique, electrophoresis, allows us to measure enzymes and protein concentration in the blood, which can serve as an indication of how far one individual's genetic make-up diverges from another's — and the same of course for populations, sub-species and full species.[6] To date, electrophoresis offers only partial and approximate measures of genetic variability. But as the technique is refined, it may prove useful to conservationists who agonise over whether to allocate funds towards saving species X while implicitly consigning species Y and Z to oblivion. Already electrophoresis has revealed that the average polymorphism and heterozygocity (two indexes of variability) for plants is 17 percent, for invertebrates 13.4, for man 6.7, for vertebrates in general 6.6, for reptiles 5, and for birds less than 5. Least variability appears among polar-region species, not much among large marine vertebrates such as porpoises and tuna fish and probably the great whales, an intermediate amount among temperate-zone species, and the greatest degree among tropical species. These findings tend to confirm that the tropical rainforests, with their plethora of plant and insect species, deserve to be at the top of the conservationist's shopping list.

Which groups of species can best maintain the processes of evolution?

There are other ways to hedge our bets in favor of maintaining the planet's genetic diversity. The reduced array of species that survives by the end of the century will probably contain a disproportionate number of opportunistic or "clever" species. Examples include the common rat and the house sparrow — species that seem able to "learn" how to get along with man. There is no great harm in a trend that favors clever species, insofar as they are slow to settle into specialized lifestyles and contain much potential for evolutionary adaptation. To this extent, then, the genetic variability of an opportunistic species can be considered to be greater than that of a more "developed" species. So should we look after the interests of species with greatest potential for adaptive radiation in the future? Or should we help the likely "losers", and thereby restore some kind of balance between different categories of species? These are questions that need to be investigated urgently, and that have hardly been looked at. About all that can be said right now is that "specialist" species, particularly parasites and predators, are often the creatures that keep down the numbers of opportunistic species, notably the ones that are likely to become pests. To date, probably less than 5 percent of all insect species can be considered pests. However, if selective patterns of extinction were to result in a disproportionate total of clever species surviving, this could mean that the relative number of harmful species could eventually expand beyond the capacity of natural enemies to control them.

Approaching the situation another way, it may make sense to favor groups of species such as insects which, with their rapid reproductive rates, possess high potential for speciation. From this perspective, there is little point in assisting a group of species that is, by comparison, an evolutionary dead-end, the whales. True, whales contribute much to the healthy functioning of their ocean ecosystems. They do not compete with man for living space. If their numbers were allowed to recover, they could eventually serve as a major sustainable source of protein. They are highly developed representatives of the most advanced creatures on earth, the mammals: so able are whales to record experience in their "memories" before recalling them years later, and so capable are whales in communicating with each other, that in destroying whales we may be destroying a kind of "culture" dating back 50 million years. There are abundant good reasons why whales deserve the best efforts of conservationists. However, whales' longevity and low reproductive rates mean that it takes decades for one generation to give way to another. In turn, this means that whales' scope to respond to environmental changes via selection pressures and adaptive variations — the forerunner processes of speciation — is more limited than for almost any other form of life, except for similar higher mammals such as elephants and rhinos, also man. So for purposes of evolutionary processes that lead to new species and greater genetic diversity, whales have little to offer as compared with virtually all other of earth's stock of species.

Many insects, on the other hand, can produce dozens of generations within a single season. This is a principal reason why there is almost certainly 100 and perhaps 200 times as many insect as vertebrate species. If a pair of cabbage aphids in north-eastern United States start producing progeny at the onset of warm weather in early April, and if they produce an average of 41 young per female, and if all their descendants live and reproduce normally, they will, through the course of 16 generations by late September, throw off progeny totalling 1,560,000,000,000,000,000,000,000 (Sobrowsky, 1962). During this process there is vast scope for the forces of natural selection to pick out "fitter" variations. Although it is not known how long it takes for one species of animal to throw off another or several species, the time-scale for insects could amount to only a few dozen years, by contrast with thousands of years for most vertebrates and hundreds of thousands for large mammals such as whales. Thus insects, with their quick-response adaptability, are, compared with most species, well suited to survive the environmental upheavals of man's activities, whereas the whales will be caught at extreme disadvantage.

It is a mistake, then, to deplore the extinction of a species on the grounds that it leads to the disappearance of unique genetic material, without considering the vast scope available for man to engender greater variety among present organisms. The number of individuals of any species is tiny compared to the diversity that is theoretically on the cards. Suppose there are only 1000 kinds of genes in the world, each existing in ten different alleles or variants. With this material, the number of gametes that is potentially possible, each featuring a different combination of genes, would be 10^{1000}, a total to be compared with the number of subatomic particles in the universe, estimated at 10^{78}.[7] In a human population of just over 4 billion, and only 100 variable gene loci known for the human species (probably a considerable under-estimate of the actual numbers), the huge majority of possible genetypes is not going to be realized. Earth's array of insect species, totalling somewhere between 3 and 8.5 million, is not generating anything beyond a mere fraction of their genetic potential, since most of them die before they go through a full reproductive cycle. If conservation postulates the maintenance of genetic variety as a leading rationale for preservation of species, should we not lend a helping hand to the evolutionary processes for insects, along the lines of what we have been doing for dogs and their breeds?

It appears, then, that some species are more "important" than others, and thus deserve greater efforts to preserve them. It is also plain that we are not going to save all species, not by a long way. How do we assess species in a hierarchy of priorities? As yet there is all too little guidance offered by the science of applied ecology. An urgent need lies in developing conservation as a predictive discipline — a challenge that is only starting to be recognized.

What is already recognized is that the genetic resources of species serve many pragmatic purposes of humankind. These purposes bring immediate utilitarian benefit to society, through contributions to modernized agriculture (e.g. new foods), medicine and pharmaceuticals (drugs from plants) and industrial processes (raw materials). This constitutes a realistic rationale for conservation of species in the practical work-a-day world. By contrast, the first three arguments, while worthy in themselves, are unlikely to stand up against man-made pressures to modify and disrupt natural environments on every side. This applies even to the diversity/stability argument, since the time horizons in question are too long when compared with the immediate urge to exploit natural environments for purposes of everyday living — a factor that is especially compelling in developing regions.

So the strongest argument is that which generates most practical muscle for conservation where it counts, on the ground. If species can prove their worth through their contributions to agriculture, technology and other down-to-earth activities, they can stake a strong claim to survival space in a crowded world. Fortunately, species have already demonstrated thousands of ways in which they serve humanity's immediate needs. So significant are these utilitarian benefits, that they deserve separate treatment in Chapter 5.

5 Utilitarian Benefits of Species Preservation

Protection of species is not merely an objective for idealist preservationists. It serves strictly utilitarian purposes of immediate value to society. Present uses of genetic resources run into many thousands of forms, the main categories being modern agriculture, medicine and pharmaceuticals, and industrial processes. In view of the benefits derived from the small segment of species investigated thus far, the planetary spectrum of species can be considered among society's most valuable raw materials. Conversely, the erosion of genetic resources is not only a loss to future generations, but an impoverishment for present society.

This chapter documents a selection of these utilitarian benefits. The emphasis is heavily on plants, largely because only a few of the 46,000 known vertebrates among animals have been subjected to research, while hardly any attention has been given to the millions of invertebrate animal species. By contrast, an appreciable number — though still only a very small proportion — of 250,000 higher plants have been investigated.

A.1 Agriculture: plants

Wild plants, together with primitive cultivars, contribute markedly to new forms of food production and to advances in conventional agriculture.[1]

A whole range of entirely new food plants is available. The planet is believed to contain 80,000 edible plants, of which man has, at one time or another, used at least 3000 for food. Yet only about 150 have ever been cultivated on a large scale, and less than twenty produce 90 percent of the world's food.[2] We are essentially using the same limited number of plant species as have served humankind for centuries.

Examples abound of under-exploited food plants with proven potential.[3] Aborigines in Australia have used scores and possibly hundreds of plants, especially fruits and bulbs, as food. They favor certain yams that are well adapted to dry conditions, opening up the possibility that cross-breeds with forms in other parts of the tropics could allow this important crop to be extended to several further regions of the tropics. The leguminous tamarugo tree of the Atacama Desert in Chile can survive in soil covered with 1 m of salt, so it could be grown in naturally salty soils and in the 1250 km² of land made saline each year through inappropriate irrigation; its highly nutritious pods and leaves allow sheep to be stocked at rates approaching those of the best grasslands anywhere. A considerable number of wild arid-zone shrubs — saltbush, mesquite, spineless cacti, atriplex and bush alfalfa, among many others — could supply protein-rich fodder for livestock, also fuelwood, fibres and oil; not only can they make desert lands productive, but they can help to halt desertification which is overtaking 60,000 km² of cropland and much larger areas of grassland each year.[4]

Much the same applies to plants from other ecological zones. A marine plant from the west coast of Mexico produces grain that can be ground for flour, opening up the prospect of using the seas to produce bread (U.S. National Academy of Sciences, 1975). From the highlands of Ethiopia, a leafy grassy vegetable seems a promising source of plant protein, yielding 120 kg per hectare, or as much as alfalfa and soybean.[5] It is worth recalling that a single wild plant of the same genus has provided us, through genetic engineering, with cabbage, kale, broccoli, cauliflower and brussels sprouts. Many other food plants are locally important while unknown elsewhere.[6] Systematic investigation could indicate many hundreds of plant species with potential as food.

Let us take a quick look at a couple of examples.[3] The Wax Gourd vegetable grows in the Asian tropics, but could be extended to many parts of Africa and Latin America. A creeping vine that looks somewhat like a pumpkin, it can be raised more easily than any other cucurbit (pumpkin, squash, melon, etc.). It grows rapidly: one shoot produces 2.3 cm every 3 hours during the course of 4 days, a prolific rate of growth that allows three or four crops to be produced each year. A full-grown gourd reaches 35 kg in weight and measures 2 m long and 1 m in diameter. However, the fruit's pulp — a thick white flesh that is crisp and juicy — can be eaten at any stage of growth. It has a mild flavor, and is used as a cooked vegetable, as a base for soup, as a sweet when mixed with syrup and as a food extender. A unique feature of the plant that is very pertinent to the humid tropics is that the gourd's waxy coating preserves the food inside from attack by micro-organisms, thus allowing the vegetable to be stored for as long as 1 year without refrigeration.

Secondly, a novelty food. A blue-green algae, called *Spirulina,* grows around the shores of Lake Tchad in Africa. Like related species of algae, it flourishes in saline, often alkaline, waters, which suits it to arid zones. If mutant varieties could be found with tolerance for magnesium, Spirulina could be grown in seawater. At temperatures of 30-35°C the algae produces at least 12 g per m^2 per day, while a trial project in Mexico shows that 1 hectare can produce 85 kg of protein per day. Spirulina is larger than other micro-organisms that have been promoted as protein sources, which allows villagers around Lake Tchad to harvest it by filtering the water through muslin. The villagers then dry the residue in the sand and eat it as a cooked green vegetable. As much as 60-70 percent of Spirulina is good-quality protein; it is rich in vitamins and it appears to contain nothing harmful to humans. It can be added, up to 10 percent by volume, to cereals and other food products without altering their tastes. The only other locality where Spirulina is known to have been eaten by local people is in Mexico, where the sixteenth-century Spanish Conquistadores found the Aztecs using Spirulina as their main source of protein. A pilot plant has been set up at Texcoco near Mexico City, producing about 1 ton of dry Spirulina daily. When dried, Spirulina does not ferment, so it can be easily stored.

As for established crops, their productivity cannot be maintained, let alone expanded, without fresh variations from wild relatives and primitive cultivars. There is as much "genetic plasticity" in many crop species as in the domestic dog, allowing man to produce numerous variants according to his needs — a factor that points up the need to safeguard genetic variability *within* species as well as *among* species.[7] It is the skills of plant geneticists, rather than large amounts of artifical additives such as pesticides and fertilizers, that have led to one record after another in crop yields in North America and other regions of both temperate and tropical zones.

This applies especially to the principal crops of the Green Revolution, wheat, rice and corn. Together with sorghum, these crops account for half of the world's land under food crops. Moreover, sorghum has recently taken a big leap forward in productivity, following an analysis of 9000 forms that produced two types rich in lysine (an amino acid).[8] Similarly, a strain of barley has been developed that can grow in sand dunes and be irrigated with seawater.[9] By drawing on sufficient wild varieties of other crops, geneticists may be able to achieve parallel breakthroughs with other crops. Geneticists have produced an entirely new crop plant, triticale, a cross between wheat and rye (the name is derived from the scientific terms for wheat, *Triticum,* and rye, *Secale*). Triticale is not only highly nutritious, but it inherits from rye a capacity to withstand cold and to grow in sandy, infertile soil — a characteristic that may enable farmers to put many marginal lands to food production. This triticale breakthrough points the way to other possible new crops, notably by crossing wheat or rye with barley.

But without sufficient stocks of wild strains and primitive cultivars of major crops, there is little prospect of extending the Green Revolution and other recent advances in agriculture. Forms of commercial wheat, for example, have evolved from genes of primitive wheats found in Asia Minor, where disease-resistant varieties have likewise evolved. Yet in Asia Minor, as in many other centers of wild crop varieties, genetic resources are being rapidly eroded. In part, the problem lies with sheer attrition of natural environments through increase in human numbers and human aspirations. In part too, a major threat lies with the trend for subsistence farming to give way to commercial agriculture, whereupon food plants that over centuries have evolved adaptations to their local ecological conditions are supplanted by a small range of highly-productive varieties, often from outside sources. In this latter sense, the Green Revolution, while an admirable achievement in many respects, is proving a disaster for local genetic diversity. According to crop experts of the U.N. Food and Agriculture Organization and the International Board for Plant Genetic Resources, the prospects for genetic reservoirs are extremely serious and growing worse.[10] For example, in Mexico, many wild relatives of maize have been supplanted by high-yielding varieties, by hybrid sorghum, by strawberry farms that export to the United States and by an eight-lane freeway across the Central Plateau.[11]

Furthermore, specialist strains of modern crops are unusually vulnerable to disease. Despite present efforts at control, diseases cause annual losses to world crops worth around $25 billion.[12] Without further supplies of resistant genes from the wild, blight could sweep through any of humanity's main food crops. Four crops — wheat, rice, maize and potatoes — contribute more food than the next twenty-six most important crops combined. Were a blight to get in among one crop, the results would be far worse than the 2 million people who died in Ireland in the mid-1800s as a result of potato disease. Crop geneticists believe that between 5 and 15 years after they introduce a crop strain and fresh resistance to diseases, the resistance collapses in the face of newly evolved forms of disease. So there is constant need to "top up" a plant's genetic constitution with new germ plasm.

The challenge is a race that can never be finally won. In fact, it is a race that will become even more complex and difficult even were there plentiful stocks of germ plasm in the wild. The dilemma is illustrated by a recent story of rice. A few years ago, the famous "miracle strain" of rice in the Philippines, IR-8, was hit by tungro disease. Rice growers switched to a further form, IR-20, whereupon this hybrid soon proved fatally vulnerable to grassy stunt virus and brown hopper insects. So farmers moved on to IR-26, a super-hybrid that turned out to be exceptionally resistant to almost all Philippines diseases and insect pests. But it proved too fragile for the islands' strong winds, whereupon plant breeders decided to try an original Taiwan strain that had shown unusual capacity to stand up to winds — only to find that it had been all but eliminated by Taiwan farmers as they planted virtually all their ricelands with IR-8.

Similar problems apply to other conventional crops. Coffee was badly hit in Brazil in 1970 not only by unfavorable weather but by leaf rust disease, a consequence of the extremely restricted genetic base of coffee breeds. If Africa's forests — the original home of coffee — were to become grossly disrupted or were to be largely eliminated, there would be far fewer wild reservoirs of coffee germ plasm. Monoculture plantations of other crops such as cocoa, rubber, cotton, groundnuts and bananas are exceptionally vulnerable to new pests and diseases. Monocultures must also be able to cope with changes in climate, such as unexpected increases in aridity or cold. This attribute is all the more significant insofar as present high-yielding grains with their narrow-response capacities are adapted to what may have been the most moist 30-year period during the past 1000 years.[13] If in fact the climate of northern temperate zones, with their huge grain-growing territories, is becoming drier, agriculture will require large inputs of new germ plasm to cope with less moist growing seasons. Similarly, a global fall in temperature of only 1°C could cause world rice production to fall by 45 percent.

Yet plant breeders face virtual wipe-out of endemic genetic diversity of several crops. Many strains of wild wheat have all but disappeared from their ancestral homes, from the Atlas mountains through the Mediterranean basin as far as Ethiopia and Nepal. Even in the remotest valleys, native wheats are becoming rare. In Turkey, wild progenitors of several cereals find sanctuary from grazing animals only in graveyards and castle ruins. Many ancient forms of maize in Colombia are now hard to trace, while tens of thousands of varieties in Bolivia have completely disappeared. The same applies to rice throughout Southeast and South Asia; recent cross-breeding has increased rice yields from 1.5 tons per hectare to 6 or even 8 tons, by virtue of indigenous varieties from Borneo — an island now being rapidly disrupted through commercial logging and through floods of human migrants from Java (see Chapter 10). A high-protein strain of barley was recently identified in Ethiopia, shortly before the area with the last remnants was scheduled for settlement. In fact, in Ethiopia, the situation across the board is growing critical. The country has been the gene centre for many African crops, but during the course of centuries its flora has undergone widespread impoverishment through deforestation, overgrazing and other misuse of biotic resources. In recent years two Ethiopian strains of sorghum, rich in an essential protein-making chemical, have improved the nutritional content of sorghum in many lands. Possibly Ethiopian gene pools could have done the same for wheat, barley and other crops, formerly available in the country in thousands of forms but now virtually eliminated.

There are various other opportunities to enhance productivity of existing crops. For instance, genetic manipulation now allows breeders to increase fixation of naturally occurring nitrogen on the part of legumes.[14] A five-fold increase has been achieved for soybeans, following atmospheric enrichment and carbon dioxide. Breeders can develop other plants with unusual capacity for nitrogen fixation; a number of tropical grasses feature a form of intracellular root symbiosis that allows them to fix up to 1.7 kg of nitrogen per hectare per day. This would relieve the need to use artificial nitrogenous fertilizer — a costly commodity. To produce 1 ton requires natural gas equivalent to 6 barrels of oil. If nitrogen-fixing plants cannot be developed, the world will need, within the next two decades, an additional 500 ammonia factories costing $40-50 billion.

Similarly, there is scope to improve photosynthesis, the process by which water and carbon dioxide are energized by sunlight and converted into plant foods.[15] Certain plants are 2 or 3 times more efficient than others at photosynthesis. Maize is highly efficient, a few such as sugarcane are moderately efficient, but most, including cereal grains, soybeans, peanuts and cotton, are decidedly inefficient. In fact, most food crops capture only 1 percent, and often less, of the sunlight that illuminates their leaves. Geneticists can increase photosynthesis by rearranging the leaf configuration to allow greater intake of sunlight. In the tropics, where sunlight is an abundant natural resource, the productivity of certain food crops can probably be doubled through this technique alone.[16]

The United States is especially dependent on exotic genetic reservoirs. The country has a dearth of native crop germ plasms and a shallow base of primitive cultivars, leaving its crop production resting on a very restricted genetic base.[17] According to the U.S. Department of Agriculture in 1973, "the situation is serious, potentially dangerous to the welfare of the nation, and appears to be getting worse rather than better". Within the parentage of seed corn used in the United States in 1970, 70 percent depended upon five in-bred lines of corn — whereupon southern corn leaf blight eliminated one-seventh of the entire crop, pushing up corn prices by 20 percent and causing losses to farmers and increased costs to customers totalling more than $2 billion.[18] Nearly all the United States' cultivated crops have such a narrow genetic base that they are highly susceptible to some new form of pathogen, insect pest, or severe environmental stress such as unusual cold or aridity (see Table 1 for details). At the same time, the United States' agriculture is essentially an imported agriculture, all its main food crops having originated in Latin America and elsewhere. So the nation is almost entirely dependent on other countries for new sets of genetic characteristics. This is why, in the past few years, American plant collectors have been searching in Ethiopia for virus-resistant barley and fresh germ plasm for peas, in Turkey and Afghanistan for new varieties of wheat and in Mexico for wild and primitive strains of corn. Yet in all these sources of genetic wealth, economic and social changes are causing rapid eradication of genetic variability.

Table 1
Some major U.S. crops: extent to which they are dominated by a few varieties

	Hectares (millions) 1976	Value ($ millions) 1976	Total varieties	Major varieties	Hectarage, % of major varieties
Corn	33,664	14,742	197	6	71
Wheat	28,662	6201	269	10	55
Soybean	20,009	8487	62	6	56
Cotton	4411	3350	50	3	53
Rice	1012	770	14	4	65
Potato	556	1182	82	4	72
Peanut	611	749	15	9	95
Peas	51	22	50	2	96

Source: Information supplied by U.S. Dept. of Agriculture, 1977.

Not only can crops be assisted through infusion of germ plasm along the lines described so far, but food output can be boosted through reduction of damage caused by insects. According to the U.S. Department of Agriculture, damage caused by insects in the United States each year accounts for one-tenth of all crops grown, and a loss estimated at around $5 billion. World-wide the amount is believed to be at least one-third. A number of wild plants, notably tropical species, produce chemical compounds that repel or inhibit the feeding of insects. There are two main groups of these natural-toxin compounds, the pyrethrins from chrysanthemum-type plants and the rotenoids from roots of rainforest Leguminosae. Both groups are bio-degradable, and they do not accumulate in organisms, and they cause little harm to higher animals such as mammals and birds. Since many plants and insects have evolved in symbiotic relationship, notably in tropical zones, many other similar substances must be available in the wild. Anti-insect defenses of this sort had been introduced into less than 1 percent of the United States' crops in 1900, but by 1965 the proportion had grown to three-quarters.[19] However, insect pests can develop new strains to overcome plant defences in only 3-10 years, so there is constant need to derive further genetic combinations to stay ahead of insect evolution. Regrettably, very few plants have been screened for these purposes (or for any other purposes), so we know next to nothing about their potential for controlling insect pests, except that almost certainly it is very large.

In addition, a number of insect pests can be controlled by other insects, notably by predators and parasites that limit populations of plant eaters by attacking their eggs, larvae, pupae and adults. Since many of these predators and parasites are highly specific in their choice of prey, they would be inclined to limit their attentions to target species of insect pests without doing damage to other harmless species. This strategy is far preferable to broad-scale use of persistent toxic chemicals.[20] Moreover, many insect species are growing resistant to chemical insecticides. Among certain insects, as little as fifteen generations are required to build up resistance. The U.S. Department of Agriculture estimates that of 500 or so species of insects that do annual damage to U.S. crops worth $2 billion, around half have developed resistance to insecticides — and something the same for 10,000 species that do significant damage world-wide.[21]

The record now indicates that more than 250 cases of partial or complete control of insect pests and weed problems have been accomplished through introduction of predators and parasites. The winter moth threatened to defoliate hardwoods in Nova Scotia and ultimately across North America, until it was controlled by two parasites brought in to tackle it; the savings in Nova Scotia alone were put at well over $12 million. In California, biological control projects during the past 45 years have reduced crop losses to insects and cut back on the need for pesticidal chemicals, to an extent of savings worth $200 million. On the island of Principe off the west coast of Africa, biological control of the coconut scale insect, that threatened the island's entire economy, was achieved through a one-time outlay of $10,000, producing savings in the first 10 years of $2 million. Many similar cases can be cited, sometimes with a gain on investment as high as 25,000 percent.

A.2.   Agriculture: animals

The number of animal species widely used for food is, to date, far smaller than the number of plant species. But, as with plants, the gene pools of species already in use are much reduced and declining rapidly.[22]

The potential consequences of a loss in genetic diversity can be illustrated by the so-called Cornish chicken. Known to have potential for extremely rapid growth, it was saved from oblivion by geneticists who crossed it with other breeds to produce the modern fast-growing broiler chicken. Similarly, a race of sheep in Finland, declining from 1 million animals in 1950 to 170,000 in 1967, has been used to breed ewes that produce three lambs at a time.[23] A parallel decline of specialist strains applies to sheep, cattle, pigs, horses and poultry in many developed countries, where the livestock industry is considered to be headed for an emergency level of homogenization. In Europe and the Mediterranean basin, 115 breeds of cattle are severely threatened, and only 30 breeds are considered to be holding their own.[24] In Scotland the Orkney sheep thrives off seaweed and nettles rather than grass; it has recently been saved from extinction through action on the part of the newly formed U.K. Rare Breeds Survival Trust.

A similar story can be told for developing countries. Around Lake Tchad, the Kuri breed of cattle is able to swim in order to feed off lake-bottom vegetation; it is threatened with "genetic swamping" through excessive cross-breeding with local zebu cattle. Also in West Africa is a dwarf shorthorn breed of cattle, the N'dama, with tolerance for trypanosomiasis disease that limits cattle raising in several million square miles of Africa; the N'dama is in danger of disappearing. Diseases world-wide account each year for 50 million cattle and buffalo and 100 million sheep and goats, or roughly 5 percent of all domestic livestock; genetic breeding could reduce this mortality by half.

Current cattle breeds could likewise be improved through hybridization with related species from the wild. In California, a cross-breeding of domestic cattle with bison has led to an animal that reputedly produces meat costing 25-40 percent less than beef because of the creature's capacity to thrive off grass without the $500-worth of feedstuffs that conventional cattle consume before slaughter. In addition, the "beefalo" can reach a weight of 450 kg in half the time that cattle usually take.[25] Similarly, the domestic goose could be improved by an infusion of genes from Arctic-breeding species of wild geese that feature short incubation period and ultra-rapid growth rates.[26] Temperate-zone breeds could also be helped through tropical species of goose with their capacity to produce eggs right around the year.

Numerous animal species could qualify as new sources of meat. The several dozen wild antelopes and other herbivores of African savannahs are a prime example,[27] as are certain species of the Amazon region.[28] Apart from these and other well-known instances, there are some less expected candidates. Snakes and lizards are relished by certain peoples for their delicate flavor and texture. Grasshoppers, locusts, termites and grubs are widely eaten in arid zones.[29] In parts of Mexico, ants are a common food:[30] they contain 30 percent protein, as compared with 21.5 for beef, 20.2 for chicken, 18.9 for fish and 6.4 for eggs. Since some ant species produce 25 generations in a year, and a single pair can generate a total of 564 million offspring, there is potential for major production of meat. Pretty soon the advertisements may read, "Don't beef about high prices, try bugburger". Who is for caterpillar cannelloni?

A.3. Economic evaluation of upgraded agriculture

What economic benefits can be derived from infusions of wild germ plasm? As a preliminary evaluation, the U.S. Department of Agriculture has produced a figure for the farm-gate value of all

America's crops, $52 billion per year. The Department has also estimated that increases in productivity due to genetic improvement have averaged around 1 percent annually. This means that advances through infusion of new germ plasm can be set at $520 million per year. To cite a specific example, an introduction of a wild strain of wheat from Turkey, with resistance to all known races of common and dwarf "bunts" and several other diseases, has conferred benefits on commercial varieties of U.S. wheat worth around $50 million annually. For three-quarters of a century onion-growers in the United States suffered severe losses through thrips disease, until a fresh strain from Persia supplied resistance estimated at a minimum of $3.5 million per year (a figure roughly equivalent to the combined annual budgets of the U.S. Agricultural Research Service, the various State Agricultural Experimental Stations and all other research agencies concerned with crop genetic resources). Conversely, were the climate in America's cornbelt to alter (according to climatologists, the temperature at the height of the growing season could increase by 2°C and the rainfall could fall off by 20 mm), the costs — were adapted corn strains not available — could reach at least $285 million per year.[31]

Colombia introduced several new dwarf strains of rice in the mid-1960s. By 1975 they had accounted for a 2½ times increase in output, estimated to be worth $350 million, as compared with a government and agency investment of only $340,000.[32] Similar large-scale benefits can be documented for groundnuts, rubber, coconut and palm oil.

B. Medicine and pharmaceuticals

Both animal and plant species present many benefits to medicine and public health. Already they have contributed a wide range of drugs and pharmaceuticals, including analgesics (pain-killers), antibiotics, heart drugs, anti-leukemic agents, enzymes, hormones and anti-coagulants.[33] As many as one-half of all prescriptions written in the United States each year contain a drug of natural origin, while the growing value of plant medicinals is presently put at well over $3 billion.[34] There is no convenient way to estimate the commercial value of drugs obtained from plants that are available to U.S. citizens without prescriptions (e.g. laxatives, cough and cold preparations and the like), but it could well amount to another $3 billion. The United States, like other advanced nations, is especially dependent upon imported plant materials for most of its botanical resources for medicines; these imports come mainly from the tropics and especially from tropical forests. Of seventy-six major pharmaceutical compounds obtained from higher plants, only seven can be commercially produced at competitive prices through synthesis. Reserpine, for example, can be commercially prepared from natural sources for about $0.75 per gram, but through synthesis for $1.25.

Many animals serve medicine in direct fashion. Bee venom is used for arthritis. Snake venoms can be put to a range of uses as non-addictive pain-killers, and offer promise for treatment of thrombotic disorders.[35] Blowfly larvae secrete a substance, alantoin, that promotes healing of deep wounds, decaying tissues and osteomyelitis. Cantharidin, prepared from the European blister beetle, is used to treat certain conditions of the uro-genital system.

In addition, animal physiology affords clues to the origins and nature of many human ailments. The stormy petrel, the albatross and other long-flying birds with highly developed heart and circulatory systems contribute a better understanding of cardiomyopathy, a failing caused by over-development of the heart muscle that obstructs blood outflow. Similar benefits might become available from hummingbirds that spend much of their waking life in flight, from butterflies that migrate 4000 km a year, and from locusts and other insects that sustain high levels of activity.[36] The desert pupfish of the United States, one of the most threatened creatures on earth, shows remarkable tolerance to extremes of temperature and salinity, an evolved attribute that could assist research into human kidney diseases. Elephants throw light on atherosclerosis and problems of fatty acids.[37] The only animal other than man that is known to contract leprosy is the armadillo, which may thereby hold a key to a cure. The Florida manatee, which has poorly clotting blood, may prove useful in research on hemophilia. Because of their close relatedness to humans, primates are especially valuable for medical research, and have contributed to the development of many drugs and vaccines. For example, chimpanzees are the only creatures on which the safety of anti-hepatitis vaccines can be tested (and there are only 50,000 chimpanzees left in the wild). Baboons assist in resolving urinary incontinence in humans. Cotton-topped marmosets, a species of monkey susceptible to cancer of the lymphatic system, help to produce a potent anti-cancer vaccine.[38] The black bear, which possesses hormonal mechanisms that enable it to "sleep" for 5 months during the winter, supplies information on development of a low-protein, low-fluid diet that helps humans suffering from kidney failure.[39] By studying the lungfish's primitive mechanisms for air breathing, and by tracking down the substance that activates aestivation (a state of suspended animation that allows the lungfish to survive well over one year without food or water), a means may be found to simulate a suspension of metabolic processes in humans who undergo long open-heart operations.

As for plants, a little-known species looks likely to assist the campaign against bilharzia or snail fever. Bilharzia has become one of the world's most widespread parasitical diseases, affecting more than 250 million people. As irrigation systems spread, the disease grows more prevalent. The main method of countering bilharzia has been to attack the parasite-bearing snails by spraying water courses with synthetic molluscicidal chemicals, an expensive approach that attacks many non-target organisms as well. Now there is prospect of utilizing a snail-killing compound isolated from an Ethiopian plant, endod.[40] The plant is little toxic to mammals, fish are affected by it to only limited extent and birds appear immune.

An exceptionally valuable group of drugs stem from organic alkaline compounds, found in almost 20 percent of all plant species, or alkaloids.[41] These alkaloids include strychnine, cocaine, narcotics such as morphine and nicotine, hallucinogens such as mescalin and LSD, and a host of medicines used as painkillers, anti-malarials, cardiac and respiratory stimulants, blood-pressure boosters, pupil dilators, muscle relaxants, local anesthetics, tumor inhibitors, and anti-leukemic drugs. To date only around 2 percent of the earth's 300,000 flowering species have been screened for alkaloids, producing nonetheless over 1000 alkaloids. The glycoside alkaloids are used for cardiac complaints, while certain other alkaloids show therapeutic promise against hypertension. An alkaloid from Lobelia is used in anti-smoking preparations. The pyrrolizidine and acronycine alkaloids look likely to prove active against several forms of cancer, and other recently discovered alkaloids help to treat leukemia. The Maytenus shrub found in East Africa provides an alkaloid compound that is highly active against leukemia and solid tumors in animals, and related plants in Ethiopia show promise as key sources for several more anti-cancer drugs.[42]

Now let us take a detailed look at two particular plant species. First of all, the well-known Purple Foxglove, a native of western Europe and Morocco. This plant yields digitalis, a drug that increases the force of systolic contractions of the heart muscle, and provides more rest between contractions, thus assisting the treatment of congestive heart failure. As a secondary effect, digitalis lowers blood pressure in hypertensive heart disease, and elevates blood pressure where necessary due to impaired heart function. The closely related Grecian Foxglove, native to central and southern Europe, serves as a source of digoxin, a drug 300 times more powerful than digitalis; it is also more stable, and is especially valuable because of its prompt action and quick elimination. Without the cardiotonic compounds produced from this Foxglove, more than 3 million Americans would find their lives cut short within as little as 72 hours.[43] Commercial sales of digoxin in the United States now amount to $14 million per year.

Secondly, the Rosy Periwinkle. Originally described from Madagascar, though thought to be a native of the West Indies, the Periwinkle now grows in many parts of the tropics. Of the seventy-five alkaloids found in this plant, two have proved to be exceptionally useful in human medicine: vincristine and vinblastine in the plant's stems and leaves have led to a breakthrough in the campaign against cancer. Used in combination with other materials such as mustard, they supply chemotherapy that achieves 80 percent remission in treating Hodgkin's Disease (before 1960, a patient had only 19 percent chance of remission), 99 percent for acute lymphocytic leukemia, and 50-80 percent for several other forms of cancer. As much as 530 tons of the plant are required to produce 1 kg of vincristine. For many years, that 1 kg was worth $1.3 million, placing it among the most valuable products in the world and roughly on a par with heroin; now it can be manufactured for $200,000 a kg. According to the U.S.

National Prescriptions Audit, world-wide sales of vincristine in 1976 totalled $22 million — a measure of the economic value of one beneficial plant species.

Plant-derived drugs for cancer could offer so much potential that the U.S. National Cancer Institute has undertaken a major research effort to identify new drugs from wild species. The annual budget for collecting plants, extracting materials, and screening them for anti-tumour activity, runs to $1.5 million a year. Since 1960 the Institute has screened about 100,000 extracts from 29,000 plant species, of which around 3000 show potential against cancer (the plants also offer potential against a wide range of other diseases and conditions). Of these 3000, fifteen have yielded materials that warrant clinical trials and the Institute expects to find at least five with sufficient potential against cancer to merit commercial development, possibly rivalling vincristine. Although this research program represents the most extensive pharmacological investigation ever undertaken, it covers only a fraction of the array of plant species that could offer startpoint materials against cancer.

A further group of drugs is of increasing importance, those that are used in treatment of mental disorders. Mescalin, from a spineless cactus of northern Mexico, helps to relieve schizophrenia.[44] Hyoscine, from a forest plant in eastern Australia, is used in the treatment of several forms of mental illness. A number of plant-derived halluciogens are useful for experimental psychiatry. The traditional raw material for codeine has been the alkaloid morphine — likewise the source of heroin; a promising new startpoint for codeine is the alkaloid thebaine from a species of *Papaver,* which would satisfy licit medical needs without fostering drugs of abuse. Research is underway to identify other substitute crops for narcotic plants — a significant initiative, considering that drug abuse and drug-related crime costs over $10 billion each year in the United States alone.

C. Industrial processes

Industry utilizes many wild species. Plants already serve the needs of the textile manufacturer, the toilet-goods producer and the icecream maker — likewise the butcher, the baker and the candlestick-maker. As technology advances, in a world growing short of just about averything except shortages, industry's need for new raw materials will grow ever more rapidly.

Examples of industrial materials from plants include latex products (e.g. rubber), pectins, resins and cleoresins, gums and other exudates, essential oils for flavors and related juices, vegetable dyes and tannins, vegetable fats and waxes, insecticides, growth regulators and other biodynamic compounds. In like manner, animals supply furs, leather goods and many other products, also fibres, glues and other substances for industrial processes.

One category of products is exceptionally important — lubricants. Because of the increasing cost of petroleum-based lubricants, there is a premium on finding substitute materials. Of 6400 plants recently screened by the U.S. Department of Agriculture for new oils and waxes among other products, promising leads were revealed by 460. Principal candidates include a number of plants with oil-rich seeds, including the Buffalo Gourd and the Jojoba shrub of the deserts of northern Mexico and southwestern United States.

The second, the Jojoba, deserves to be dealt with in some detail.[45] It produces liquid wax, a substance that, despite many efforts, still cannot be synthesized at commercially acceptable costs. A good number of plants yield solid waxes as coating on their seeds, fruits, leaves and stem, but Jojoba oil is the only liquid wax in the entire plant kingdom. Liquid wax serves numerous industrial processes, including manufacture of textiles, leather, electrical insulation, paper coatings, polishes, carbon paper, lubricants, pet foods, pharmaceuticals and cosmetics. Due to rapidly expanding demand for these products, the price of liquid wax has reached one record level after another during the past two decades.

Until recently, the only natural source of liquid wax was the sperm whale. During the late 1960s, sperm oil was considered to be so important to U.S. industry that the country imported 50-55 million tons per year, about half of it being used exclusively as an ingredient in lubricants, especially for automobile transmissions and other high-speed machinery subjected to extreme pressures and temperatures. For a time, sperm oil was even stockpiled against a national emergency. Since 1970 the sperm whale has been classified under U.S. legislation as an endangered species, so there has been a pressing search to find an economic alternative. A naturally occurring liquid wax has turned up in the Jojoba shrub, comprising 50 percent of the seeds by weight. Jojoba oil feels less oily than the usual edible oils, due to its radically different chemical structure, being composed almost entirely of unsaturated fatty acids, esterified with unsaturated fatty alcohols of high molecular weights. The oil is virtually identical with sperm oil, though more uniform in composition and with fewer impurities.

Jojoba oil appears suitable for a range of purposes. It can withstand repeated heatings to high temperatures without changes in its viscosity. It requires little refining before it can be used as a high-quality lubricant. When added to other lubricants, it serves as a fine cutting or grinding oil. It can serve as a transformer oil and as an oil for precision instruments and delicate mechanisms. When combined with sulfur chloride, it can be used in the manufacture of linoleum, printing ink, varnishes, chewing gum and adhesives. Its alcohol and acid derivatives can be used to prepare disinfectants, detergents, surfactants, driers, emulsifiers, resins, plasticizers, protective coatings, fibres, corrosion inhibitors and bases for creams and ointments. It can be used for hair oil, shampoo, soap, face creams, lipsticks, perfumes and sunscreen compounds, among other cosmetics. In pharmaceuticals, it serves as a stabilizer of penincillin products and other coatings for medicinal preparations. When hardened by hydrogenation (a process which produces margarine from vegetable oils), Jojoba oil is transformed into a dense solid of sparkling white crystals, known as Jojoba wax, resembling spermaceti (also from the sperm whale) and beeswax. The wax's hardness and high melting point (70°C) make it a rival of carnauba, the "king of waxes", that, deriving from a difficult-to-harvest Brazilian palm, is rising rapidly in price. Jojoba wax has further potential uses in polishes for floors, furniture and automobiles; as a protective coating on fruit, fruit preparations and paper containers; in candles; as a sizing for textiles and as a high-dielectric-constant material for electric insulators.

As a measure of the commercial prospects awaiting development of Jojoba's potential, its oil now sells to Japan for $3000 a barrel, as compared with an OPEC price for fossil petroleum of $12. To meet projected world demand for Jojoba oil and wax, plantations covering 100,000 hectares and yielding 2500 kg of nuts per hectare are required, laying the foundations for a $250-million industry.

A second plant worth considering in detail is the Guayule shrub.[46] Indigenous to virtually the same desert regions as the Jojoba, all parts of the Guayule contain a rubber that, when purified, is virtually indistinguishable from natural rubber from *Hevea* trees. Due to the soaring costs of its petroleum content, synthetic rubber needs to be supplemented, if not supplanted, by natural sources. Global demand for rubber of all types is expanding at over 5 percent per year, with natural rubber taking 30 percent of the market. Certain products are highly dependent on natural rubber due to its great elasticity and heat resistance. For example, lorry and bus tyres and automobile radial tyres use 40 percent, while aircraft tyres must consist almost entirely of natural rubber. The World Bank believes that the price of natural rubber may double between 1976 and 1985, after which it could go through the roof as market demand steadily outgrows the expected production of rubber plantations in Southeast Asia. Because the United States now imports almost 1 million tons of natural rubber a year, at a cost of over $500 million, Congress has appropriated $60 million for a 5-year effort to develop a domestic source of rubber. Although natural rubber occurs in some 2000 species of plants, the leading candidate for the United States is the Guayule shrub, between one-seventh and one-quarter of which consists of rubber.

Furthermore, every ton of rubber from the Guayule is accompanied by about half a ton of resin. This resin contains volatile and non-volatile terpenoids, a shellac-like gum, drying oils and cinnamic acids. So valuable are these materials that the resin might fetch a better price than the rubber. On top of all this, 1 ton of Guayule leaves contains about 25 kg of a hard wax with one of the highest melting points ever recorded, 76°C.

Thirdly, let us take a look at a tree that could generate the single most widely used of all raw materials for industry, energy. Petroleum, natural gas and other fuels are no more than plant material that has been converted, through geological processes, into their present form. How to harvest the solar energy that is currently being stored in photosynthesizing plants? The foremost technique available is pyrolysis, or heating vegetable matter in air-free containers, whereupon an oil not unlike crude petroleum is released with around 75 percent calorific value of ordinary oil, plus a mixture of gases and flaky char. One ton of tropical dry wood can yield 13½ liters of methanol (for use as a liquid fuel), 36 liters of wood oil and light tar, 330 kg of charcoal, and 140 m³ of gas (used to energize the production process), together with 25 liters of acetic acid, 11½ liters of creosote oil, 7½ liters of esters and 33 kg of pitch.

In order to "grow gasoline" in this manner, the main requirement is a steady supply of vegetable matter in large amounts. A number of fast-growing plant species appear to be suited to "biomass energy farming", including sugarcane, cassava, kenaf and trees such as eucalyptus, pines and, perhaps best of all, the giant ipilipil.[47] The ipilipil is an evergreen tropical legume whose original home is central America. It is one of the most versatile plants in the world. It grows 4 m in 6 months, almost 10 m in 2 years, and over 15 m in 6 years. A 1-hectare plantation can easily produce 35³ per year of fuelwood for pyrolytic production of fuel, or for direct use in electricity generators and industrial boilers. A rate of 35 m³ matches most other fast-growing species; trials show that the giant ipilipil can yield twice and even 3 times as much. A 12,000-hectare plantation could generate an estimated energy equivalent of 1 million barrels of oil per year.

In addition, a 1-hectare plantation of giant ipilipil can produce 90 tons per year of palatable forage for livestock. When cattle are fed on a mixture of grass and leaves from young ipilipil trees, they put on weight as fast as cattle on the best pastures anywhere. The dry leaves contain 27-34 percent protein, with a balance of amino acids much as in alfalfa, and one of the highest pro-vitamin A contents ever reported in plants. Alternatively, if the foliage is used for green manure, the leaves from 1 hectare supply 600 kg of nitrogen, 500 kg of potash and 200 kg of phosphorus fertilizer.

Fourthly, certain plant species can serve as sources of energy by virtue of their capacity to produce hydrocarbons like oil instead of carbohydrates like sugar. These hydrocarbons can be of various kinds, one of which we have long used — rubber from *Hevea brasiliensis* of the Euphorbia family, exactly the same hydrocarbons as produced by guayule. Various other Euphorbias produce significant amounts of milk-like sap, latex, that is actually an emulsion of hydrocarbons in water.[48] The hydrocarbons are similar to those produced by the rubber tree, but much lower in molecular weight, and with size distribution similar to those of hydrocarbons in petroleum. In point of fact, their hydrocarbons are superior to those of crude oil, since they are practically free of sulfur and contaminants found in fossil petroleum. All in all, some 30,000 species of plants produce latex, but the genus Euphorbia seems to be especially suitable for "growing gasoline", notably twelve Euphorbia species identified in Brazil that contain about 10 percent by dry weight of hydrocarbon-like materials. Not only do they produce valuable products, but they can be grown in areas that are too dry for other conventional purposes, or on land that is otherwise useless such as strip-mined areas. Small-scale experiments indicate that 1 hectare of Euphorbia trees could produce between 25 and 125 barrels of oil per year, at annual production costs of about $20 per barrel, to be compared with current OPEC prices of over $14. Geneticists have no doubt that production could be doubled through seed selection in the first year, while agronomists believe they could achieve similar increases in yield within a few years. After all, the rubber tree in 1945 was producing a mere 225 kg of rubber per hectare, an amount which scientists pushed upwards 10 times within the space of 20 years, and even bred a few trees that yielded 40 times as much. Commercial plantations have been established on Okinawa by two large Japanese corporations, Nippon Oil and Sekisui Plastics.

Further candidates for biomass energy could include a number of water plants, notably certain algae and marine species such as giant kelps.[49] According to trial research in California, seaweed could prove a notable source of energy: being carbonaceous, it can be processed by fermentation and anaerobic digestion into methane. In theory, a $2\frac{1}{2}$-km^2 "marine farm" could generate enough energy (plus other products such as fertilizer and plastics) to support at least 300 persons, and also grow sufficient food to feed 3000-5000 persons, at current world average consumption levels; while a 750-km^2 area could produce as much natural gas as the United States consumes in one year.

D. Other uses

Animals and plants serve many other purposes. For example, the manatee appears to hold promise for relieving the serious growing problem of aquatic weeds, which cause direct economic costs to developing countries totalling over $100 million per year.[50] Stretches of the Rivers Nile and Zaire have been covered with a solid layer of water hyacinth. In other tropical areas, the hyacinth prevents the cultivation of extensive tracts of land and reduces the efficiency of hydro-electric dams. It creates public health problems by providing favorable conditions for breeding mosquitoes and schistosome-bearing snails. Through reducing surface aeration of water, one-quarter of a hectare of hyacinth can impose an oxygen-depleting load on the water equivalent to the sewage of forty people. To tackle problems of this sort, Guyana has experimented with manatees, which eat as much as 25 percent of their bodyweight of vegetable matter in an average day. A 600-m length of canal in Georgetown required four men to work for 10 days before they could clear the weed, and then they had to put in several hours each week to keep it from recolonizing. When two manatees were introduced, they kept the canal clear without difficulty.

Recent research suggests that the water hyacinth itself could be put to good use. It offers potential as an animal feed and as a fertilizer, even as a control for water pollution and as a source of energy.[51] Hyacinth plants cultivated on domestic sewage in warm conditions can double themselves reproductively in 8-10 days and can generate 7 tons of biomass per hectare per day, with a high proportion of crude protein. Moreover, one-third of a hectare of water hyacinth can purify 2000 tons of sewage daily; the plant can also filter out toxic heavy metals such as cadmium, mercury, lead and nickel, and absorb or metabolize trace-organic compounds such as phenols.[52] As for energy, the hyacinth produces biogas in amounts that could prove economically exploitable. The same applies to a number of other aquatic plants that are frequently regarded as mere pests.[53]

Many less prominent species serve society's needs, often in unexpected ways. Several of the world's 18,000 lichen species, notably those that grow on tree trunks and walls, are exceptionally sensitive to traces of heavy metals and sulfur dioxide in the atmosphere — yet it is precisely this factor that is causing lichens to disappear in several industrialized countries.[54] The common lilac develops a disease, leaf roll necrosis, when atmospheric levels of ozone and sulfur dioxide rise, while bees' honey can be used to monitor pollution by heavy metals.[55] Snakes' organs serve to measure residues of organochlorine pesticides (DDT and others) and of industrial-waste PCBs (poly-chlorinated biphenyls, chemical cousins of the organochlorines).[56] Similarly, kinked tails in tadpoles may indicate heavy loads of pesticides in the environment.[57] A plankton in the Black Sea can apparently absorb large concentrations of uranium through its natural sugars, which opens up the prospect of synthesizing these sugars for use in cleaning up radioactive spills.[58]

E.   Genetic resources of the oceans

As a measure of our ignorance of our planetary patrimony, the largest single sector of the earth's surface remains virtually unknown — the oceans. In fact, the genetic resources of the oceans have hardly been investigated at all with regard to their potential to serve society's purposes. This is all the more significant in view of pollution threats to ocean ecosystems, especially in those areas where most marine life exists, viz. along coastlines.

The ocean provides many startpoint materials for drugs.[59] The tiny fraction of marine organisms examined to date has yielded many extracts and compounds with varying biological characteristics, including anti-microbial, anti-viral, blood-coagulant and anti-coagulant, neuro-muscular and anti-cancer capacities. A strongly neurotoxic insecticide has been isolated from the segmented seaworm. Although only one group of antibiotics has been developed from marine life, there are probably antibiotic organisms in every class of marine creatures. This is especially the case with algae, which also show promise for anti-cancer work. A number of anti-cancer compounds could well be derived from corals, sea anemones, molluscs and sponges. A palliative for terminal cancer has been found in the poisons of the porcupine fish and the puffer fish. Liver lipids from sharks appear to enhance body resistance to cancer. The sting-ray produces a potent cardiac-depressant material. An extract from the octopus relieves hypertension, the seasnake has yielded an anticoagulant and the menhaden provides an oil which may help with treatment of atherosclerosis. Sea cucumbers yield a substance that may prove better than digitalis in treatment of certain heart conditions. Sea cucumbers also yield glycosides with anti-tumor activity. Several species of seaweed contain an active agent that inhibits the growth of two forms of a virus that cause the common cold sore, severe eye infection and a widespread type of venereal disease. A Caribbean sponge yields a compound that proves effective against herpes encephalitis, a deadly brain infection that strikes many thousands of people each year and against which there has been no worthwhile drug. The sponge's compound thereby supplies a breakthrough in the treatment of diseases caused by viruses, much as penicillin did for diseases caused by bacteria. As a result of this widely hailed discovery, there is now prospect of curing a wide range of viral diseases, from the common cold upwards.

Furthermore, marine creatures assist not only with drug exploration, but they also help scientists with basic research into disease. The female octopus, with its specialized glandular mechanisms, offers clues on the aging process of body cells in humans. The hagfish does not possess a thymus gland, so has no immune system which might cause a rejection of grafts, thus making it an excellent subject for the study of skin grafts. Sea urchins, with their relatively simple life cycles, allow researchers to observe the teratological effect of drugs, since adverse reactions can be noted in a matter of days instead of weeks or months as is generally the case with conventional laboratory animals. The electric eel may one day point the way to development of a form of biological battery. Squids and the seahare, with their specialized nervous systems, are especially valuable to neuroscientists.

Of exceptional potential are the many forms of seaweed.[60] Already seaweed as a food is worth over $1 billion per year and yet most species of seaweed have yet to be analysed as food sources. Seaweed supplies startpoint materials for products that are used as anticoagulants and antibiotics and to treat stomach ulcers, bronchitis, emphysema, epilepsy, high blood pressure, cholesterol problems, atherosclerosis and hypertension. Seaweed also produces a number of gums for use in pharmaceuticals, cosmetics, detergents, emulsifiers and food processing, and it can serve as a source of fibres, plastics, waxes and lubricants.

Despite the many utilitarian benefits already produced by wild species, only limited investigations have been carried out to determine which other species could be of direct and immediate service to society. We know next to nothing of the biological, chemical and mechanical properties of most species identified by science, let alone those species awaiting discovery. As a measure of what awaits us, only around 10 percent of the world's 300,000 species of plants have been screened for any purpose, and only about 1 percent have been thoroughly screened for possible utility to humanity. Yet in view of what has been revealed to date, it seems a statistical certainty that the earth's stock of species offers many new materials of immediate benefit to society — and that these materials will repay, many times over, the costs of preserving species and of exploiting their genetic resources.

6 Disappearing Species: The Economics of Natural Resources

As indicated in the chapter on pragmatic purposes served by plants and animals, species rank among society's most valuable resources. So why does society allow species to go under so fast? This central issue is broached in this chapter, through a review of the economics of natural resources.

Species as common heritage

Species form part of the heritage of humanity. That is how many people perceive species. The general public, notably in developed regions, expresses marked interest in the tiger, gorilla, blue whale and many other species. In the United States, almost twice as many people visit zoos and aquariums each year as attend baseball, football, hockey and basketball games. Many people believe that the heritage of humanity, as well as that of Mauritius, has been impoverished by the loss of the dodo. According to a 1976 Gallup Poll, at least three-quarters of people in both developed and developing countries would like to see more done for wildlife species. Certain citizens even sense a degree of responsibility for species in far-distant lands, as part of humankind's common heritage.

True, many species occur within the territory of a single nation or a few nations, and may thus be regarded, from the strict standpoint of national sovereignty over natural resources, as the exclusive possession of the nation or nations in question. But there is more to the situation than that. For one thing, species constitute integral components of the planetary ecosystem. For another thing, genetic resources from species in one part of the world can benefit people in many other parts of the world, if not of the entire world. Similar illustrations abound. In significant senses, then, the spectrum of species can be considered an indivisible part of the global heritage, now and forever.

Species as common property

Regrettably, everybody's heritage is treated as nobody's business. However much the community may regard species as "the community's estate", it generally has no effective way to express its interest through institutional devices such as ownership. By consequence, the community cannot adopt protection measures that are promoted by ownership. An individual can own a cow, which enables and encourages him to take care of it, and induces others not to use or misuse it. But species are not subject to such "property rights" on the part of society. Nobody automatically looks out for species. If a man poaches a deer, he is far less likely to get into trouble than if he steals someone's cow. The same problems apply, of course, to species' habitats as habitats.

In short, species constitute "common property". The consequence is that, however much they might belong to everybody, they are treated as if they belong to nobody. Worse, common property tends to run into conflict with private property. The owner of a cow prefers to see grass going down his animal's throat, rather than down the throats of buffaloes or antelopes. If the private owner disposes of the wild grazers, he may leave insufficient prey for wild predators, which turn their attention to the cow. Hence the declining numbers of gazelles, tigers, wolves and zebras.

Society's needs in conflict with individual interests

Given the way that society tends to run its affairs, it would not be easy to turn around the sad situation for wild creatures. For centuries, the market-place economy, with its emphasis on private enterprise, has supported the rights of private property (much the same for the law and political systems — see Chapter 7).[1] The needs of common property, such as species, have suffered by default.

The upshot is that the common heritage in species is readily eroded. The main source of trouble lies with economic activity of various kinds. A few species are directly exploited or over-exploited for their products, e.g. furs, meat and eggs. Many more species encounter indirect trouble, through exploitation (not necessarily over-exploitation) of natural resources, e.g. grazing, water, timber, in their environments, leading to disruption of their habitats and life-support systems.

At the heart of the problem, then, lie three key factors. First, species are a legitimate concern of the community at large, as part of the global heritage. Secondly, due to deficiences in its traditional way of running its affairs, the community at large fails to take steps to safeguard its heritage in species. Third, the growing threat to species is a consequence of economic activity on the part of the citizenry at large.

The situation can be illustrated by a brief look at a country that contains an exceptional array of endemic creatures. Madagascar features no fewer than nineteen species of lemur, a special group of primates, all of them threatened. No person or organization in Madagascar exercises ownership over the lemurs. Nor can any authority readily be charged with responsibility to make certain the lemurs survive — not, at any rate, with sufficient power to withstand the economic forces tending towards the lemurs' destruction (principally forest depletion; Madagascar's forests are only one-fifth of what they once were). True, Madagascar can assert that it seeks to exercise ownership rights by declaring legal protection for the lemurs as national resources. But Madagascar cannot adequately enforce this assertion, since too many citizens have a strong interest in seeing the lemurs' forest environments give way to cultivation, and the country has too little capacity to enforce its laws in every last corner of the land.

Much the same applies to the cheetah in Africa.[2] Neither the communities in the dozen principal countries concerned, nor the world community, can exercise property rights or any other form of protective authority to prevent the cheetah being depleted by stockmen who are unwilling to see their domestic herds marauded by a predator with which they share savannah grasslands. Rhinos in Africa face similar problems: in big demand for their horns which purportedly offer aphrodisiacal powers, they are hunted far and wide by poachers who earn as much from one rhino horn as from one year of growing maize. African governments pass laws to protect "their" cheetah and rhinos, but they do not have sufficient enforcement powers to protect scattered groups of cheetah and rhinos across thousands of square kilometers of savannah Africa. So the stockman who disposes of cheetah to prevent commercial loss and the poacher who kills rhino for commercial gain have good hope of getting away with their illegal actions. Still more to the point, the cultivator who digs up cheetah or rhino habitats can hardly be charged with any offence at all, either legal or moral.

Other natural resources of common heritage, such as the atmosphere and large water bodies, similarly constitute common property and are similarly degraded. They are available to any exploiter who wishes to use a patch of sky as a costless garbage can or a river as a no-charge sewer. Species are different only insofar as it is generally their habitats, rather than the creatures themselves, that are appropriated by the private exploiter. In principle, the consequences are the same.

Not that this state of affairs has mattered much until recently. Common-heritage resources have required little protection as long as they were little used, let alone abused. Now that community resources are widely depleted through misuse and over-use, the community finds itself with its institutional pants down. True, a number of developed countries have taken belated steps to tackle the grosser forms of pollution, with the result that the Los Angeles sky and the River Thames are cleaner. As regards species, however, the best that can generally be said is that the situation is no longer declining so fast in developed countries, while in developing countries conservation measures of sufficient scope are in critically short supply.

As common property resources, then, species and their habitats are up for grabs by any exploiter who wishes to make use of them. To use the economist's term, they are subject to "open-access" exploitation. A live animal is usually common property, a dead one readily becomes private property. Species' habitats may belong to nobody as such, but they can be eliminated by a private entrepreneur who exploits associated resources, for example timber from a forest environment. Thus an individual can exploit a tiger for its skin, or more likely (and even worse for the species), he can exploit the tiger's habitat for a variety of purposes — timber, fuelwood, livestock grazing, or cultivation.

Furthermore, whereas other natural resources, such as the atmosphere and large water bodies, can generally be restored after ill treatment, a species is susceptible to terminal misuse. When an excessive amount of a species' numbers or habitat have been converted to restricted purpose through exploitation by private persons, society permanently loses something of unique value. There is no substitute for a species, and there is no turning back from extinction.

Species as "free goods"

Because of the irreversible injury to which a species is prone, and because of its unique genetic attributes, a species is often regarded as beyond normal estimations of value, i.e. as priceless. Yet, because no private owner can trade a species in the market-place and thus establish a dollar price to reflect its economic worth, it is usually treated as if it is price-less, i.e. worthless. True, genetic resources are occasionally exploited via the market-place; for instance, and as documented in Chapter 5, the pharmaceutical industry trades in certain plants and animals as source materials for drugs. But the industry generally exploits only specimens of a species, rarely a species in its entirety, and thus establishes no economic evaluation for the species in itself.

This "worthless" evaluation encourages private entrepreneurs to over-exploit a species as a "free good". This is all the more regrettable in that the good is free only to the few individuals who exploit it, while of considerable scarcity value to society. The peasant who kills a clouded leopard pushes a threated species one step closer to the brink of extinction, even though, when he sells the skin, he may double his annual income. And whereas the benefits accrue to a single person, viz. the hunter, the costs fall on the entire community. If the leopard's continued existence as a species means something because of its intrinsic value, it potentially means the same "something" to everybody. Nobody can be deprived of enjoying this something, just as nobody can be excluded from enjoying a clear sky. To cite the economist's way of looking at the situation, the leopard's value is spread equally among society at large: it represents an indivisible asset of all members of society. So long as the leopard survives, we all win together — and if it disappears, we all lose together.

Conservationists sometimes protest that it should be as unthinkable to destroy a species for whatever passing benefits as it would be to burn a Rembrandt painting to keep warm for an hour. The analogy is correct, but it misses a vital point. The painting is highly unlikely to be burnt, since it will either be in the private possession of an individual citizen (which encourages him to take sufficient care of it), or it will be safeguarded, as a common possession of the general public, in an art gallery (which enables it to be adequately protected). Hence a further dichotomy: a painting of a tiger, as a single "resource" that is subject to a high degree of protection, can fetch $1 million on the art market, whereas it has proved difficult to raise $1 million to protect the high-value resource represented by the tiger species in the wild.

The conflict between priceless and price-less evaluations can be illustrated by one of the most endangered mammals on earth, living in one of the most conservation-minded nations on earth. The black-footed ferret barely survives in the United States. It once occupied a range of 1½ million km², but today it is confined to a few patches of farming country in South Dakota, and still rarer and smaller habitats in neighboring states. It subsists primarily off a single species of prey, the prairie dog. Being a grass eater, the prairie dog competes with man's domestic stock for grazing. The farmers who poison prairie dog populations are not likely to forfeit a significant slice of private income for the sake of an endangered species in their midst. To be sure, if they were to act with extreme public spirit, they would thereby safeguard society's interest. But that is precisely the point. The farmers do not see why they should accept uncompensated sacrifice on behalf of their fellow citizens of the United States, let alone the rest of the world or of future generations. True, the U.S. government has taken out "easements" on a few ferret localities. This arrangement compensates farmers for refraining from poisoning prairie dogs. But the easement initiative, while sound in principle, is far too limited in practice to have much effect on the ferret's survival prospects. Easements worth $18,790 have been taken out on a mere 794 hectares. In other areas, where ferrets are presumed to have disappeared, no compensation is available — and in certain of these localities, where poisoning continues, ferrets have subsequently been discovered.

As is so often the case with natural environment values, the asymmetry of institutional mechanisms promotes farming/market-place interests against wildlife/non-market-place interests. Since no market exists for the "goods and services" which the ferret's survival makes available to society, no one can trade in the ferret's continued existence. If such trading opportunity existed, customers could demonstrate by their dollar votes how far they opt for the ferret's survival in preference to other goods and services such as cheap food or a new set of clothes. The lack of opportunity for the consumer to indicate a preference means the ferret's worth cannot be priced in the way most goods and services are. Conversely, competitive activities in the ferret's farmland habitats are sensitively evaluated in the market-place. Markets pay profits for these competitive activities when they produce beef and bread, whereas next to nothing is paid for the benefits of the ferret's existence.

Although it would be difficult to demonstrate the point, it is possible that the community at large in the United States would like to see its black-footed ferret better protected. To achieve this would mean that present efforts to make the ferret more secure in its last corner of living space would have to be complemented by efforts to get it out of its corner. In turn, this would mean that additional farmers would have to be persuaded to refrain from poisoning prairie dogs, in the hope that this would extend the ferret's range. Were the ferret to be thus accorded better protection, the total economic cost to the United States of foregoing a few extra tons of agricultural produce would be trifling. But within the American system, with its emphasis on private profit to be derived from private property, common property of society's heritage gets short shrift: farmer's interests are allowed precedence over the nation's needs. Millions of American citizens may be willing to pay an additional one-hundredth part of a cent for their beef or bread in order to offset agricultural losses arising from protection for the ferret — just as a nation of 225 million persons may be willing to pay out more than one-hundredth part of a cent per head in annual compensation to save one of the most imperilled creatures on earth. But the private-enterprise system gives them scant opportunity to express their preference on a scale to withstand market forces, since they lack collective mechanisms through which to safeguard collective goods.

In short, it is the dual nature of species — the fact that they constitute resources of common heritage and common property — that lies at the heart of the problem. Yet conservationists do not always recognize this conflict inherent in the situation, together with the need for society-level measures on sufficient scale to counteract the pressures of private interests.

The conflict can be further illustrated by a hypothetical situation. Suppose a conservationist finds himself on a desert island. He notices a huge animal haul itself out of the sea on to the beach. He is relieved to see it, since it represents a large stock of meat — until he is surprised to find it is a Steller's sea-cow, a creature long thought extinct.

As a measure of the sizeable commitment required from conservation bodies to achieve results, let us look at a few recent success stories for threatened species. The whooping crane in North America, which in prehistoric times enjoyed a range throughout most of the continent, and which as late as the mid-1800s probably totalled around 1400 birds, declined, through loss of habitat and hunting among other factors, to only fifteen in 1941. By virtue of massive efforts on the part of conservation bodies, and through governmental outlays that reached $50,000 in 1965 and at least $400,000 in 1978 (more than has been spent on any other threatened species), the crane recovered to 126 individuals in 1977. The vicuna in Peru and patches of neighboring countries, was reduced, through gross over-hunting, to way below 10,000 animals by 1965, and seemed set for a speedy decline into oblivion. Following a series of major initiatives — financial, legal, political — on the part of governments concerned,

and with exceptionally strong support from conservation groups, the
vicuna has now recovered to 60,000. The tiger in India, having fallen
well below 2000 by the early 1970s, is now building up its numbers
once more, but only as a result of a $1 million campaign to save it.

The parable of the grazing commons

The guts of the issue is that private interests do not necessarily run
parallel with public interests. In certain circumstances, private
interests undermine public interests. This runs counter to much
conventional wisdom concerning a free-market economy, as
exemplified by Adam Smith's dictum that, through pursuing his own
interests, an individual is "led by an invisible hand to promote the
public interest".

The problem is well illustrated by the parable of the grazing
commons.[3] The setting is Medieval England. In accord with
traditional practice, herdsmen graze their cattle on common
pastureland. One particular area might be used by ten herdsmen, each
with one cow, the animals not being so numerous as to over-graze the
commons. This means that the herdsmen exploit the pastureland on a
sustainable basis, and they all thrive there. One dismal day, however,
an enterprising herdsmen reckons that it will serve his best interest to
bring another cow on to the commons. This means slightly less grazing
per cow, but for the herdsman in question this loss is heavily offset by
the fact that he now receives two shares of grazing. Exactly the same
argument can be offered by each of the other nine herdsmen to bring a
second cow on to the commons; then for a third cow, and so on. The
outcome will be that each herdsman finds himself poorer and poorer.
But unless the community of herdsmen can agree on a way to share
out the grazing fairly, each individual will reasonably react by trying
to put still more cattle on to the commons, before the others beat him
to it. Thus the tragedy of the commons: while each herdsman works
out a plan for himself that, within the framework of his own needs as
he sees them, is rational, the collective result is that the commons are
wrecked, with disaster for each herdsman.

This story, deriving from Medieval England, is played out time and
again by modern cattle-owners who share communal grazing. For

example, the Masai in East Africa build up their individual cattle herds until the savannah grasslands are on the way to becoming worthless scrub. When crisis point arrives, a larger number of cattle die of starvation. The lesson that each Masai cattle-owner learns from his experience is that when the grasslands recover he should build up his cattle holding as fast as he can before his fellow tribesmen do the same.[4] The overall result is an up-dated tragedy of the commons. The débâcle will be repeated over and over again until the Masai community devises a rationing system that ensure fair shares for all.

In circumstances such as these, there is little mileage in appeals to individuals to "behave better" or to accept a "conservation ethic", an approach that has been urged with respect to stock-raisers, forest cutters, wildlife hunters and many others who over-exploit natural resources. Meanwhile, the situation continues to deteriorate. The trouble does not lie with the moral degeneracy of the individual, however "short-sighted" or "greedy" his actions may appear. Rather the deficiency lies with the way society chooses to regulate — or not to regulate — its affairs.

In face of this dilemma, an institutional initiative is required whereby all members of the community accept a code of "mutual coercion mutually agreed on".[5] This would amount to an arrangement that looks out for the best long-term interests of both the private citizen and of the community at the same time. It would also represent a challenge that human beings, with their traditionally narrow-visioned approach to their individual welfare, would find hard to tackle.

To press the point further, "irrational" activities such as these are not confined to exploiters in the conventional sense, viz. whose who harvest natural resources. It applies to many other persons who use, or misuse, natural resources during the course of their daily lives.[6] Many an enlightened citizen owns an automobile, which enables him to pursue his activities through quick and convenient travel from place to place. He has only to look around him to see that the use of automobiles by many of his fellow citizens causes serious problems, such as traffic snarl-ups, air pollution, road accidents, urban noise and so forth. Yet he values the individual benefits of his own automobile higher than the social costs of adding one more car ("cow") to the road ("commons"). To relieve these problems, the community now asserts itself through various forms of "mutual coercion mutually agreed on", in the form of road tolls, parking meters and the like. These legal constraints do not represent arbitrary authoritarianism on the part of the community. Rather they are accepted by auto owners as a form of necessary organization, and amount to no more "loss of freedom" for the citizen than readiness to drive only on the same side of the road as all other drivers.

Being simple to perceive, these regulations are readily accepted. Not so simply perceived, and not yet readily accepted by car owners, is the wasteful use of petroleum to power automobiles. The world's petroleum stocks are expected to run out within another four decades or so, principally due to the increasing use of petroleum for automobiles. It is already apparent, however, that a far more efficient use of petroleum's unique attributes lies with petro-chemicals, synthetic fertilizers and several other specialist applications for which substitutes are not readily available. The value added for petro-chemicals is 10 times that of gasoline. Automobiles can be powered by means other than burning petroleum. According to this argument, use of petroleum for automobiles should be limited at least by far higher prices for gasoline. However, automobile owners are very reluctant to accept a higher price than the "super-high" prices already in force. Thus automobile owners contribute to the prodigal waste of one of earth's most precious resources.

Direct misappropriation of species

Species can be misappropriated both directly and indirectly. Direct misappropriation arises when man takes an excessive amount of their meat, eggs, hides, horns and other products. Indirect misappropriation arises when man extracts goods from their environments (e.g. timber from the tiger's habitats) in such a way as to undercut their life-support systems.

Direct misappropriation has endangered or extirpated a good number of species. They include the dodo, the great auk, several seal and turtle species, the manatee and the dugong, all five species of rhinoceros, many deer species, certain spotted cats and several crocodilians. These instances are not such clear-cut cases of man's greed and short-sightedness as is sometimes suggested. The depletive process is due more to these species' status as common property. Not only can an exploiter avail himself of a "free" resource, but he sees the resource as available to all comers — a circumstance that encourages him to seize as much as he can before others take their chance. All his fellow exploiters view the resource in the same spirit, each of them seeking to outdo the rest. The self-defeating process compounds itself as the competition grows evermore severe. Too often, the overall result is that the exploiters find it makes economic sense to over-harvest the resource to exhaustion, i.e. to commercial if not biological extinction.

This "irrational" dissipation of a potentially renewable resource is illustrated by the story of the American buffalo.[7] At the end of the Civil War, the buffalo roamed the plains west of the River Mississippi in herds 60 million strong. When the white man started to exploit this "free good", the railroad had not yet reached beyond the Mississippi, so there was no way to get buffalo hides and meat to the markets of the Mid-West and the East. However, a tiny part of each carcass, the tongue, was regarded as a delicacy. The slaughter began. Each animal dispatched resulted in a fine profit for the hunter by virtue of the tongue, while the remainder of the carcass, 500 kg of meat, was left to rot on the plain. After a few years, markets became available for the hides, whereupon the slaughter intensified. For every penny profit on a hide, at least 2 kg of meat were left to rot. During a single decade, millions of buffalo were accounted for, and millions of tons of meat were written off.

There would have been little use in pointing out to an individual hunter that he should limit his exploitation in order to leave sufficient stocks of buffalo for the time only a few years hence when, thanks to the extended railroad, there would be a several-times larger profit through marketing the meat. In response to this argument, he would have commented that if he sacrificed part of his immediate gain in order to cater to his own future needs (let alone the needs of the community), he would almost certainly find that, when the future arrived, other hunters would have finished off the buffalo herds. In fact, he would feel incentive to seize as much as he could before his competitors took ever larger slices of a dwindling pie. Even when he saw the great herds being reduced to final remnants, he would perceive no benefit in slackening his part in the "senseless" slaughter. Rather, he would perceive still more compelling incentive to grab the last scraps of the resource before it completely gave out.

The essence of this sad story is that the buffalo's products could be exploited at a cost which did not reflect society's loss. Buffalo hunters created greater public detriment than private reward. But, as is the case when individuals exploit resources of the community's estate, the advantages accrued to a small group of people concentrated in place and time. This allowed each member of the group to reap appreciable benefit. By contrast, the losses were spread among the collectivity of society, causing each citizen's immediate perceived loss to be small (future members of society had no say in the matter). The upshot was that in just a couple of decades, the once great herds were reduced to a few hundred animals.

Human nature having remained what it is, and society having done little to tackle the "tragedy of the commons", the story of the buffalo is played out with other species, time after time. The only difference is that man can now employ modern techniques of exploitation to enable him to over-harvest more resources faster.

The oceans as a commons environment

A notable instance of intensified over-exploitation arises with those commercial concerns that fish the oceans. The oceans present a classic "commons" environment, a situation that encourages each fisherman to invest in ever-more sophisticated equipment in order to seize a larger slice of the cake than other exploiters. His rivals respond through similar escalation of effort, thus exacerbating the conflict between short-term economic advantage for individuals and long-term husbandry of ocean species for all.[8] In these circumstances, each exploiter soon sees that the path of individual wisdom lies in once-and-for-all exploitation. The inevitable outcome is demonstrated by the recent record in the North Atlantic, where fishing enterprises from a dozen European nations have severely over-harvested twenty-two major varieties of fish.

An equally pertinent case in point lies with the whales.[9] Although the whales may appear an exceptional example of man's feckless attitude to species' survival, whalers are motivated by incentives no different from those who over-exploit fisheries, who over-cut forests, who over-load highways. A whale swimming in the oceans belongs to nobody; when it is killed it becomes the private property of the whaler, and the profit therefrom accrues to the whaler alone. The whaler's action leads to costs of various sorts. All whalers, both present and future, are left with a reduced whale stock, and they will have to spend extra time in finding their next target. Worse still, all people face an aggravated risk of a whale species going extinct. While these costs fall also on the individual whaler who caught the whale, his share of the costs is fractional compared to the sum total of costs.

Obviously it is in the interests of all whalers, as well as all humanity, to find a way to restrict, if not to suspend, whaling. Until such an agreement can be achieved, however, the individual whaler sees clearly where his own best interest lies — to grab another whale before other whalers snatch it away. He sees little merit in isolated sacrifice of his own whaling prospects through holding back from catching more whales. Thus the whaler's exploitation rationale accords with standard practice as regards common property resources — and the whales' reduced status is a cause rather than a consequence of present prodigal-seeming exploitation practices.

A further factor encourages gross over-harvesting of whales. Not only advancing technology, but sky-high interest rates on capital induce the entrepreneur to aim to recover his investment, plus profits, within a foreshortened time span, often as little as half a decade. This militates against considerations of long-term sustainable harvest of resources with lengthy self-renewal periods, such as whales. A whale population may grow at only 5-7 percent a year, a rate way below a typical rate of discount on capital investment, now generally 10 percent or more. In fact, the circumscribed and short-term purview of money markets are so out of kilter with certain of society's needs that it would not make financial sense to invest in conservation of the oceans themselves, with their oxygen-producing capacities.[10] Nor, from a strictly economic standpoint, is it "rational" to bring one's children.

The situation can be illustrated by considering, say, a single stock of 75,000 whales.[11] In biological terms, the maximum sustainable yield from this stock could be around 2000 whales per year. If an average whale is worth $10,000, a sustainable harvest of the stock will yield $20 million per year. Suppose, however, that whalers chose to rule out the prospect of sustained exploitation for the future, preferring instead to kill off the entire stock at one go. They would then derive a lumpsum revenue of $750 million, which, invested at a conservative rate of 5 percent per year, would produce an annual return of $37.5 million. Simplified as these calculations are, they indicate how it would be considerably more profitable to knock off the entire stock forthwith, rather than to plan for a sustained-yield harvest.

Indirect misappropriation of species

So much for direct and deliberate over-exploitation of wild creatures. Most species in trouble suffer indirectly, through heedless exploitation of natural resources (timber, water supplies, etc.) that form part of their habitats.

The golden lion marmoset once inhabited 6500 km² of forest in south-east Brazil. Now the last 600 wild marmosets are confined to a 550 km² path. This forest remnant will not, where exploited to elimination, produce overall economic benefits greater than those which could be generated were the mormoset found to possess medicinal properties similar to the cotton-topped marmoset, a source of a potent anti-cancer vaccine.[12] But forest clearing brings immediate profit to a limited number of individuals, hence the benefits to each are concentrated, appreciable, and readily recognized. By contrast, adequate protection for the marmoset would bring benefits, which, though they would extend over a far longer term, would be spread among many beneficiaries, hence would be diffused and difficult to perceive. Given the way society's institutions weight the choice, short-term benefits for private persons win the day.

The rationale for the marmoset applies, on a larger scale, to forest clearing in Amazonia (see also Chapters 9 and 10). Various projects for smallholder settlements and cattle ranchers may already have caused the extinction of a number of insect species with highly localized distribution in the Amazonian rainforest. The benefits of saving these species would be dispersed, delayed and difficult to evaluate concisely, whereas the benefits of agriculture are immediate, apparent and quantifiable. True, a difference lies in the fact that exploiters of the marmoset's habitat may be aware of their activities' significance for an endangered species (but they have continued their forest clearing since they are unwilling to accept uncompensated sacrifice to safeguard part of society's heritage). By contrast, cultivators and ranchers in Amazonia have almost certainly been unaware of the consequences of their actions for vulnerable species. Fortunately, the Brazilian authorities are now giving more careful thought to their grandiose ambitions for opening up Amazonia.

Similar loss of habitat and disruption of life-support systems occurs in other ecological zones. In grasslands, for example, the needs of man's domestic stock often clash with those of wild herbivores. In South Africa, ranchers shot out the quagga and the blue buck in order to restrict veldt grazing for their cattle and sheep. In Botswana and Namibia, formerly great herds of wildebeest, totalling half a million animals, have been reduced by 90 percent as rangelands are increasingly given over to competitive use by domestic stock. The same story can be told for livestock lands throughout savannah Africa, and in other grassland territories in both developing and developed regions.[13] The problem is not that stock-raisers are callous toward wild creatures, but that society has not yet sufficiently woken up to the idea that it must take stronger steps to protect its heritage.

Institutional deficiences are all the more critical at a time when there are more entrepreneurs than ever who aim for intensified exploitation of natural resources, in implicit indifference to other values at stake. A forest exploiter in Southeast Asia now encounters growing economic incentive to over-harvest the forests in disregard not only of society's needs, but apparently of his own long-term interest. As is the case with marine fisheries and whales, much of the blame lies with exceptionally high discount rates and inflationary fluctuations in money markets, impelling the exploiter to go for quick-return investments (see Chapter 13). The upshot is a headlong harvest of Southeast Asia's forests, exploited through a once-and-for-all operation. As the forests are felled, they take with them the habitats not only of the orangutan and a few other well-known creatures, but many thousands of other species.

A similar process arises with respect to other natural resources. Farmers around the world are frequently criticised for poor cultivation practices that cause valuable topsoil to be eroded away, thus undercutting not only their own means of livelihood but society's eventual capacity to feed itself. Yet farmers do not neglect to protect the soil because they are unusually ignorant or worse. They feel a compulsion to grow as much food as they can with each season that goes by, leaving aside the need to maintain cropland productivity for the longer-term future. This was the rationale followed by American farmers 40 years ago when they brought on the great dust bowl. Even the U.S. Soil Conservation Program has not helped much, despite its financial incentives to individual farmers to look out for the collective good as well as their own private good.[14] After outlays of nearly $15 billion during the 40 years of the Program, no more than one-quarter of U.S. farmlands are adequately protected against erosion. Farmlands overall now lose an average of 22 tons of topsoil per hectare per year, almost twice as much as the Soil Conservation Service considers "acceptable". Altogether this amounts to 3 billions tons (together with 50 million tons of plant nutrients, worth around $7 billion). The loss represents about one-sixth of 1 cm of topsoil, to re-create which can take decades. Far from becoming more "enlightened", many U.S. farmers have recently become more negligent than ever about soil conservation, on the grounds that, at a time of soaring crop prices, they do not want to allocate time and money to any activity that will mean less than record crops. The Soil Conservation Service believes that if U.S. crop output is to be maintained, erosion must be cut by half.

In developing countries, the problem of soil erosion is considered to be twice as bad as in advanced nations. World-wide, the loss of cropland to erosion, plus related problems such as salinization that stem from poor farming, amounts to 50,000-70,000 km^2 per year, an area roughly the size of Holland and Belgium, or West Virginia.

Similar conflicts between individual and community needs, and between short- and long-term interest, afflict people of all sorts and conditions in virtually every part of the earth. Few problems are so pervasive and so demanding of urgent solution, yet so little recognized and understood, as those of common property resources.

Externalities

All through this analysis of the common heritage/common property conflict, there keeps cropping up a central factor: the unwitting "spillover consequences" of people's economic activities when directed at a hundred and one goals other than destruction of wildlife species. To use the economist's language, people unknowingly inflict effects external to their intended context of action, or "externalities".[15] Just as the externalities are almost always unintended, so they almost always remain unremedied. When an economy grows larger, more complex, and more integrated, there is increasing chance of participants treading, however accidentally, on each other's toes — or on unusually vulnerable parts of their surroundings, such as natural environments (the atmosphere, water bodies, species' habitats). The accumulative impact of externalities tends to concentrate at weak points in the mechanisms by which society runs its affairs. Especially susceptible to spillover injury are common property resources, notably species.

Affluent sectors of the global community are responsible for much of the disruptive economic activity that occurs around the world. They thereby trigger many externalities in other countries,[16] and stimulate disruption of remote species' habitats. For example, shoppers in European supermarkets seek beef from Africa at "reasonable" prices, i.e. prices competitive with those of beef from other sources. All unwittingly, they thereby encourage stockmen in African savannah-lands to eliminate a major source of profit loss in the form of the cheetah and other predators.[2] The American consumer of hamburgers wants best quality at least price. Without knowing it, he thereby connives at the destruction of Central America's forests, with mass elimination of species' habitats (for details, see Chapter 10). The timber harvester in tropical forests seeks to meet growing demand on the part of affluent nations for specialist hardwoods. As a profit-oriented entrepreneur, he is reluctant to undertake environmental safeguards as part of his logging operations since his customers might consider the extra costs "inflationary" (for details, see Chapter 13).

As the global economy grows steadily more developed and integrated, international externalities will tend to generate increased impact on species' habitats. In response, conservationists will need to devise strategies that counter externality effects (see Chapter 16). After all, habitat disruption is an unwitting consequence, not an intended cause, of an exploiter's activities, and there is little gain in wagging a finger at him: better ways will have to be found. A daunting task, since it will depart from much conventional wisdom of conservationist circles in the past. But a far from intractable task.

Conclusion

In summary, species constitute unique resources of society's heritage. As such, they deserve exceptional measures for their protection. Regrettably, they tend to be treated as common property resources. As such, they become subject to exceptional degrees of destruction.

Yet an exploiter who misuses a common property resource is not being blind to everybody's ultimate needs including his own. He is pursuing his own immediate self-interest within the rules of the game as laid down by society's inadequate institutions. It is not the exploiter who is to blame, so much as society for not devising better rules. Society's efforts to conserve its heritage should include measures of a nature and a scale to match the individual's incentive to look after his own needs. We shall return to this topic, and consider some practical possibilities, in Chapter 16 and 17.

7 Political and Legal Dimensions of Species Conservation

As the previous chapter has emphasized, the concept of species as part of humanity's natural heritage is little recognized by market-place mechanisms. In fact, species are threatened for the most part because inadequate economic institutions encourage misuse of species and their habitats as common property resources.[1] When private good does not run parallel with public good — both of which are rational interests as perceived by respective proponents — economic systems tend to tilt the balance in favor of private interests. In face of this conflict, there is need for the community to assert itself on behalf of its long-term welfare. A principal means is for public authority to lift the problem beyond the scope of economic mechanisms into the sphere of political and legal initiatives.

The problem of species conservation thus becomes a question of what political scientists call public policy. This opens the way to formulating a consensus about species as part of the common heritage: how far are they worth conserving, at what cost to the collective pocket in comparison with other collective purposes, and so on? This in turn can lead to practical proposals for species' conservation, notably legal measures that establish land-use controls, environmental regulations, taxes, subsidies and the like.

So, at any rate, runs the public-policy process in individual countries. In the United States, for example, various legal doctrines articulate community concern for community values. They enable society's wishes as regards species to over-ride private interests that seek to over-harvest certain species or to cut away the habitat from under other species. At international level, however, the process straightway runs into major difficulties. While global society might want to see species better conserved, it cannot readily over-ride

sectoral interests in the form of individual nations within whose
territories species exist. Thus arises the dilemma of national
sovereignty over natural resources that form part of humankind's
patrimony. This core conflict lies at the heart of much of the species
problem, and is worth dealing with in some detail.

National sovereignty and the global community

The concept of national sovereignty has been steadily reinforced for
practically the entire time since the term was first coined 400 years
ago. It implies that nations, as independent political units, have a
sovereign right to do as they wish within their national boundaries.
The concept is especially appealing to those many developing nations
that have only recently won independent nationhood after lengthy
periods under alien control. These nations are understandably
sensitive about any encroachment on their sovereign freedom to go
their own way. And it is in developing nations that most species exist.

Yet only two decades after the number of independent nations
around the globe has grown from around 60 to over 150, the practice
of sovereign independence is, in certain respects, becoming something
of a charade. However much this may sound an unrealistic
interpretation of the current scene, it increasingly reflects the actual
nature of nations' dealings with each other by contrast with
national leaders' rhetoric about independence. By virtue of trade
patterns, monetary systems and myriad other international
relationships, nations are becoming ever-more intricately involved in
each others' affairs. As long as governments and private
entrepreneurs engage in transactions with organizations from outside
their national borders, foreigners are in a position to affect their
national interests. It is an inescapable fact that every international
transaction is subject to the influence of more than one sovereign
state; and a hundred solemn declarations by governments to the
opposite effect do nothing to alter the objective facts.

This growing limitation on sovereignty applies clearly to developed
nations, with their push for endless economic growth. It applies at
least equally to developing nations, which, though they frequently
wave the flag for their new-found political independence, seek rapid

economic advancement for their impoverished peoples, and thereby need to play a growing role in the international economy. These nations are increasingly aware that many of their natural resources acquire value only by virtue of international markets. They also recognize that these resources can often be exploited only through highly complex technology, for which they must turn to foreign capital and expertise. In short, developing nations, like developed nations, are swapping certain images of independence for the benefits of interdependence.

Increasingly, then, it is a fact of international life that a nation's sovereignty can be permeated through inflation, currency fluctuations, shifts in trade patterns, and so forth. As a result, it is less and less the case that the nation as an expanding economic unit, and the nation as an independent political unit, pursue identical goals. In addition, nations are affected by common predicaments that are political as much as economic in nature: the population question, international terrorism, the threat of nuclear war and the energy and food crises (both oil and grain can be used as political weapons). However much politicians around the world may proclaim the ideal of sovereignty, the course of their daily dealings with each other often demonstrates the converse.

These new trends could make it easier for the global community to assert itself in support of its global heritage. It is scarcely realistic any longer to assert that just because species exist within the territories of individual nations, they therefore constitute natural resources over which the nations exercise sovereign rights. The world hardly works in such absolute terms any more. For the community of nations to express an interest in what happens to species within the jurisdiction of a single nation need not be construed as unjustified interference. It is no more an "encroachment on sovereignty" than international measures to regulate trade patterns, investment flows, inflation, health controls, even the international mailing system and transportation networks.

As global society grows more interdependent it grows more vulnerable to disruption through externality effects. As indicated in the previous chapter, the accumulative impact of externalities tends to concentrate at weak points in the mechanisms by which society runs its affairs — notably at linkages in the "resource relationships" that reflect the common heritage/common property conflict. A decline in global grain supplies, especially in the world's main bread basket, North America, induces more peasants in tropical countries to break new land on which to plant their subsistence crops. In turn, expanding subsistence agriculture eliminates wild or primitive forms of crop genetic resources that are needed to maintain the productivity of North America's croplands.

This recent undermining of national sovereignty represents a basic change in the international scene. It is one of the greatest changes ever to confront nations since the emergence of sovereignty as an acknowledged concept. It is probably a greater change than those precipitated in the past by widespread wars. It is in recognition of this change that nations increasingly engage in new international structures to supercede the old system of independent nations. Nations cede slivers of sovereignty to international bodies such as the United Nations and the Organization for Economic Cooperation and Development; they cede significant slices of sovereignty to regional groupings such as the North Atlantic Treaty Organization and the Association of Southeast Asian Nations, and to trade organizations such as OPEC; and they cede considerable chunks of sovereignty to integrative units such as the European Economic Community. As President Carter has asserted, the main problems confronting the world "lie beyond the reach of the individual nation-state, no matter how powerful it might be .... A central concern of (the United States') foreign policy in the remaining years of this century must be the building of more effective international bodies such as the U.N. system".

These voluntary steps toward broader political orderings reflect a growing acknowledgment of interdependence. Increasingly, people perceive new needs and opportunities of the shifting international scene. According to a 1976 Gallup Poll, citizens in many countries recognize that certain major national problems are related to, and can be partly caused by, what is happening in other nations: in the United States, 62 percent of persons questioned agreed, in Western Europe, 61 percent, and in Japan, 45 percent. In Brazil, however, only 29 percent assented, suggesting that people in a developing nation are less inclined to recognize that interdependence has become an established phenomenon of late twentieth-century life. In fact, only a few developing-world leaders will openly go along with the idea that, while the nation is still the main political and administrative unit at international level, it is less and less a functional unit in terms of its economic, social, cultural and environmental activities. Yet without perception of the new state of affairs, there will be little urgency to devise new political mechanisms for the global community. Regrettably, certain nations continue to insist that the best way to tackle international questions is through national institutions alone, rather than in conjunction with broader-scope mechanisms to meet the new challenges.

Exclusive and inclusive rights and activities

In these circumstances, a central dilemma lies with rights and activities that can be either exclusive or inclusive. This is a basic issue of international law — and, like the concept of sovereignty, it is in a state of flux, however little that fact may be recognized in some sectors of the global community.

"Exclusive" refers to those rights and activities that affect predominantly only one nation. The term is thus associated with national independence. "Inclusive" refers to those rights and activities that have significant effects for other nations, or externality effects. Thus the term links up with interdependence. By implication, "inclusive" refers especially to those resources that are, in whatever degree, resources of common heritage (generally resources of common property, too). Examples include the earth's air mantle, the oceans and major water bodies, marine fisheries, rare geomorphological features, exceptional ecosystems, and species. Some of these, e.g. the earth's air mantle and the high seas, are clearly resources that belong entirely to the entire community. Yet they are sometimes subject to exploitation by individual countries with severe repercussions for all humankind. France or China explodes a nuclear device in the atmosphere, and thereby exposes people in far-away lands to radioactive fallout. Virtually all industrialized nations use the open oceans as dumping grounds for huge amounts of toxic chemical wastes.

Other categories of resources, such as exceptional ecosystems and species, "belong" to individual nations on the grounds that they are located within territorial jurisdictions. At the same time, they are clearly of legitimate interest to the community at large. This applies equally to major tracts of forests, with their "watershed services" for territories far beyond the forestlands themselves. A nation may exploit its forests as resources over which it believes it exercises sovereign rights; and the nation thereby engages in what is, from certain standpoints, an apparently exclusive activity. Yet the forest exploitation, if not strictly regulated, may precipitate severe spillover consequences for other nations. Deforestation in Nepal leads to disruption of river systems (flash floods, followed by reduced flow) for nations downstream, viz. India and Bangladesh, causing $2 billion of damage in mid-1978. Widespread forest exploitation in Indonesia or Brazil can lead to extinction of untold stocks of species. As economic and technological activities grow evermore advanced and complex, they trigger off growing numbers of externalities within an increasingly integrated global community. In turn, the adverse impact of these activities on common heritage/common property resources becomes more pervasive and acute.

The situation has been graphically expressed by two Yale law professors, McDougall and Schneider:[2]

"It is today widely recognized that the globe — or, more precisely, the entire earthspace environment — is an ecological unity both in a basic scientific sense and in the interdependencies of the social processes by which man uses it. All living creatures, including man, that inhabit the planet, are united with each other and with their non-living surroundings by a network of complex and interdependent natural and cultural components known as the "planetary ecosystem". . . . It is the more specific ecological unities or interdependencies of this comprehensive ecosystem which make it a single shareable, and necessarily shared, resource. What is true about interdependencies in the enjoyment of the atmosphere, the oceans, the air space and outer space, drainage basins, and land masses when considered separately, is equally true of the indivisible whole which they comprise."

This illuminates the dilemma of inclusive and exclusive rights and activities of nations, with particular regard to environmental resources. Certain resources, due to their outstanding importance for the community at large, deserve to be maintained as shared resources under inclusive competence, as free as possible of exclusive competence or dominance. These resources include the atmosphere, the climate and weather, and the oceans and major water bodies. Almost all species occur within the territories of individual nations, yet they should, in some sense, be considered as an inclusive interest of the entire community. Thus species straddle both exclusive and inclusive concepts, a situation that raises complex difficulties for their conservation. Much the same applies to tropical moist forests, as was acknowledged by a pioneering statement of the Eighth World Forestry Congress in Jakarta, Indonesia, at the conclusion of its deliberations in October 1978:

> "The many goods and services which flow from forests . . . are increasingly needed by all peoples of the world, whether they are urban or rural dwellers, whether they live in the tropics or in temperate zones, and whether they inhabit forested regions or treeless deserts and tundras. . . . The Congress therefore declares that the world's forests are for all people, irrespective of longitude and latitude, irrespective of income, irrespective of age or sex, irrespective of race, religion and color, and irrespective of political boundaries."

The community of nations is faced, then, with a growing problem of resource exploitation and environmental spillovers. The problem has not been ignored by international bodies, even though they have taken few practical steps to face up to the challenge. The 1972 Stockholm Conference on the Human Environment came up with a Declaration that asserted, under Principle 21, that

> "States have, in accordance with the Charter of the United Nations and the principles of international law, the sovereign right to exploit their own resources pursuant to their own environmental policies, and the responsibility to ensure that activities within their jurisdictional control do not cause damage to the environment of other states or of areas beyond the limits of national jurisdiction."

Similarly, the recent Charter on Economic Rights and Duties of States proclaimed, under Resolution 3281 of the U.N. General Assembly, that

> "The protection, preservation and enhancement of the environment for the present and future generations is the responsibility of all States. All States shall endeavour to establish their own environmental and developmental policies in conformity with such responsibility. The environmental policies of all States should enhance and not adversely affect the present and future development potential of developing countries. All States have the responsibility to ensure that activities within their jurisdictional control do not cause damage to the environment of other States or of areas beyond the limits of national jurisdiction. All States should cooperate in evolving international norms and regulations in the field of the environment."

Significantly, both these last two statements stress the responsibility of nations to make sure that their own activities do not harm the environment of "downstream nations". It is clear how this responsibility applies to the environment of nations in close ecological association. How about nations further afield, with which the relationships may not be so direct and plain? If a nation is to avoid activities that may harm "the environment of other nations", may this not mean the planetary ecosystem in the sense referred to by McDougall and Schneider? Were a nation to cut down a sector of its forests that included the sole habitat of some bird species, could this not be construed as eliminating an integral component of the planetary ecosystem, and thus inflicting a degree of environmental injury on all nations?

High-value resources: rights and interests

The argument can be carried further. A number of resources, notably oil reservoirs, are located, through geographical accident, within the territories of only a few nations. Oil is of such critical importance to the welfare of all nations that the entire global community can assert a strong legitimate interest in how it is made available. A case can even be made for "rights of access" on the part of all needy nations, as well as "rights of possession" on the part of the fortunate few. A similar case can be made for a range of high-value resources, such as grain reserves, fertilizer stocks and other scarce commodities.

Indeed, the time may be coming when the earth's endowment of high-value resources will be seen as an asset to be handled for the benefit of all mankind. This will mean that the community of nations will have to reconsider what is implied by ownership, management, use, allocation and conservation of these resources. This would be a tough and virtually unprecedented challenge. Yet some step of this sort may become necessary as global society grows ever-more hungry for critical resources. As long as there seemed to be plenty of oil to meet everybody's needs for ever, there was no need for a commonly agreed way to share out earth's bounty. Now that we are into a fundamentally different scene, the ways of the past no longer measure up.

It is within this perspective that the problem of species can be looked at afresh. The guts of the situation boils down to this: outright possession of an individual species is generally limited to a few nations (if not a single nation), whereas significant benefits can accrue to all nations (through modernized agriculture, medicine and other pragmatic purposes). Much the same applies to tropical moist forests: if the forests continue to decline through over-exploitation on the part of possessor nations, the adverse repercussions will fall not only on the nations in question and on neighboring nations (through degradation of watersheds, river systems and the like), but on nations far and wide (through disruption of climatic paterns, elimination of exceptional concentrations of species, etc.). As already pointed out, the two sets of problems are inter-related. The principal cocoa-growing nations are located in West Africa, while the genetic resources on which modern cocoa plantations depend for their continued productivity are found in cocoa's original source areas, the forests of Central and South America. The principal banana-growing nations are in Central America and the West Indies, while the genetic base is in the forests of South-east Asia.

In sum, then, the challenge of conservation of species, as of tropical moist forests, is of special concern to the entire global comunity. Even though almost all species exist within national jurisdictions, their survival can hardly be viewed as a matter solely for the nations in question. This implies two forms of responsibility — highly compelling responsibility, considering what is at stake. First, any nation faces a duty to safeguard the species within its territory, on behalf of all humankind. Second, all humankind faces a duty to offer whatever support is required — finance, skills, etc. — to enable individual nations to discharge their duties. What these responsibilities could mean in practical terms is considered in Chapter 16.

Part II

TROPICAL MOIST FORESTS

8 The Special Case of Tropical Moist Forests

The biome with greatest abundance and diversity of species is the tropical moist forests.[1] Estimates for the numbers of species range from two-fifths to one-half of the planet's total, i.e. somewhere between 2 and 5 million. Moreover, tropical moist forests are being more rapidly disrupted than any other biome, to the extent that many observers believe that large sectors may not survive, except in grossly degenerate form, by the end of the century. At the same time, the biome is less known than virtually any other. We understand little of these forests' ecological workings, and most of their species have yet to be identified, let alone documented. In 1972 the Tasaday tribe was discovered in the Philippines' rainforests, separated from the outside world by a mere 25 km of forest and apparently isolated since Neolithic times.

Actually, there are two main types of tropical moist forest. Some receive at least 400 cm of rainfall per year (occasionally as much as 1000 cm), making them very wet areas. These are properly known as rainforests, or wet evergreen forests. Other areas receive "only" 200-400 cm of rainfall (and at least 12 cm in the driest month), which still makes them much wetter than, say, New York with 105 cm. These are known as moist deciduous forests. Both types together make up "tropical moist forests". The richest forests are the wettest ones. In various parts of Latin America, a patch of rainforest is likely to contain half as many species again as a patch of moist forest (and three times as many as a dry forest).[2] Rainforests cover a large proportion of the moist forest zone in Latin America, but a relatively small part of Southeast Asia and very little of tropical Africa.

Of the 12 percent or so of the earth's land area that enjoys a warm damp climate all year round, tropical moist forests still occupy well over half (Table 2). Probably once covering about 16 million km², the total extent now amounts to 9.35 million km² at most.³ Somewhat over 5 million km² occur in Latin America, 2.2 million in Asia (largely in Southeast Asia), and 1.75 million in Africa, with patches in a few Indian Ocean and Pacific Ocean Islands. So far as is known, Latin America has lost around 37 percent of its original tropical moist forests, Southeast Asia 38 percent and Africa almost 52 percent.⁴

Table 2
Tropical moist forest areas
(millions of km²)

Region	Present moist forest area	Percent of total land area	Percent of total tropical moist forest area	Total moist forest climax area	Percentage regression of climax area
Total Africa	1.75	36.2	22.6	3.62	51.6
East Africa	0.07	10.6	1.6	0.25	72.0
Central Africa	1.49	65.9	16.8	2.69	44.6
West Africa	0.19	19.1	4.2	0.68	72.0
Total Latin America	5.06	51.2	50.2	8.03	37.0
South America	4.72	53.5	46.9	7.50	37.1
Central America/ Caribbean	0.34	31.9	3.3	0.53	35.8
Total Asia/Pacific	2.54	37.2	27.2	4.35	41.6
Southeast Asia	1.87	67.4	18.9	3.02	38.1
South Asia	0.31	24.4	5.3	0.85	63.5
Pacific	0.36	12.8	3.0	0.48	25.0
Total Humid Tropics	9.35	42.8	100.00	16.00	41.6

Source: After Sommer, A., 1976.³

Although tropical moist forests comprise only one-third at most of the world's forests, they contain four-fifths of the earth's vegetation on land.⁵ One hectare of primary forest may comprise plant material weighing 650-1000 tons (the animal biomass may be only one-five-hundredth as much). With year-round growth, a forest can produce as much as 70 tons of plant material per hectare per year — almost twice as much additional biomass as is generated in the earth's forests as a whole, and a higher level of productivity than for any other vegetation type except for a few forestry plantations and high-yielding agricultural crops such as sugarcane and irrigated rice. Because organic matter is speedily decomposed, however, annual net increment in an undisturbed forest is usually nil.

Not only do tropical moist forests feature many local variations, due to different altitudes or to soils with different fertility and drainage systems, but many of them underwent fundamental transformations during the late Pleistocene, when glaciations in the northern hemisphere were matched by repeated expansion and contraction of tropical forest ecosystems, producing marked local differentiation in conditions. So these forests, some of which date back 60 million years and are the oldest ecosystems on earth, have experienced exceptional stability and continuity at times, with opportunity for evolution to go its way undisturbed, while at other times they have undergone sufficient "creative disorder" to stimulate fresh evolutionary trends.

The result is that tropical moist forests have developed extreme ecological richness. Southeast Asia, for example, with only 2.5 million km², or less than Western Europe, is conservatively reckoned to comprise 25,000 species of flowering plants, or about one in ten of the world's flora. The Malay Peninsula alone has 7900 such plants in its 132,000 km², while Great Britain, with an area almost twice as large, has only 1430 species. A single hectare of forest near Manaus in the heart of Brazil's sector of Amazonia has been found to feature 235 tree species,[6] whereas one hectare of temperate forest normally features no more than ten species. Moreover, of 100 tree species in a typical hectare of Amazonia's forest, as many as half may be different from the array in another hectare only 1 km away. This means that many tropical tree species are comparatively rare — a situation that makes certain species liable to local extinction when the forest is subject to intensive exploitation. In Amazonia, one specimen of each of two trees was located more than 50 years ago, and neither has been encountered since.[7]

The same richness applies to animals. The Sunda Shelf sector of Southeast Asia, roughly the western part of the region, harbors 297 species of land mammals and 732 species of birds, whereas Europe west of the Soviet Union, an area nearly four times as large, totals only 134 and 398 respectively.[7]

Self-perpetuation and regeneration

A tropical forest has not had to cope with annual feast-and-famine conditions such as characterize temperate zones with their seasonal changes. Instead, tropical trees reflect an environment with much continuity.[8] As a result, a tropical forest is little able to tolerate the abrupt and broad-scale disruptions that modern man can inflict.

As an example of tropical trees' adaptations to little-varying conditions, let us consider their systems of regeneration. Tropical-tree seeds generally feature little or no capacity to remain dormant. Whereas the seeds of a temperate-zone tree may well lie unchanged for 10 years before finally sprouting into life, the seeds of trees in tropical Latin America sometimes survive no more than 25 days. Moreover, tropical tree seeds are acutely sensitive to changes in environmental conditions. The dipterocarp family of trees in Southeast Asia produces seeds that germinate only as long as the micro-climate does not vary outside 23-26°C. This means that when a timber exploiter breaks open the canopy and allows the soil to heat up to over 40°, most if not all seedlings die.[9] By contrast, temperate-tree seeds survive the heat of summer and the cold of winter year after year. Although some tropical trees flower and seed almost continuously, certain species have flowers that complete their cycle in one day, or are receptive for only a few hours around the middle of each day, while other trees seed heavily only every third year, a few only every 10th year, and an occasional species only every 35th year.

Moreover, since there is not much air movement beneath the dense forest canopy, there is little wind-borne pollination. For instance, in 40 hectares of forest in Brunei, only 1 out of 760 tree species is wind pollinated.[10] So most tree and plant species rely on insects, birds, bats and other creatures to transport their pollen. In some localities of Southeast Asia, teak tree pollen is carried by only two bee species. Since many pollinators must operate across wide stretches of forest, many tree species are acutely susceptible to disruptions of the scale that man inflicts: the chance extinction of a small population of pollinators can lead to the local elimination of a tree species, which in turn can lead to the elimination of certain insects that depend on it for food — which in turn can lead to further elimination of tree populations, and so on. In Central America, every one of forty species of fig trees has its own pollen vector;[11] if a local ecosystem is so disrupted that a vector cannot survive in sufficient numbers to ensure pollination, the population of the tree species in question is similarly doomed.

Nutrients and soils

Central to the functioning of tropical moist forests is the cycling of nutrients through their ecosystems, a vital sector of the cycle occurring within the soil and its humus layer. Except for recent alluvial and rich organic soils, tropical forest soils are very old, and hence poor.[12] Because of high rainfall that leaches away minerals, it is "inefficient" for the forest ecosystem to leave nutrients lying around in the soil. So evolutionary processes have responded by developing a virtually leak-proof system. Many forest trees have tap roots reaching 30 m below ground, while lateral roots can extend 100 m from the trunk. The network of roots, 3 times as dense as in a temperate forest and amounting in some instances to as much as one-quarter of the tree biomass,[13] absorbs nutrient washed into the soil from rotting vegetation on the forest floor, allowing far less than 1 percent of nutrients to be lost to the cycling process.

In addition, the continuously high temperatures and humidity of forest environments make for a high rate of decomposition. Leaf litter can be broken down in 6 weeks, as compared with 1 year in temperate deciduous forests, and 7 years in boreal conifer forests.[14] By virtue of this ultra-rapid cycling, the forest stores as much as 75 and even 90 percent of its nutrient stock in its vegetation. The result is that forest soils have virtually no exchangeable minerals such as calcium, magnesium, potassium and phosphorus, which leaves them highly acid and infertile. Contrary to popular reputation, the forest thrives despite its soil rather than because of it.

Because the ecosystem's nutrients are held almost entirely in the vegetation, felling or burning of the forest triggers a flood of minerals into the soil. After 1 or 2 years of heavy-rainfall leaching, this stock may be washed so deeply into the soil that it is beyond the reach of the new plants — grasses, shrubs, etc. — that replace the forest trees and that feature only short roots. The nutrient cycle being broken, fertility disappears fast, and can be restored only by increasing amounts of fertilizer. Moreover, when the forest cover is eliminated, the exposed ground often bakes under the tropical sun into a concrete-like surface, causing massive water runoff and soil erosion. Generally speaking, a forest ecosystem, even on undulating terrain, allows erosion of way under 1 ton of soil per hectare per year, whereas the same area can lose 20-160 tons if the forest is replaced with dense tea plantations, 20-200 tons in the case of man-established pasturelands and 1000 tons or more for field crops.[15] Forests also help to prevent erosion in areas far removed from their location, through their "sponge effect". While the forest cover is intact, rivers run clear and clean, and, more importantly, they flow regularly throughout the year. When the forest is cleared, rivers start to turn muddy, and swollen or shrunken.

As experience has demonstrated time after time, clearing of the forest can readily lead to a chain of degradation. Within a few years there remains an impoverished land on which the forest would have great difficulty in re-establishing itself.

Secondary forest

Hitherto this account has dealt only with old and mature forest, what is commonly known as "primary" or "virgin" forest. When this form of forest is removed, and natural vegetation is allowed to regenerate in its own way, the immediate result is a formation which differs fundamentally from the original ecosystem. The make-up of plant species is different, the structure and functioning of the community is different, the ecosystem is less diverse. However, the secondary forest tends to develop slowly toward a formation akin to that of primary forest and in time, provided all the necessary complex factors are available, the primary forest takes over again. But secondary forests tend to hold their ground for long periods; after 600 years, the vegetation of cleared areas around Angkor in Kampuchea (Cambodia) reputedly does not fully resemble the surrounding areas of undisturbed "climax forest". When certain lowland rainforest ecosystems are grossly disrupted or destroyed, the successional process to a mature primary forest ecosystem may take as much as 1000 years.[16] By contrast, a temperate-zone forest recovers much more quickly. By the mid-1800s there was not much original forest left in West Virginia. Now a large part of the state is covered with forest again, and in another 300 years the forest ecosystem will probably be very similar to the original one, except that there will be no elms or chestnuts or passenger pigeons.

Man's impact

Man has exerted profound impact on tropical moist forests for millennia. This is apparent from the fact that suitable climatic conditions are available in roughly 12 percent of the earth's land surface, yet only 58 percent of this zone supports forests (true, part of the discrepancy lies in soil factors). Much of the deforestation was caused by primitive man, who burned back the forest-edges century after century. This was the case especially in Africa, where prior to modern times the forest may have been reduced by as much as 1 million km², or an area 4 times the size of Great Britain or as large as Texas and New Mexico.[17] Through this lengthy destructive process, many thousands of species have almost certainly been eliminated by the forebears of modern man.

In recent times, forests in all three main tropical regions have been steadily reduced. The predominant factor has been peasant agriculture, coupled with the use of wood for fuel. In addition, the last 20 years have seen two further major factors. First, and especially in Central and South America, large tracts of forest have been burned to make way for modern agriculture, notably stock-raising pasturelands. Second, forests have been increasingly exploited for their highly valued hardwoods. This has been particularly significant in Southeast Asia and in the West African sector of Africa's forests, and it is becoming important in Amazonia. The accelerated rate of timber exploitation has been fostered by expanding technology. Instead of the man-powered saw and axe of the 1950s, a modern chainsaw can slice through a tree in a matter of minutes. Caterpillar tractors with cable-winch and blade handle outsize logs with ease. A tree-crusher can topple and pulp several forest giants in 1 hour, while a complex of modern machinery can clear a whole hectare of forest in just a couple of hours.

The overall impact of this expanding exploitation of forests and forestlands is that we could be losing as much as 245,000 km² of tropical forests each year, or almost 50 hectares per minute (see Chapter 11). While these are very rough-and-ready figures, they give an idea of the scale of present destruction. When the figures are extrapolated, they suggest that all tropical moist forests could be destroyed within less than 40 years.

This is a crude reckoning, since advanced technology could encourage more intensive and efficient use of forests and forestlands, thus relieving pressure on virgin areas. Conversely, as human populations increase, the urge to clear forests will grow progressively. Population growth in most of the countries in question is exceptionally high. Whereas the United Nations estimates a growth rate for the world of 1.6 percent per year, and for developing countries as a whole of a little over 2 percent, West and Central Africa is put at 2.6 percent, Southeast Asia's at 2.7 percent, and tropical America's at around 3 percent. By the end of the century, Nigeria's populace is projected to grow from its present 76 million to 135 million, Indonesia's from 142 million to 235 million, and Brazil's from 114 million to 212 million. Still more critical than the upsurge in human numbers could be the upsurge in human aspirations. Per capita GNP in these three countries amounts respectively to only U.S. $140, 120 and 580 per year. Crudely expressed, almost twice as many people by the end of the century are likely to generate at least twice as much pressure, and far more than that in view of their growing aspirations. It is not unrealistic, then, to surmise with IUCN[18] and many other authorities, that the end of the century could see the elimination of large areas of tropical moist forests.

At the same time, of course, it is important to recognize that the devastation will not be evenly spread throughout the biome. At the one extreme, most lowland forests of the Philippines and Peninsular Malaysia are likely to have been logged over by 1985; much the same applies to West Africa. Little could remain of Central America's forests within another 10 years. Virtually all of Indonesia's lowland forests seem certain to have been exploited for timber by the year 2000; something similar could well hold good for Colombia and Peru, where, together with extensive areas of eastern Amazonia in Brazil, cattle ranching could claim large tracts of virgin forest. In Central Africa, however, where low human densities and an abundance of mineral resources induce far less incentive to convert the forests into quick cash, there could well be large expenses of little disturbed forest by the end of the century; and because of its remoteness, the same could apply to western Amazonia in Brazil. The overall outcome, then, is likely to be "patchy", and a figure for average rates of forest conversion throughout the biome should be considered from the standpoint of individual countries.

Certain it is, however, that if present patterns of exploitation persist, the foreseeable future will witness the elimination of vast tracts of tropical moist forests. This would not be the first time that extensive sectors of earth's forest cover have been removed. Europe used to be forested for 90 percent of its area until around A.D. 900 when steady conversion of forestlands to agriculture gained momentum. Now Europe's forests account for only 20 percent of the continent. At the time of Columbus' arrival in North America, the moist eastern portion of what is now the United States was covered with dense forests, covering 1.6 million km^2 to the edge of the great plains; now less than 5 percent remain in virgin form. Some of this forest clearing did not have adverse repercussions for the agricultural communities that thereby developed; and so far as is known, very few species were eliminated, since many non-tropical creatures prove adaptable to the intrusions of man. By contrast, broad-scale elimination of forests in the tropics will have a far-reaching impact, through soil erosion, etc., on agricultural communities; it will disrupt various other forms of development, e.g. generation of energy through hydropower facilities (dams will silt up as a consequence of deforestation); and the fallout of species could well reach hundreds of thousands if not millions.

Loss of species

The elimination of species in such numbers would represent a distinct loss to society. Already tropical-forest species have made a major contribution to human welfare.[19] They have supplied the origins of many staple foods, rice, millet, cassava, pigeon pea, mung bean, yam, taro, banana, pineapple and sugarcane, to name but the better known. A huge cornucopia of further foods waits to be investigated. In Indonesia alone, around 4000 plant species are thought to have proved useful to native peoples as food of one sort or another, yet less than one-tenth have come into wide use. At least 1650 plants of tropical forests offer highly nutritious leaves. In New Guinea, 251 tree species bear edible fruit, though only 43 have been brought into cultivation; a hitherto uncultivated fruit of Southeast Asia, the mangosteen, has been described as "perhaps the world's best tasting fruit".[20] A vine from tropical forests of southern China, known as the Chinese gooseberry, bears fruit with juice 15-18 times richer in vitamin C than orange juice. Nor are all these foods limited to local consumption; high-protein beans from Nigeria have found favor with Wisconsin farmers.

Moreover, tropical moist forests contain many wild relatives of modern food crops. These crops, the refined products of genetic engineering, require constant "topping up" with fresh germ plasm in order to resist new types of diseases and pests, environmental stresses and the like, as well as to increase productivity and nutritive content. During this century, genetic resources from the wild have saved a number of important crops, including bananas, sugarcane, cocoa and coffee. To give an idea of economic values involved, groundnuts worldwide have suffered from leaf-spot diseases — a problem that proved surmountable through resistant varieties from wild forms in the rainforests of Amazonia among other areas. The annual value of eliminating the disease is estimated, by the International Crop Research Institute for the Semi-Arid Tropics, at $500 million. Similar large-scale benefits could be documented for rubber, coconut and palm oil.

Forest animals too can assist modern agriculture. Within the forests of the Thailand/Kampuchea (Cambodia) border lives a secretive cow-like creature, the kouprey. This animal is believed to have been one of the wild ancestors of the humped zebu cattle of southern Asia. So fresh cross-breeding between the two bovids could boost cattle raising throughout an entire region. Regrettably, the kouprey's survival is doubtful, due to military activities within its habitats during the past 15 years. Other wild bovids of Southeast Asia's forests, such as the selatang, the tamarau and the anoa, could possibly help cattle raising. Like the kouprey, their numbers have all been severely reduced through man's disruption of their life-support systems.

Not only can tropical moist forests serve as sources of new and improved foods, but they can help to keep down the numerous pests that reduce the amount of food already grown around the world.[21] Despite an annual pesticide bill of several billion dollars, at least 40 percent of our crops are lost each year to insects and similar pests, both in the fields and in storage. A sound way to control pests is to utilize chemicals from plants that have developed mechanisms to repel insects. The main source for these plants is the tropical moist forests, with their extraordinary variety of plant forms that have co-evolved in balance with their insect associates. Pest control can also be advanced through selective breeding of adapted species of insects — a method that could prove more effective and economic in the long run and result in less environmental disruption than broad-scale application of persistent toxic chemicals. For instance, the little-documented ichneumonid wasps, comprising many thousands of species in tropical moist forests, could offer much potential as predators and parasites of insect pests. According to a recent study by the U.S. Department of Agriculture, biological control programmes that entail importation of counter-pests from abroad into the United States are believed to return $30 for every $1 invested. For example, citrus growers in Florida have been able to save their industry $25-35 million a year through a one-time outlay of $35,000 for the importation of three types of parasitic wasps.

In addition to providing a hefty boost to agriculture, tropical moist forests are earth's main repository of drug-yielding plants. The highest percentage of alkaloid-bearing plants is to be found in lowland rainforests, and the yield of these plants is the highest.[22] At least 70 percent of plants that are known to possess anti-cancer properties, 3000 species in all, exist in the tropics, and a similar proportion in tropical moist forests. The huge stock of tropical forest plants that has still to be investigated from scratch could well supply a similar proportion of anti-cancer drugs. In addition, recent research suggests that many insects, notably butterflies, offer potential for anti-cancer compounds — and tropical moist forests harbour between 1.5 and 3.5 million insect species. It is on these grounds that the U.S. National Cancer Institute believes that the widespread elimination of tropical moist forests could represent a serious setback to the anti-cancer campaign.

To grasp what a single species can contribute to medicine, let us take a look at a small shrub of deciduous moist forests from India to Southeast Asia, the Serpentine Root. This plant has been used for 4000 years to treat snakebites, nervous disorders, dysentry, cholera and fever. In the late 1940s the plant turned out to be a fine hypotensive agent, and by 1953 it was used to relieve hypertension and schizophrenia. Shortly after that, its extract reserpine became the principal source of materials for tranquillizers. Before that time, high blood pressure strongly disposed a patient toward stroke, heart failure or kidney failure, but today this one plant helps many millions of people to lead a reasonably normal and healthy life, partially freed from a set of ailments — hypertension — that constitute the single greatest and fastest-growing source of mortality in advanced societies. As long ago as the early 1960s, this first modern tranquillizer generated sales in the United States worth $30 million per year.[23]

In the developing world, the most widespread disease is malaria, afflicting 350 million people a year. Resistance to synthetic insecticides has been developed by fifty-seven species of mosquito (mosquitoes also spread filariasis, encephalitis, yellow fever and several other viral diseases). This means that at least one-third of all people exposed to malaria are now subject to increased risk. India, which reduced its 100 million cases in 1952 to 60,000 in 1962, recorded 6 million cases in 1976. This opens up renewed scope for the cinchona tree of Amazonia, whose bark yields quinine.

Let us also look briefly at a category of drugs that is of growing importance — those that serve as contraceptives and abortifacients. The rhizomes of a climbing vine, the Mexican yam, yield virtually the world's entire supply of diosgenin, from which a variety of sex-hormone combinations are prepared, including "the pill". (Apart from its exceptional role in regulating global population, diosgenin leads to manufacture of cortisone and hydrocortisone, used against rheumatoid arthritis, rheumatic fever, sciatica, certain allergies, Addison's disease and several skin diseases including contact dermatitis.) By the mid-1970s the world was using up to 180 tons of diosgenin per year; by 1985 the amount could rise to as much as 500 tons, and by 1995 to 3000 tons, if the contraceptive needs of all women at risk are to be met. Right now, 80 million pills are used each day, and if total needs were recognized and catered for the figure would probably be 2½ times higher. Current sales of Mexican yam materials for contraceptive pills amount to $7 million per year; when chemical compounds have been made up, the figure rises to $70 million, and when cross-counter sales for final products are totalled, the figure amounts to $700 million. In view of this end-product turnover in the commercial market-place, and in view of the fact that the yam has not been persuaded to grow anywhere but in tropical moist forests, the Mexican government decided in 1974 to seize a larger part of the action through jacking up export prices. As a result, 1 kg of diosgenin, that cost $11.25 in 1970, cost $152 in 1976.[24]

A third category of products derives from tropical moist forests — specialist materials for industrial use. The range is wide. From Southeast Asia's forests alone come latex, gums, camphor, damnor, resins, dyes and ethereal oils.[25] In the wake of the cyclamate and saccarin controversies, there is urgent need for a non-nutritive sweetening agent, and many plant pigments, such as carotenoids in sweet-tasting fruits, serve as attractants in nature, so almost certainly are non-toxic to mammals, including man; there is prospect of several sources of sweeteners among forest plants of Southeast Asia, where many fruits are exceptionally sweet tasting.

One group of industrial products is especially important, oils and lubricants. Many forest plants bear oil-rich seeds, e.g. the Babassu palm, the Seje palm, several species of the *Caryocar* genus, and a number of other trees that grow wild in Amazonia.[20] The Babassu's fruit contain up to 72 percent oil, which can be used to produce fibres, cattlefeed, soap, detergents, starch and general edibles, and can serve as a substitute for diesel oil.[26] Similarly, the "petroleum nut" of the

Philippines produces a highly volatile oil, and was used by the Japanese as fuel during World War II.

Many other plants of tropical moist forests could offer utilitarian benefits to man, if their economic potential is investigated before their forest habitats are eliminated. Until fairly recently, the ramin and kuku trees of Southeast Asia were considered weeds. One hundred years ago the value of the rubber tree was not remotely recognized. Who knows what new "rubber tree" now stands in the way of some settlement project in Borneo or a ranching enterprise in Amazonia? How many tree species are there like the Monterrey Pine which existed in four local sites in California, and was undergoing steady reduction in numbers, until it was tried out as a plantation species, whereupon it became possibly the most important timber tree in the southern hemisphere? Tropical moist forests could contain many thousands of local endemic species like the Monterrey Pine, any of which could be forever lost in a single month's cutting for a forestland development project. This is not an unduly pessimistic prognosis. A tree that was once a major source of timber in Ecuador's lowland forests swiftly lost its native habitats to plantations of bananas and oil palms after its wildland home was opened up by a road in 1960; it is now reduced to twelve reproducing individuals in less than 1 km^2 of forest at the Rio Palenque Biological Centre — the Centre itself being the last surviving patch of lowland wet forest along the western base of the Andes in central Ecuador, and containing almost fifty species of flowering plants no longer known anywhere else.

Not only wild species quickly disappear in their hundreds of thousands as tropical moist forests are cut and burned, but also another valuable "resource" is likewise headed for oblivion, and that is the large number of forest-dwelling tribes who still pursue their traditional way of life. The number used to be much larger. In 1900 there were 230 tribal groups living in Brazil's sector of Amazonia, totalling 1 million people, but now there are only 143 groups numbering 50,000 people. On humanitarian grounds alone, forest tribes should be permitted to adapt to the outside world at their own pace. These considerations apart, the demise of forest peoples is all the more regrettable in that they represent a fund of experience whose value can hardly be estimated. Amerindians of Amazonia know of 750 plant species with medicinal properties.[27] It was from Amazonian tribesmen who use curare, a muscle relaxant, on their arrow tips as a hunting poison, that Western-world surgeons learned of the substance's potential for human operations.[28] A single village of forest dwellers in northern Thailand uses 119 plant varieties for medicine and 295 for food.[29] Forest tribes of Southeast Asia also supplied knowledge about the winged bean, a protein-rich plant that is now upgrading diets in over fifty countries. Many tribal peoples are aware of plant products that serve as contraceptives and abortifacients.[30] Indonesia's National Biological Institute tells of a tribe that utilizes a forest tree as a spermicide, while certain South Pacific islands feature a number of forest plants that are used as first-month abortifacients.[31] The World Health Organization is searching for safer and more effective materials from which to manufacture an improved "pill", and believes the most likely source lies with tribal peoples who have used 3000 plant species for their anti-fertility properties.[32]

Global climatic consequences of deforestation in the tropics

As this book has already pointed out, destruction of species and tropical forests reflects the way both developing and developed nations go about their affairs. All are implicated; all will lose. It is appropriate therefore to end this chapter with a further dimension to the prospect of disappearing tropical forests. Due to climatic effects, there could be broad-ranging consequences for lands far outside the tropics, on a scale that would generate significant changes in lifestyle for many developed nations.

Although no conclusive scientific evidence has been presented as yet, a number of scientists believe that widespread clearing of tropical moist forests might affect climatic patterns in temperate zones.[33] For one thing, cleared forestlands could start to reflect greater solar heat than before (the "albedo effect") and in turn, this could lead to changes in global patterns of air circulation, wind currents and convection processes. So far as climatologists can tell, a not unlikely outcome would be a decrease in rainfall in the equatorial zone, an increase of rainfall for lands between 5 and 25 degrees North and

South, and a decrease for lands between 40 and 85 degrees in the North (not so much change in the southern hemisphere because of the greater extent of oceans). These climatic changes could prove critical for forest-growing territories of the northern temperate zones, notably the U.S./Canada grainlands.

Secondly, widespread elimination of tropical moist forests could contribute to a build-up of carbon dioxide in the earth's atmosphere (though it would make little or no difference to oxygen stocks). Carbon dioxide now amounts to about 0.03 percent of the atmosphere, as compared with 78 percent for nitrogen and 20 percent for oxygen. The concentration of carbon dioxide has recently been increasing. Until 1860, when the Industrial Revolution stepped up the burning of fossil fuels, the concentration amounted, at most, to 290 parts per million. During the next 100 years it expanded by 20 parts or so, and the past 20 years have seen an increase of a further 20 parts. At the current rate of increase, which is itself increasing, the pre-1860 "natural" amount could well double by the year 2050 or soon afterwards.

Until recently it was thought that the increase was being absorbed partly by the oceans and partly by the earth's forests, especially by tropical moist forests with their huge capacity to soak up carbon dioxide through photosynthesis. Now, however, as forest burning overtakes the tropics, tropical forests probably serve no longer as a great natural "sink"; rather they could become a net source of carbon dioxide.[34] It has been estimated that if tropical forests were to be converted into carbon dioxide during the next 50 years, and to be replaced by no other vegetation that stores carbon dioxide on a similar scale, the process could dump carbon dioxide into the atmosphere at about the same rate for fossil fuels.

The consequences of carbon dioxide build-up could be severe. Carbon dioxide traps sunlight in the atmosphere and, through the "greenhouse effect", causes the earth's temperature to rise. Twice as much carbon dioxide in the atmosphere seems likely to cause an average global increase of 2-3°C, a greater temperature change than has occurred during the past 10,000 years. As with the albedo effect, one result would be warmer and drier weather in the North American grain-growing region. A temperature increase of only 1°C could decrease U.S. corn production by 11 percent and could cut the gross income of spring wheat farmers by $268 million (at 1977 prices).[35]

In addition, burning of huge amounts of tropical forest timber could lead to a great deal of particulate matter being released into the atmosphere. This troposphere dust could increase atmosphere subsidence, again leading to less rainfall.

In sum, then, elimination of tropical moist forests affects not only developing countries in question, but it could precipitate severe if not critical consequences for countries of the developed world as well. In other words, we either all lose together or, through sufficient conservation measures, we all gain together.

9 Regional Review

In view of important differences between the three main regions of the tropical moist forest biome, let us take a good look at each.

(a) Amazonia

Of tropical America's moist forests, around 6 out of 8 million km^2 lie in Amazonia — "Amazonia" here being taken to mean the lowland-forested parts of the 7.8 million-km^2 drainage. This forest tract, 85 percent of which is dense lowland rainforest, comprises well over half of all moist forests in the tropics. It covers an area equal to the United States east of the Rockies; on its own it would be the ninth largest nation on earth. Over three-fifths of Amazonia lies in Brazil, making up almost half the country. Of the seven other countries that share the basin, Peru, Ecuador and Bolivia have over half their national territories in Amazonia.

Although Amazonia is reputed to comprise the richest biological system on earth, it remains a scientific vacuum. From the 1850s, when Bates undertook a preliminary exploration and catalogued over 8000 new insect species, virtually no broad-scale investigation was conducted until the early 1970s. As a measure of our ignorance about Amazonia, a major new tributary hundreds of kilometres long has just become widely known, while entire mountain ranges are proving to be far away from where they were thought to exist.[1] We are also learning that Amazonia is far from being one vast wet rainforest. In fact, only limited areas receive year-round rainfall. There are at least three main ecological zones; namely, the "varzea" floodplains, the "igapo" swampforests and the "terra firme" upland forests. As much as 300,000 km² contain little or no forest and another 500,000 km² can be counted as "transitional zones".

Without doubt, Amazonia is, biologically speaking, the richest area on earth. As mentioned in Chapter 2, Amazonia contains at least 50,000 species of higher plants, or one in five of all such plant species on earth.[2] It also features one in five of all birds on earth. While all too little is known about most animal species in Amazonia, it is reasonable to suppose that the region features a similar proportion of the planetary spectrum. It is known to contain not only the largest reptile on earth, the 12-m anaconda, but the largest insect, a 15-cm beetle.

Fortunately, we are now forming a good idea about which localities in this huge region deserve priority conservation. As a consequence of Amazonia's evolutionary ecology, a number of lowland areas feature high concentrations of species.[3] During the Pleistocene, a period which lasted from around 3½ million years ago to a mere 10,000 years ago, Amazonia underwent a series of climatic fluctuations. Sometimes the region was as wet as now, other times the rainfall was much less, and extensive sectors of the forest disappeared for a while. This cycle of advance and retreat of the forest probably occurred at least twice and perhaps four times. During the drying-out phases, forest species were confined to a number of isolated patches of damper climate, or "refuges", from which surviving species could later re-colonise the expanding spread of forest when wetter times returned. Certain areas of forest have now been identified as centres of diversity, with exceptional concentrations of species, many of them endemics. These areas could well correspond to the Pleistocene refuges. Clearly, conservation programs should concentrate on these areas, sixteen of them in all.

During the past 10 years, several of the countries of Amazonia have begun to open up their forestlands for exploitation and settlement. (For details of Brazil's major effort, see Chapter 10.) Amazonia contains the world's largest stocks of timber; Brazil's stocks alone are reputed to be worth $1 trillion. Although timber exploitation has hitherto been negligible compared with Southeast Asia, tropical America's forest exports are projected to increase from 3 percent of world trade in 1967 to about 10 percent in 1985, or from 1.1 million m³ of logs to 6.4 million.⁴ Peru, for example, which currently imports much of its timber and paperpulp, hopes to produce 50 times more wood than at present through exploitation of its 650,000 km² of Amazonia forests. To achieve this, Peru is considering an investment offer of $500 million from Japanese wood-chip corporations.⁵

Amazonia also contains the world's most extensive reserves of minerals. These minerals occur primarily in peripheral areas such as the eastern slopes of the Andes, a factor that has prompted the countries concerned to settle their border territories in order to secure their deposits. In addition, a sharp increase in demand for beef, both from within and outside Latin America, has fostered a growing urge to convert forests into man-made pasturelands (see Chapters 10 and 11).

At the same time, there has been something of a spirit that believes that Amazonia's forestlands should be exploited merely because they are there, and exploited only for their commercial products. In certain extreme instances there has even been the pioneer's response to the forest, that the only good tree is a cut one. Far more forestlands have been cleared than are needed to meet the needs of expanding agriculture and little attempt has been made to utilize the vast amounts of timber felled to open up lands for crops and pastures. This is not to say, of course, that Amazonia should not be developed and exploited. The question is: what is the best way to achieve highest sustainable use of the region's natural resources, for greatest benefit to people concerned, both now and in the future?

So far as we know — and the picture is very unclear — around one-third of Amazonia's forests have already disappeared, much of them during the past 25 years. The present rate of clearing is estimated by the Food and Agriculture Organization to have reached 125,000 km² per year, an area almost half the size of Great Britain, or the size of Virginia. Of this clearing, the great bulk, at least 100,000 km² occurs in Brazil, while Colombia loses 10,000 km² per year, and Peru and Ecuador appreciable areas. Venezuela, with large oil revenues to fund its development programs, has decided that it will stop exploiting its Amazonian territories until it has carried out scientific surveys to determine the best ways to tackle the challenge.

Clearing of this order means that, even if the rate were not to increase, Amazonia's forests would be eliminated in little over 50 years. Considering that the rate itself has been accelerating since the late 1960s, the speed of exploitation could increase more and more until the 1990s could see as much clearing as all past years put together. So it is not unrealistic to suppose that a large portion of Amazonia's forests could disappear as early as the end of this century.

What would be the ecological repercussions of this clearing? To date, scientists have little clear idea. The main thing that they know is that man tampers with such a large and complex ecosystem only at risk of some potentially severe consequences. Let us consider a single possibility. Through Amazonia's vast hydrological systems flow two-thirds of all fresh water on earth. Less than half of the region's rainfall drains away into rivers, the rest being returned to the atmosphere through evapotranspiration. Equally, a good part of the rainfall derives from moisture circulation patterns within the region, rather than from outside, e.g. from the Atlantic. This means that the region serves as a source of much of its own moisture.[6] The implications are profound. When a part of the rainforest is cut down, the remainder could probably be less capable of evapotranspiring as much as was circulating through the ecosystem before. In turn, this could mean a steadily desiccating ecosystem. And so on, with each reduction of the forest expanse. At what stage could the lowland rainforest start to be transformed into a different kind of forest? Has the process already begun? If so, how far has it gone? Could it still be reversed?

To date, we scarcely know how to formulate the correct questions about what is probably the most complex ecosystem on earth, let alone supply the right answers.

(b) Southeast Asia

The wettest and richest of Southeast Asia's forests are located mostly in Indonesia, Malaysia and the Philippines. The rest of Southeast Asia, viz. Indo-China, Burma and Thailand, tends to feature mixed and semi-dry deciduous forests.

The three countries in question cover 2.5 million km², of which 1.87 million are reputed to be still under primary forest. This amounts to one-fifth of all tropical moist forests. Malaysia's and Philippines' forests have been heavily exploited for commercial timber for at least 25 years and the bulk of their primary forests have been grossly disrupted or eliminated. Indonesia's forests have been exploited for only the past 10 years or so and the country still believes it possesses 1.2 million km² of forest.

Extensive as Southeast Asia's forests are, they amount to less than one-third the size of Amazonia's. Yet in terms of abundance and diversity of species, Southeast Asia is at least half as rich as Amazonia, and it greatly surpasses any other similar-sized region on earth. Unit area for unit area, Southeast Asia is probably the richest region on earth. This is largely because its rainforests have been able to evolve continuously over a period of at least 60 million years. During the dry stages of the late Pleistocene, when the forests of tropical America and Africa contracted to fragments, Southeast Asia did not suffer a heavy fallout of species: its archipelago, lying in a maritime rather than a continental setting, proved less prone to desiccation. As a result, the main sectors of Southeast Asia contain a remarkable number of plant species: Java 4500, Sumatra 6000, Sulawesi 5000-6000, Philippines 7000, the Malay Peninsula 8000, New Guinea 8000, and Borneo 9000-10,000 (less than half of them overlap). Each area is likely to feature a proportionate number of animal species, roughly ten to thirty for each plant species. The tiny state of Brunei in northwestern Borneo, only 5000 km², is believed to contain 2000 tree species, whereas Holland, 7 times as large, possesses only thirty.

Not only does Southeast Asia feature large numbers of species, but it features a high degree of endemism. The region comprises more than 20,000 islands. This implies that many of its biotic communities have enjoyed a fair period of ecological separation. In turn, this means plenty of opportunity for speciation in those power-houses of evolutionary adaptation, the moist forests. Whereas Amazonia features localized centres of diversity and endemism that are believed to indicate the sites of Pleistocene refuges, much of the western sector of the Southeast Asia archipelago can be regarded as one vast refuge that recently became fragmented into islands by the rising sea levels of a few thousands years ago.[7] In the present Malay Peninsula, which, being a long narrow extension of a continental land mass, supplies much of the genetic isolation found on islands, 152 of 317 bird species are endemic (whereas only 10 of 108 non-forest birds are endemic).[8] Something the same applies to the eastern sector of the archipelago. Of Papua New Guinea's 670 bird species, 320 are endemic; of the Philippines' 180 mammal species, more than half are endemic. In the region overall, many species are confined to small islands, which makes them vulnerable to swift destruction as forests are given over to exploitation (virtually the whole of 4480 km² Siberut Island off the west coast of Sumatra, with four endemic primates, is scheduled for logging). To this extent, Southeast Asia deserves priority attention over Amazonia and tropical Africa — all the more so in view of the rapid rate at which its forests are being disrupted.

From an economic standpoint, the most important trees of the region — and indeed of the tropics as a whole — are the dipterocarp family of trees, with over 500 species. Supplying high-quality timber that is exceptionally light and suitable for plywood and veneer, the dipterocarp forests have been widely exploited since World War II, and particularly so since 1960. This trend has been due mainly to growing developed-world demand for tropical hardwoods, now earning $2 billion a year for Southeast Asia.[9] By the early 1970s the region was accounting for 70 percent of all exports of tropical hardwoods and in 1976 Southeast Asia exported 23 million m³ of logs, mostly to Japan. Moreover, being located close to the most populous region of the world (1.7 billion people live within 5000 km of Singapore), Southeast Asia can look forward to a vast future market right on its doorstep.

If present exploitation trends persist, pretty well all the lowland forests of Peninsular Malaysia and the Philippines will be logged within another 10 years. The same will apply to most lowland forests throughout the region by the end of the century. In addition, many tracts of logged forests are being steadily converted to agriculture, both through shifting cultivation and through organized settlement. Indonesia is converting 180,000 km² of forest to permanent agriculture during the period 1976-85, Peninsular Malaysia plans to convert 20,000 km² over the next 20 years and the Philippines loses 10,000 km² to a combination of organized agriculture and shifting cultivation each year. In late 1977 the Deputy Premier for Peninsular Malaysia, Mr. Datuk M. Mohamed, acknowledged that by about 1990 Peninsular Malaysia will have to import hardwood timber. In the Philippines, President Marcos has proclaimed a virtual crisis in forestry. He has restricted the export of unprocessed logs and seeks to impose a complete ban as soon as possible. Through a recent decree, he requires every male over 10 years of age to plant 1 tree per month for the next 5 years. For a detailed treatment of Indonesia, see Chapter 10.

(c) Tropical Africa

Tropical Africa[10] contains, so far as can be ascertained, about 1.75 million km² of moist forests, an expanse a little less than Southeast Asia's and less than one-third as large as Amazonia's. Of this total, almost 1.5 million lie in Central Africa (Zaire, 1.1 million) and 190,000 in West Africa.

Africa's moist forests, like those of the other two regions, contain localities of high species endemism. At certain stages of the Pleistocene, the forest dwindled to a few isolated patches.[11] In fact, it was not until around 12,000 years ago that they expanded again to stretch right across the continent. During the times of greatest contraction, four main areas survived as "refuges", to serve as reservoirs of plant and animal species from which the forests were later able to re-establish themselves. The four areas are the Upper Guinea Refuge, comprising parts of Liberia, Ivory Coast and Western Ghana; the Cameroon-Gabon Refuge, extending into eastern Nigeria and parts of Congo; the Central Refuge, located in northern and eastern Zaire; and a Mountain Refuge complex, comprising the highlands of Cameroon and the East African mountains. Clearly, these areas deserve priority conservation, though the planning of parks and reserves in the countries in question rarely appears to take account of this "refuges rationale".

Fortunately, extensive sectors of Africa's moist forests are not under nearly so much threat as their counterparts in the other two regions. In fact, it is thought that, whereas 0.4 million km² have already undergone some exploitation, and another 1.1 million km² are potentially exploitable, a large proportion, perhaps as much as half, could remain little affected by the year 2000. In Central Africa, the equatorial forest is expected to lose only 350,000 km² or 23 percent of its 1.5 million km². This positive prognosis is due to low population pressure: Zaire has almost 5 hectares of forest per head of its populace, Congo 17, and Gabon 43. Moreover, these countries possess appreciable deposits of minerals, so they sense little compulsion to exploit their forests for timber, cash-crop agriculture or stock raising.

By contrast, a major loss of forest is likely to occur in West Africa, with critical consequences for certain of the species refuges. The West African forest has already declined from perhaps 700,000 km² to 190,000 or less, and is likely to drop well below 100,000 by the year 2000. The destruction will be partly due to commercial logging; in a number of countries, notably Nigeria and Ghana, virtually all remaining forest has been allocated for concessional exploitation. At least as much, and possibly far more, destruction will be due to slash-and-burn cultivation. Ghana has only 0.2 hectare of forest per head of population, and Nigeria 0.07, so pressure to exploit the last remnants of forest is great and growing.

All in all, Africa's moist forests lose at least 25,000 km², and conceivably as much as 40,000 km², each year.[12] At least 400,000 km², or one-half of tropical Africa's zone of cultivated crops, are located in the rainforest region. If, as is likely, each of 8 million new people per year needs half a hectare of cultivated land, the forest loss does indeed reach 40,000 km² per year.[13]

Tropical Africa's output of commercial wood has been steadily increasing. In 1976 production of industrial timber amounted to 32 million m³, of which almost 6 million were exported, three-fifths from West Africa. As a measure of rapid destruction taking place in West Africa, Ivory Coast, according to aerial surveys, has already lost between one-third and one-half of its virgin forests and is currently losing over 5000 km² each year, a rate that is accelerating. In 1964 the country exported forest products totalling 1.5 million m³ and worth $49 million, and in 1976 3.3 million m³ worth, $280 million. If present patterns persist, Ivory Coast will lose virtually all its primary forest by 1985.

10 Four Country Profiles

Let us now look in more detail at exploitation trends in four countries of the tropical moist forest zone: Brazil, Costa Rica, Indonesia and Kenya.

Brazil

Of the Amazon basin's 6 million km² of forests, 3.6 million lie in Brazil. Thus Brazil contains a far greater expanse of tropical moist forests than any other nation on earth, 3 times larger than Indonesia's or Zaire's. At the same time, the Amazonia sector of Brazil, while comprising 42 percent of the country's area, contains only 5 percent of its 121 million people; an area as large as the Sahara, it contains as few people as the Sahara. Moreover, it contributes less than 5 percent to GNP; its timber stocks have been estimated at $1 trillion, yet they contribute only 10 percent to Brazil's output of industrial timber. The region also contains the world's largest reserves of high-grade iron ore, plus appreciable deposits of bauxite, tin, uranium, diamonds, coal and gold, the last worth perhaps $30 billion.

So Brazil tends to look upon its tract of Amazonia as a valuable asset going to waste, lacking people, capital, technology and, above all, a spirit of enterprise. Little wonder that opening up Amazonia is looked upon by many Brazilians as "our moon shot". Politicians, economists, planners, entrepreneurs, all become euphoric at prospects for speedy development: "Amazonia cannot wait, Brazil cannot stop".

To exploit Amazonia, Brazil has embarked on an ambitious program to criss-cross the region with roads.[1] The Transamazon Highway, begun in 1970, extends for around 6000 km, a distance greater than from New York to San Francisco. Subsidiary roads will total another 12,000 km. (Similar road-building programs are underway in Ecuador and Peru.) Ironically, Amazonia contains the largest continuous network of rivers on earth, with 50,000 km of navigable waterways. To dredge this system would cost less than to construct major roads, and would cause far less environmental injury.

Along the roads of the Highway system, a 20-km belt of forestland has been designated for agricultural development. The settlers were originally supposed to come mostly from Brazil's famine-stricken northeast, with its 37 million impoverished people; Amazonia was to be, in the words of former President Medici, "a land without men for men without land". But the settlement program now envisages an immigration rate of only 100,000 persons per year, which would amount to less than the annual increase of the northeast's population. Settlers have been offered 100 hectares of free land, plus crop seed, the equivalent of 6 months wages and a rough wooden house. Yet only 1 in 15 of the 100,000 families expected has so far arrived and by 1975 the total of 50,000 "colonists" had almost stopped growing. Many homesteaders have tried to grow unsuitable crops. Many have been immobilized by diseases of the forest to which they have no resistance (conversely, they have introduced bilharzia and Chagas' disease into the region). Worst of all, the soils have proved poor. Preliminary results from Brazil's remote-sensing survey reveal that only 4 percent of Amazonia's soils have medium to high fertility. A good number of settlers have abandoned the plots allocated to them and turned to slash-and-burn cultivation — the type of uncontrolled settlement that was to be expressly avoided. Wildcat fires started by shifting cultivators acount for 10,000 km^2 of forest every year.

All in all, it is now reckoned that less than 7 percent of the planned settlement can be called successful. Due to a plethora of problems, including widespread soil erosion and threats from hostile forest tribes, government support for the settlement program is falling off, and officials are taking a longer look at the ecological aspects of developing Amazonia. As a result, funds are dwindling and construction of certain side-sectors of the Highway has been halted for the time being.

A more realistic settlement program could focus on high-fertility areas within Amazonia. The periodically flooded zones, with their rich alluvial deposits, amount to only a small fraction of the region, yet altogether they cover around 60,000 km², an area almost the size of Ireland or West Virginia. These "varzeas" could support an agriculture as rich as any known on the River Nile, costing not a penny in fertilizer. Moreover, they do not feature such biotic complexity, or diversity of species, as the upland forests. They are well suited to fast-maturing crops such as beans and corn and especially to crops which favor floodplains such as rice. Whereas irrigated lands outside Amazonia produce 4-5 tons of rice per hectare per year, a number of commercial plantings in varzeas yield 18 tons per hectare through three crops per year.[2]

The emphasis in Amazonia agriculture has now shifted almost entirely away from small-scale pioneers toward large agro-business entrepreneurs, most of them ranching operations. A potential rancher, like other investors, is attracted by generous terms. He receives a rebate of 50 percent of his income tax on activities elsewhere in Brazil. Certain forms of equipment and other capital can be imported into the country duty-free. Tax holidays abound. An investor from overseas can repatriate his profits and capital. Yet the new herds will supply only a mere fraction of Brazil's demand for meat, and in fact much of the beef will be exported (see following chapter).

The largest foreign enterprise in Amazonia is at Jarilandia, on the River Jari near Belem.[3] In 1967 Daniel K. Ludwig, head of the American corporation National Bulk Carriers, purchased 15,000 km², a tract larger than Connecticut, for a reported $10 million. In this multiple-activity project, varzea soils produce an average of 10-12 tons of rice per hectare per year, 2½-3 times the United States' average. Jarilandia also includes plantation forestry and stock raising. By 1976, 73,000 hectares, out of an eventual 100,000 hectares, had been planted with gmelina and pine trees, to feed a $275-million pulpmill that will produce 750 tons a day by 1981 — enough to make a single strand of toilet paper stretching 6½ times round the world (though the pulp will be used for other products as well). Stock raising is a marginal enterprise, undertaken through a herd of 12,400 head of cattle to supply meat to a present labour force of 4,200 persons and an anticipated labour force of 30,000 by 1985. Eventually the workers, plus ancilliary-service personnel and families, could add up to a community of one-quarter of a million people. As luck would have it, the property contains one of the world's largest deposits of kaolin, used in bleach printing of paper. Ludwig's investment has reputedly reached $650 million, and the ultimate total could be far greater.

Although Amazonia's timber industry is small-scale compared with Southeast Asia's and tropical Africa's, an estimated 1 million trees are felled each day.[4] In 1971 a single area of the Territory of Rondonia featured five sawmills; by 1978, thirty. Major corporations include Eldal of Japan, Bruynzeel of Holland, and National Bulk Carriers, Georgia Pacific and Atlantic Veneer of the United States, with a total investment just short of $15 million.

Such, then, are some patterns of forestland exploitation in Brazil's Amazonia. Between 1966 and 1975, 44,000 km² (or 38 percent of total deforestation) were accounted for through cattle ranching, 35,000 (31 percent) through smallholder settlement and other agricultural colonisation, 30,000 (26 percent) through highway construction and 5000 (4 percent) through timber extraction, making up a total of 115,000 km².[5] Of these activities, cattle ranching, although the least appropriate since poorly productive and hardly sustainable, is growing the fastest. Brazil envisages that eventually 400,000 km² of forest will be cleared for agriculture and almost as much again for other purposes. How far this ambitious program of forestland exploitation will be carried through depends in major measure on how much capital is pumped into the region. Overseas capital brought into Amazonia by over fifty foreign firms, one-quarter of them North American, already totals more than $200 billion.[6] Future investment will be required on such a large scale that Brazil is making ever-greater efforts to attract the foreign entrepreneur.

Thus exploitation patterns in Amazonia point up the economic-ecologic linkages that operate among the global community. Amazonia is being exploited in part to supply natural resources to international trade. In addition, much exploitation is being carried out through the medium of multinational corporations that supply the capital, skills and technology without which Amazonia could not be developed so rapidly. In one part of the region, only 30 percent of purchasing capital stems from within Brazil, the rest comprising 30 percent American, 20 percent West Germany, 10 percent Japanese and 10 percent other foreigners.

Costa Rica

A remarkable record in conservation is presented by Costa Rica. A small country of only 49,900 km², or little larger than Denmark, it possesses one of the richest biological endowments of any country on earth — and is taking solid steps to protect its heritage.

The country features 758 bird species (only 138 of which are migrants) or more than North America north of the Tropic of Cancer. A mere 2.6 km² of lowland forest have been found to contain 269 bird species, about twice as many as in all broad-leaved forests of eastern North America.[7] Over 8000 plant species have been recorded, with at least 1000 orchids. The La Selva Forest Reserve, 730 hectares, contains 320 tree species, 42 fish, 394 birds, 104 mammals (of which 63 bats), 76 reptiles, 46 amphibians and 143 butterflies.

The number one factor in elimination of all types of forest in Costa Rica — as is the case for several other countries of Central America and Amazonia — is the cattle rancher. Beef is produced mainly for export (see Tables 3,4). Almost all the beef is despatched to the United States, where, according to the Grupo Ganadero Industria of Costa Rica (a ranchers' organisation) and the Meat Importers Council of America, most of it makes its way into the hamburger and frankfurter trade. From the early 1960s, fast-food chains in the United States have boomed, until they grew in 1974 alone by 20 percent, or 2½ times as fast as the restaurant industry overall.[8] Over half of all sales are accounted for by only eight firms, notably the major hamburger corporations. The largest, Macdonalds, sells 3 billion hamburgers each year with total sales worth $3 billion; in the process, it accounts for the equivalent of 300,000 head of cattle.

As a result of this booming business, the fast-food trade has looked for additional supplies of meat, finding a source of cheap beef in Central America. The beef is "cheap" only in relation to supplies within the United States, which, with high land and labor costs, is over

Table 3

Central America exports of beef

Country	Cattle numbers ('000 head)	Slaughter ('000 head)	Production (million kg)	Export* (million kg)
Guatemala				
1964	n.a.	n.a.	n.a.	4.8
1971	1585	361	63.9	22.1
1977	2270	456	80.8	25.4
Honduras				
1964	n.a.	n.a.	n.a.	4.0
1971	1598	317	38.1	20.9
1977	1712	338	46.4	23.9
Nicaragua				
1964	n.a.	n.a.	n.a.	11.0
1971	2102	325	63.5	34.2
1977	2719	380	72.7	32.9
Costa Rica				
1964	n.a.	n.a.	n.a.	8.7
1971	1573	229	50.2	24.9
1977	1970	285	66.1	44.0
Central America, total **				
1964	n.a.	n.a.	n.a.	28.4
1970	9174	1379	245.8	79.2
1980 (projected)	12,940	2268	404.2	128.4

* Exports are almost entirely made up of better-quality parts of cattle. Local consumption is mainly confined to viscera and other less desirable parts. FAO projections for Central American consumption of beef indicate that it will increase from 8.2 kg per head in 1970 to 10 kg in 1980 — as compared with similar figures for the main foreign-market country, the United States, of 53 kg and 61 kg.

** Figures for El Salvador, Panama and Belize are too small to be detailed separately.

Source: Information supplied by Dairy, Livestock and Poultry Division, Foreign Agricultural Service, U.S. Department of Agriculture, Washington D.C., January 1977.

Table 4

U.S. imports of beef

Country of origin	1971 ('000s of kg)	1976 ('000s of kg)
Guatemala	14,955	15,486
Honduras	15,066	18,430
Costa Rica	18,648	25,416
Nicaragua	23,869	22,670
Mexico	n.a.	18,040
Brazil	28,631	33,196
Total, from all countries	595,751* (of which Australia and New Zealand 339,625)	675,522 (of which Australia and New Zealand 431,781)

Note: The Meat Importers Council of America states that the bulk of these imports go into processed meat products, notably hamburgers, frankfurters and other convenience foods.

* Amounts to about 1 percent of U.S. domestic production.

Source: Information supplied by Dairy, Livestock and Poultry Division, Foreign Agricultural Service, U.S. Department of Agriculture, Washington D.C., January 1977.

twice as expensive as beef grown in Costa Rica. Thus the price of a U.S. hamburger does not reflect the environmental costs of its production in Costa Rica. The American consumer, seeking a good-quality hamburger at "reasonable", i.e. non-inflationary, price, is not aware of the spinoff consequences of his actions far away from his homeland.

Since 1950 the area of man-established pasturelands and the number of beef cattle in Central America have more than doubled.[9] This expansion has occurred almost entirely at the expense of natural forests, of which two-thirds have now been cleared. Costa Rica's pasturelands, which in 1950 covered one-eighth of the country, have expanded until they now cover almost one-third. At the present clearing rate of 500 km² per year, the remaining primary forests will be finished by 1900.

Costa Rica's cattle herds, that in 1960 totalled slightly over 900,000, increased by 1976 to 1.9 million.[10] During the 1960s, beef production expanded by 92 percent. In the course of the same decade, however, local consumption of beef declined by 26 percent, to a mere 8 kg per head per year, almost all the extra output being despatched overseas. Costa Rica now exports around 45 million kg of beef per year, of which well over half goes to the United States, for a 1976 value of $34 million.

This trade is of considerable benefit to the United States. It generates sizeable profits for the U.S. corporations involved, and it enables the American consumer to enjoy ample supplies of cheap beef. Beef imported from Central America in 1978 averaged $1.47 per kg, compared with a wholesale price of $3.3 for grass-fed beef produced in the United States. Even more important, the cost of U.S. beef has been climbing far faster than the overall cost of living. This is partly due to Americans' insatiable demand for beef, and partly due to declining numbers of American cattle from 132 million in 1976 to 116 million in 1978 (stockmen have been disposing of their cattle on the grounds that they could not make sufficient profit). During the first 5 months of 1978 beef prices jumped by 35 percent. Faced with this calamitous increase, the U.S. government decided to step up beef imports by 7.6 percent. Although this contributed less than 1 percent to the country's consumption of beef, the government estimated it would trim one nickel off the price of a hamburger. Hardly any other initiative, it was said, could do as much to stem inflation — and nothing was said about what the measure would do to Central America's forests.

On top of the external-trade stimulus, the beef industry in Costa Rica, as in several other Central American countries, is fostered by a national oligarchy whose cultural background views cattle raising as a prestige activity. In 1973 Costa Rica's beef industry was dominated by only 2134 ranchers, holding an average of 750 hectares each and controlling 51 percent of Costa Rica's agricultural land in use.[11] To own land and cattle fosters both social standing and political power;

ranchers include many professional persons who retire to their
country estates at weekends to ride horseback and enjoy an image as
gentlemen stock-raisers — they prove they have "made-it".

Since 1972 Costa Rica's cattlelands have been suffering from
drought. A major cause is forest devastation, leading to decreased
rainfall and increased runoff. According to Costa Rica's Livestock
Owners Association, ranchers in one of the principal stock-raising
areas, Guanacaste Province, have lost many of their cattle to
starvation, while most of the survivors are emaciated. A number of
ranchers have gone out of business. Total agricultural losses in
Guanacaste are put at $250 million. Following this disaster, certain
sectors of the Province are to be re-forested, albeit with exotic tree
species. The drought has had other consequences. Increased soil
erosion, likewise blamed on deforestation, has caused dams to silt up,
in turn bringing shortages of drinking water and electricity. So
widespread is the problem that the utility companies have gone into
the business of selling tree seedlings.

Against this record of forest destruction must be considered Costa
Rica's recent efforts at conservation. Through the inspired initiatives
of President Daniel Oduber, a great deal has been accomplished in
just a few years. A Natural Resources Institute has been established to
conduct ecological evaluation studies of the entire country and to
come up with a program of integrated land-use planning. The network
of National Parks now contains more units, and covers a greater
proportion of national territory, than is the case in any other Latin
American country. Thirteen units total 1260 km², an area that is
scheduled to be expanded several times over. If the expansion is
approved, the parks network will then amount to 10 percent of
national territory — equivalent to the United States setting aside the
whole of Alaska. Together with Forest Reserves, either established or
proposed, this will bring the total of protected areas in Costa Rica to
37 percent of national territory.

A notable addition to the parks system has been the Corcovado
Park in the Osa Peninsula on the Pacific Coast. The park covers 290
km² or one-third of the Peninsula, and encompasses virtually the only
appreciable remaining patch of undisturbed lowland rainforest on the
Pacific Coast in Central America. When the park was declared in

1975, it was hailed by conservationists around the world as one of the most significant advances in recent years. The park has not been established without cost. First, the squatter families had to be bought out; $750,000 has been paid for alternative land for them to settle on and $1 million for their tree-felling "improvements". Second, the costs of setting up the park (administration, roads, etc.) have run to $300,000. A number of foreign organizations, notably the U.S. Nature Conservancy, the U.S. National Appeal of the World Wildlife Fund and the U.S.-based Rare Animal Relief Effort, have contributed $163,000. The remaining funds, almost $2 million, have been raised by Costa Rica's own citizens, who have contributed around $1 per head from their impoverished incomes.

In comparative terms, the Corcovado effort is the equivalent of the United States raising $225 million from its taxpayers (or $1.7 billion, if proportionate wealth is taken into account) in order to set aside a park the size of West Virginia. When the U.S. Nature Conservancy launched a public appeal for funds to purchase trout-fishing land in Idaho, it received $600,000, or enough to acquire 200 hectares at $3000 per hectare. If the $2.1 million raised for Corcovado had secured land at that price, it would have set aside a mere 700 hectares. Corcovado is more than 400 times as large an area, and it safeguards ecosystems that could well be 400 times more diverse than Idaho wilderness — a bargain indeed. Moreover, the contribution on the part of the United States could turn out to be a sound investment for Americans: when a botanist from South Carolina, Dr. Monie S. Hudson, screened 1500 tree species in Costa Rica's forests for activity against cancer, he found around 15 percent to be positive.

Several conclusions arise. One is that Costa Rica has made a significant contribution to conservation of tropical moist forests, not only in Central America but throughout the biome. Another is that conservationists outside Costa Rica should pause before blaming the slash-and-burn cultivators (or the impoverished "campesino" peasant in other parts of tropical Latin America) for chopping down tropical forests; what else is he to do if he is to earn a living for himself and his family? Still more to the point, outside conservationists might hesitate before pointing a finger at Costa Rica's privileged élite that engage in cattle ranching as a genteel spare-time activity to prove they have "arrived": which American conservationist has not taken satisfaction at the "humble hamburger" with its humble price?

Indonesia

Indonesia[12] comprises around 3000 inhabited islands, and another 10,000 uninhabited islands, strung out in a 5000 km chain astride the equator between Asia and Australia. This location gives Indonesia special importance from the standpoint of the planet's stock of species. The islands in the western part of the country, notably Sumatra, Borneo (Indonesia's sector, known as Kalimantan, makes up almost three-quarters of the island) and Java, plus many smaller islands, were once joined to the Asian mainland, and thus belong with the Asian biogeographical realm. New Guinea, including Indonesia's half of the island, Irian Jaya, was formerly attached to Australia, and thus lies within the Australasian ecological zone. The islands in between, notably Sulawesi (Celebes) and the Moluccas among others, represent an intermediate region where the two great flora-fauna complexes meet.

The result is an exceptional amount of biotic diversity within a single country, almost all of it to be found in the forests that reputedly still cover almost two-thirds of national territory, or a good one-eighth of the whole biome of tropical moist forests. Moreover, Indonesia's forests are probably richer in species, area for area, than any other surviving forests of the biome. (Peninsular Malaysia's may once have been richer, but they are mostly down to their last few years.) So Indonesia has a magnificient opportunity to safeguard a sizeable sector of the global natural heritage. During the past 12 years, however, Indonesia has embarked on broad-scale exploitation of its forests that could lead to gross impoverishment of the country's biotic endowment before the end of the century.

Indonesia's forests are estimated to cover 1.2 million km². At least, that is the figure that the government gives out. In point of fact, the same official statistic was being used in the mid-1960s before the country's forests began to be widely exploited by timber corporations, before a population transmigration project from over-crowded Java to the sparsely populated outer islands got under way, and before shifting cultivation became so widespread. The present area of undisturbed forest could now be a good deal less, possibly only 1 million km² or even lower.

Whatever figure is to be accepted, around two-fifths are considered to be lowland rainforests, the forest type that is ecologically richest to the conservationist and commercially most attractive to the logger. Rough estimates suggest that Indonesia's forests contain at least 2.5 billion m³ of merchantable timber, equivalent to almost one-quarter of exploitable industrial wood in the United States.

When Indonesia decided, in the mid-1960s, to exploit its huge timber stocks, it found it lacked the finance and technology to do the job itself. So it looked to foreign enterprise and capital. The 1966 Investors Incentive Act offered many attractions to overseas corporations, including guaranteed repatriation of investment, tax holidays, duty-free import of equipment and auxiliary goods, accelerated depreciation rates on capital investment, compensation in the event of nationalization, and government financing of some infrastructure development such as aerial surveys and forest roads. The result has been a flood of foreign timber corporations, including a good number from the United States and Japan. Most of these outside interests operate through joint ventures in conjunction with Indonesian "front names", notably military personnel on boards of directors.

By early 1978 commercial loggers had applied for, and had generally taken out, 683 concession agreements accounting for 602,000 km². This area amounts to virtually all accessible lowland forests, plus some supposedly protection-forest sectors in upland zones. Of the total concessions, almost one-quarter are held by only 40 companies. The largest is held by the Djajanti Group, over 20,000 km² in the middle of Borneo (a Massachusetts-sized area), with an authorized capital of $50 million. At least one-fifth of the forestlands allocated are exploited by Japanese concerns and one-sixth by Americans. Total investment has already surpassed $1.3 billion, the great bulk of it from outside Indonesia. Although the area actually exploited to date is relatively small, the loggers are moving in as quickly as they can go. Conservative estimates suggest that Sumatra and Sulawesi will have been logged out within 5-10 years, Kalimantan and most of the smaller islands within 10-15 years and Irian Jaya within 15-20 years. Given that present rates of exploitation are likely to speed up progressively, these time horizons could well telescope.

During the 12 years since broad-scale commercial exploitation of Indonesia's forests began, timber exports have boomed. In 1965 the country exported 140,000 m^3 of logs, worth $2.8 million; and in 1978, 21.1 million m^3 (over three-quarters of all logs cut), worth $1.2 billion. Indonesia now exports far more than the Philippines and Malaysia put together. The aim is to export 30 million, out of 50 million cut, by 1990. Whereas the export price in the late 1960s was $20 or less, it rose in 1974, and again in late 1976 and 1978, as high as $80-90.

A logger expects to take at least 10-15 trees per hectare, with an average of 6 m^3 of harvestable wood per tree. Given the disruptive impact of logging practices (see Chapter 11), a level of harvest between 60 and 90 m^3 leaves the forest with little capacity to regenerate within what is supposed to be a sustainable harvest cycle, viz. 35 years. In fact, there is no documented case on record of a logged dipterocarp forest recovering to its original state. Although the logging damage could be reduced by, for example, cutting lianas before felling, no individual corporation is going to take a step of that sort on its own initiative (see Chapter 13). A corporation will exercise exceptional care only if all exploiters are required to do the same, in order that each can maintain its competitive edge — whereupon Indonesia could well lose its market to cheaper sources of hardwood logs in other parts of the tropics. As a measure to prevent over-harvest, the government requires that a logger may cut only trees of diameter 60 cm or more. But the log ponds of several major corporations at one of the main export centres, Samarinda in East Kalimantan, contain many smaller logs. The corporations in question protest that this cutting of young timber is necessary in order to ensure an adequate profit. Whether the financial arithmetic supports this attitude or not (see Chapter 13), entrepreneurs with 20-year concession agreements feel scant inclination to ensure a future harvest through careful logging. On the contrary, they tend to go for a cut-and-run operation within 10 years at the most.

Indonesia now derives export dues, taxes and other levies from its log exports totalling around $350 million. Of these earnings, however, the government ploughs little back into forestry and even less into environmental conservation. In the fiscal year 1978-79, Indonesia is to spend about $92 million on forestry, yet this sum is to be mostly directed to reafforestation of critically denuded areas, especially in Java. Very limited funds are available for government control of timber corporations, let alone management of forests, or training and research. As a consequence, the government's squad of professional foresters totals only 400, or one to every 3000 km² of forest and less than one to each concessionaire. A result of this understaffing is the under-sized logs being harvested, among many other items of inadequate supervision. Moreover, a university-trained forester earns only half of what a private-sector bulldozer operator or a tree feller earns, a situation that fosters corruption.

In face of a pattern of increasing disruption if not destruction of its forests, Indonesia plans to increase its parks and reserves. The present system of protected areas covers about 37,000 km². It comprises 166 units, ranging in size from a 1-hectare locality that preserves a single fig tree, to over 4000 km² in the Gunung Leuser Reserve. The government aims to expand the present network of protected areas to a total of 100,000 km² by 1983, and over 5 percent of the country — equivalent to the United States setting aside an area larger than California. It envisages that all the additional parks and reserves will be in moist forest zones, with a large proportion in West Irian — many of them, however, in poor-grade forestlands.

Regrettably, many of the present protected areas amount to little more than "paper parks". Over half of the 166 units are Game Reserves, in which wildlife is theoretically protected but "management of the forests" — in reality, exploitation of timber — is permitted, leading to much disruption of wildlife habitat. The rest are Nature Reserves, fully protected by law, though, as in the case of Game Reserves, featuring much logging. In the Kutai Reserve of East Kalimantan, an area with one of the largest known orangutan populations, 1000 out of 3000 km² have been logged by "informal operators". A similar story could be told for many other parks and reserves, some of which are being blatantly logged, some designated for settlement projects and some exploited for hydropower purposes.

The year 1978, however, has seen some promising initiatives. The government has beefed up its wildlife-and-parks budget to $2.4 million per year. It has cancelled one timber concession of 10,000 km² and reduced another from 30,000 km² to 10,000, largely in order to protect watersheds and to safeguard exceptional forest ecosystems. It has appointed a Berkeley-trained man to be Minister for Development Control and the Environment, responsible directly to President Soeharto. A new day may be dawning for Indonesia's conservation scene — not before time.

Kenya

Kenya's forests cover around 20,000 km², or less than 3 percent of national territory.[13] Of these, no more than 11,000 km² can be considered to be moist forests — and seasonally moist, hence deciduous, at that. Despite their small area, however, they are important for earth's spectrum of species. Being mainly montane forests, in long isolated patches, they feature much biotic diversity, with many endemic species. Together with other relict areas of moist forests in neighbouring Tanzania and Uganda, they rank, area for area, among the richest forests of all tropical Africa.

Equally to the point, they used to be much more extensive. Within living memory, Kenya's forest cover is reputed to have been 4 times as large as today, while climatic patterns suggest that 200 years ago there could have been twice as much again. Something the same goes for other forests in East Africa. The Usambara Mountain forests in Tanzania, considered by many to be a biological phenomenon, have been reduced by over 70 percent in just the past 20 years.

East Africa's forests possess greater variety of species, with more endemics than the vast forests of Canada, Scandinavia and Russia. Forest-living bird species that are endemics or "near-endemics" (virtually confined to the region) total thirty-five.[14] Forests offer quite the richest habitats for mammals, ninety-two species, or one-quarter of all East Africa's mammals. Uganda's forests, covering 7500 km², feature over 800 species of trees and shrubs, compared with 130 in the whole of Europe; in less than 200 km² of the Semliki Forest, 380 birds have been recorded, while in a few square kilometers of another Forest Reserve, 284 species of birds have been listed within 2 months, about as many as would be recorded during a lifetime's search throughout Britain.[15] Uganda's forests also feature abundant species of flowers, ferns, amphibians, reptiles and insects. Similar statistics would almost certainly apply to Kenya's forests, though they have been less documented.

Of Kenya's forest patches, two are outstandingly important. One is the Kakamega Forest, located at 1500 m altitude in western Kenya. As the eastern-most relict of the great equatorial forest that stretches across the Zaire basin, it presumably contains variations of species that, being on the extreme fringes of their range, are adapted to environments different from their parent stocks. In short, the forest must be a crucible of evolutionary adaptation and speciation. Officially, it covers 230 km², but actual forest now amounts to little over 100 km². These last remnants are being steadily destroyed by timber cutters, charcoal burners and developers who wish to replace the virgin ecosystem with plantations of exotic trees and for agriculture. At the present rate of clearing, the forest will be completely gone by 2010.

The other important forest is the Arabuko-Sokoke Forest on Kenya's coast. A trifling fraction of what was once a forest extending for hundreds of kilometers along East Africa's coast, it has been reduced to 360 km². It is the only known home of the Scop's Owl, discovered as recently as 1964, with perhaps 2600-3000 individuals in a range of 150 km². The Forest is also the sole home of the Sokoke Pipit and the Clarke's Weaver, whose numbers are unknown. In addition, the forest very likely contains a good number of endemic insects, plants, reptiles and other creatures. It is being destroyed for much the same reasons as the Kakamega Forest.

In recent times, Kenya has been importing forest products, mainly paper and paperboard, worth about $30 million a year. In the wake of steady over-exploitation of its forests for at least half a century, the country now finds itself with insufficient natural-forest materials to supply its needs. So in the past few years, it has been establishing man-made forests, almost 3000 km² of exotic-tree plantations. The urgent aim now is to establish a further 400 km². Regrettably, part of these additional 400 km² are planned to be located in each of the two forests mentioned.

It may seem curious that Kenya, with a mere 20,000 km² of natural forests, could not choose other areas for its man-made forests. But the two forests in question, being located in good rainfall zones, not only feature vigorous natural growth (with all the ecological diversity that implies), but offer exceptional opportunity for fast-growing plantations. From many angles it would make sense to establish the plantations in border zones surrounding each of the two forests rather than in the forests themselves, i.e. in the localities that have recently been cleared of their forest cover. Such zones would be especially suitable for eucalyptus plantations, that help to rehabilitate over-cultivated and eroded lands. But to follow this course of action would mean removing the human communities that have recently put down roots there — a political complication that, in a country whose population far exceeds the arable land available, would be problematical indeed.

Kenya's plantation program costs $55.5 million. Of this, $20 million comes from the World Bank. A World Bank study has reviewed the program, and looked at Nature Reserves in each of the two forests in question. According to earlier assessments, the Kakamega Nature Reserve of 7½ km² is far too small for its task,[16] and the World Bank agrees that further research should be undertaken to determine whether additional forest, probably at least twice as much again, should be added to the Reserve. The Arabuko-Sokoke's Nature Reserve of 30 km² is to be supplemented with another Nature Reserve of 10 km²; but the area at issue contains little red soil, the only known habitat of the threatened owl. Nevertheless, the World Bank considers that "Each of these areas (Nature Reserves) will be large enough to sustain on a viable basis their particular ecosystems". The Bank's statement does not explain the basis for its evaluation, it does not define the "particular ecosystems", it does not say what is implied by "sustain on a viable basis", and it does not mention anything with regard to the dimensions and design of reserves. Certain Nature Reserves in other forests of Kenya now feature a rapidly growing tide of human settlements.

So significant is the Arabuko-Sokoke Forest that a number of scientists have proposed it for a Biosphere Reserve under the UNESCO plan for a global network of outstanding natural areas. The merit of this view could lie not only in the Arabuko-Sokoke's outstanding scientific value, but in its potential utilitarian benefits. A few dozen kilometers to the south along the Kenya coast, in the Shimba Hills forest, lives a shrub with materials of possible use for anti-cancer drugs.

While the siting of the new plantations is to be regretted from a conservation standpoint, the additional wood supplies will certainly aid Kenya's economy. Kenya is one of the more prosperous of Africa's developing nations, and its economic progress means that demand for industrial timber will expand far more rapidly than is accounted for by population growth alone. The country's requirements for this sort of timber are projected to increase at least 8 times by the year 2000 — by which time there could be a timber surplus of 700,000 m^3 for export, notably to regions with burgeoning demand such as the Middle East. (Ironically, the Middle East, with its massive supplies of oil, has been a major market for Kenya's exports of charcoal, 58,000 tons in 1971 out of Africa's total charcoal exports of 60,000 tons.) Timber exports on this scale could earn for Kenya around $40 million per year, at today's prices. So the export surplus could be said, roughly speaking, to correspond to the proportion of additional plantations to be sited in the two forests at issue. This means the conflict can be posed in the form of the question: Is Kenya warranted in running the risk of signing away a number of species in return for $40 million a year? The extra income will share out at approximately $1¼ per head of Kenya's citizens in the year 2000. While no great sum, this is not insignificant for rural communities whose per-capita cash income for a year may not average more than $70.

11 Patterns of Exploitation

In what ways are tropical moist forests being exploited? How far does this cause them to be disrupted and depleted? This chapter reviews a range of exploitation patterns.

Forests supply many goods, of both immediate and long-term benefit to society. Certain goods, notably timber and paperpulp, can be supplied through exploitation of the standing forest. Alternatively, the land on which the forest stands can be put to various uses, such as man-made forests of exotic trees, slash-and-burn cultivation, modern food growing, plantations of rubber, oil palms, bananas and other cash crops, and stock-raising on man-established pastures — all of which uses require the complete removal of the original forest.

Commercial exploitation of timber

A main reason why forests on every side are increasingly exploited, and sometimes over-exploited, is that more people want more wood. Wood serves many purposes. It is one of the first raw materials that a person uses, and it is likely to be his last. It plays a part in more activities of a modern economy than any other commodity, and almost every major industry depends on forest products in at least one of its processes. It is applied in several forms of construction, notably housing. A house wall built of wood requires about 20 percent less energy for heating and 30 percent less for cooling than does a house made of other construction materials. Three-quarters of U.S. houses are mostly wood; on average, each of the 2 million houses started in 1978 contained over $7000 worth of wood. Wood is also used for furniture and fittings, and for papers of many kinds. It serves a multitude of purposes as plywood, veneer, hardboard, particleboard and chipboard. It contributes to a number of beverages and foods (including alcohol and synthetic hamburgers), photographic film, explosives and clothing including paper swimsuits. Wood is a competitive material, since substitutes such as steel, aluminum, cement and plastics need more energy in their production.

Rough estimates suggest that the amount of wood cut worldwide in 1974 was over 2500 million m³. Of this amount, roughly 47 percent was used as fuel (over four-fifths of it to meet the needs of the developing world) (Table 5). Around 43 percent was used as timber for construction needs, for panels, and for "solid wood" purposes (two-thirds to meet the needs of the developed world). One-tenth was manufactured into pulp products (seven-eighths for the developed world). By the year 2000 total wood use could approach 6000 million m³, with fuelwood accounting for about one-third, solid wood for over half, and pulp products for at least one-sixth.

So if, as is likely, consumption of wood increases, very roughly speaking, by 130-140 percent during the last quarter of the century, growing pressures for exploitation will be directed at the world's forests — and especially at those forests that have been relatively little exploited for wood to date, tropical moist forests. Although they contain about as much wood as their larger temperate counterparts, tropical forests contribute little more than one-tenth of the world's wood used for construction and for paperpulp.

To consider industrial wood first, it is convenient to differentiate between two types: hardwoods and softwoods.

Table 5
World consumption of wood: present and projected estimates
(million m³)

	1974	%	2000	%
Fuelwood	1170	47	1950	33
Poles, sawnwood, panel products	1078	43	3010	51
Wood-pulp products	263	10	910	16
Total	2511	100	5870	100

Sources: FAO documents.

(a) Global trade in hardwoods

In recent years there has been a booming demand on the part of the developed world for tropical hardwoods (Table 6). Hardwood is favored for housing construction and for finished products such as furniture and for wood-based panels such as plywood, veneer, particleboard and fiberboard. Most hardwood forests, comprising broad-leaved or non-coniferous tree species, are located in the tropics (Table 6). Hardwood forests of temperate zones have been steadily depleted, or are coming under greater protection in order to meet environmental interests; as a result, exploitation pressure is increasingly directed toward tropical forests.

In 1950 the developed world imported 4.2 million m³ of tropical hardwood timber (Table 7). By 1973 the amount had grown to 53.3 million. By 1980 it could expand to 66 million m³, and by the year 2000 to 95 million. Of course, tropical regions use a lot of hardwood timber themselves, but the amount has little more than doubled since 1950, whereas developed-world imports have increased 14 times, until the total has recently surpassed consumption by all tropical countries combined.

The United States in particular has been expanding its consumption of tropical hardwoods at a rate far above its growth rates for population and living standards. This has been partly due to the soaring costs of high-quality hardwoods from within the United States, now that the country's hardwood forests are prized for their aesthetic and recreation values. It has also been due to the fact that plywood panelling can be obtained relatively cheaply from the Far East — over four-fifths of U.S. imports of tropical hardwoods come in the form of plywood and veneer via Japan, the so-called "Philippine mahogany" that originates in Southeast Asia's forests. Between 1950 and 1973 U.S. imports of tropical hardwoods increased 9 times, to top 7 million m³, including about 70 percent of all tropical plywood and veneer in world trade. There seems little doubt that U.S. imports of tropical hardwoods has made it easier for American environmentalists to urge greater preservation of America's own hardwood forests.

Yet the United States could easily become self-sufficient in hardwood timber. It grows much more hardwood than it uses, and the

Table 6
Hardwood and softwood forests of the world
('000 square kilometers)

Region	Total land area	Total forests (and percentage of land area)	Hardwood forests* (and percentage of all forests)	Softwood forests (and percentage of all forests)
All of Asia (except Japan and U.S.S.R.	26,320	4797 (18)	4065 (85)	732 (15)
Southeast Asia	4640	2638 (57)	2570 (97)	68 (3)
Pacific Area	8324	868 (10)	840 (97)	28 (3)
Latin America	20,100	7664 (38)	7320 (96)	344 (4)
Africa	29,360	6840 (23)	6800 (99)	40 (1)
North America	18,532	6918 (37)	2570 (37)	4348 (63)
Europe (Western Europe contains over four-fifths of forests)	4520	1462 (32)	610 (42)	852 (58)
U.S.S.R.	21,200	7194 (34)	1730 (24)	5464 (76)
Japan	989	228 (23)	128 (56)	100 (44)
World	129,345	35,971 (28)	24,063 (67)	11,908 (33)

* Includes both moist and dry hardwood forests; hardwood forests cover 19 million km², of which only around 9 million are tropical moist forests.
Sources: FAO documents.

Table 7
Consumption of tropical industrial timber

Country/Region	1950	1960	1970	1973	1980	1990	2000
		(million cubic metres)			(......projected......)		
Japan	1.5	4.6	20.1	28.9	35	38	48
United States	0.8	2.2	5.1	7.2	10	15	20
Europe	1.9	6.2	10.5	17.2	21	27	35
Total three importing regions	4.2	13.0	35.7	53.3	66	80	95
Tropical producing regions	21.0	34.0	42.6	46.5	66	117	185
Rest of world	1.0	2.1	4.2	9.0	13	18	23
Grand total	26.2	49.1	82.5	108.8	145	215	303

Sources: FAO documents.

hardwood standing stock is expanding rapidly — much of it in non-commercial forests and unmanaged natural areas that are increasingly retained for recreational and other "non-consumptive" uses. According to recent reports,[1] the sustainable output from U.S. commercial hardwood forests could be doubled quite readily, and tripled within 50 years, through widespread application of proven silvicultural methods and intensive management techniques such as complete-tree utilization.

Of course, looking at the situation this way leads to a difficult question of tradeoffs. Were, say, 1000 km^2 of a U.S. hardwood forest to be preserved in response to environmental interests, the gain for the global natural heritage could hardly be commensurate with the loss of a similar-sized area in a tropical region, bearing in mind the ecological diversity and genetic variability of the two areas. To be sure, there would almost certainly be no direct causative tradeoff in practical terms. But the question points up a dimension of the overall problem that could grow increasingly significant.

Europe increased its imports of tropical hardwoods between 1950 and 1973 by 9 times (Table 6). The timber derives mostly from West and Central Africa. As is the case for the United States, Europe could produce more of its own timber, were it not that environmental considerations are becoming increasingly important.

By far the largest consumer of tropical hardwoods is Japan, accounting for two-thirds of the Western world's imports. With a population of 115 million people living in a space less than California, Japan is critically dependent on foreign sources of raw materials of many kinds.[2] Moreover, each of its citizens consumes more wood than any other nation on earth. Between 1950 and 1973 Japan's imports of tropical hardwoods increased 19 times (Table 6), three-quarters of the supply coming from Southeast Asia. Among all Japan's imports, wood now ranks a strong second to oil; the country foresees that timber shortages could eventually amount to "another oil crisis". In 1963 Japan was dependent on overseas sources for only one-quarter of its wood, but by 1975 for over one-half, a ratio that could even rise to four-fifths by 1985. Japan's forests, covering two-thirds of national territory, do not contribute to the country's needs nearly so much as they might, due partly to increasing concern with environmental requirements, partly to the fact that plentiful supplies of cheap timber are available in the tropics.

By far the major source of tropical hardwoods is the Asia-Pacific region, especially Southeast Asia (Table 8). Between 1950 and 1973 the region increased its exports 24 times, to account for three-quarters of the world market. Latin America, with 3 times as many hardwood stocks as Southeast Asia, produces only 10 percent of the world's hardwood timber, and exports very little, due to the difficult location of many of its hardwood forests. Tropical Africa tripled its hardwood exports, mainly to Europe, during the decade 1967-76.[3]

(b) Global trade in softwoods and other sources of pulp

Softwoods are utilized in the manufacture of that group of products for which consumer demand is likely to grow most strongly, viz. paper products. World consumption of paper products is made up about 15 percent of newsprint, about 20 percent of printing and other writing papers, and about 65 percent of industrial paper such as packaging materials, tissues and convenience products such as paper cups and plates.

Tropical forests contain relatively few softwoods (Table 7). Nonetheless, the international paper trade is growing important for the future of tropical forests, in view of changes in forestry technology. Until the mid-1970s it was thought that hardwood forests of the tropics, with their multiplicity of species, could not readily be pulped after the manner of softwoods. New techniques are now showing the way to put every tree from the forest through the hopper, whereupon the woodchips from 100 species at a time can be converted into useable pulp. Developing regions, with 55 percent of the world's forests, have been producing only 6.5 percent of the world's paper and paperboard.

During the period 1950-1970, world output of paper products increased from 40 to 130 million metric tons, for a growth rate twice that of population. If recent trends continue, world demand could rise from 160 million tons in 1976 to 280 million in 1985, and to 400 million tons by the year 2000 — and to twice as much again after only a further 20 years.[4] In 1974 the developed world utilized just over 140

Table 8
Supply of tropical hardwood timber, actual and projected
(million cubic meters, roundwood log equivalent)

Region (with area of hardwood forests in '000 km²)	1950		1973		1980		1990		2000	
	Prod.	Export (%)	Prod.	Export (%)	Prod.	Export (%)	Prod.	Export (%)	Prod.	Export (%)
Asia-Pacific (3200)*	14.3	2 (14)	72.5	48.5 (67)	93	65 (70)	130	82 (63)	150	80 (53)
Latin America (7320)	15.5	0.8 (5)	20	3 (15)	32	4 (13)	60	7 (12)	118	28 (24)
Africa (6800)	4.7	1.5 (32)	16.5	11 (67)	20	12 (60)	25	9 (36)	35	10 (29)
Total (17,320; world total 24,000**)	34.5	4.3 (13)	109	62.5 (57)	145	81 (56)	215	98 (46)	303	118 (39)

* Over two-thirds in Southeast Asia.
** North America's hardwood forests account for just over one-tenth of this total.
Note: As tropical developing countries themselves start to consume more of their hardwood output, there will be (except in the eventual case of Latin America) a smaller share available for export to developed countries. At the same time, developed countries' demand will steadily expand. So there will be compounded pressure to exploit tropical hardwood forests.
Sources: FAO documents.

million tons of pulp, the developing world less than 20 million. An average citizen of the developed world now consumes over 150 kg of paper and paperboard per year (in the United States, 320 kg), while in the developing world a citizen is unlikely to go much beyond 5 kg, and may not even account for 1 kg — around half of one copy of the Sunday edition of the *New York Times*. If consumption continues to grow as in recent years, the United States will increase its present share of world output, around 70 million out of 165 million tons, to around 200 out of 400 million by the end of the century. By contrast, Africa will expand from 2.5 to 5-10 million, Asia (excluding Japan) from 8.3 to 24.5, and Latin America from 5.6 to 14.4. Thus, while developing nations are likely to expand their consumption roughly 3 times as compared with a 2¾-times increase on the part of advanced nations, by far the largest share of total consumption will remain with the developed world — again, the sector most responsible for increasing pressure on forests around the globe.

Especially dependent on outside sources of pulp is Japan. The country is expected to expand its present consumption of almost 20 million metric tons to 31 million by 1985, by which time almost half its pulpwood will come from overseas. In view of recent increases in prices of U.S. softwood chips, Japan is turning to Southeast Asia and tropical America for hardwood chips; well over half its pulpwood chips now come from hardwoods.[5]

Despite their relatively low consumption, developing countries encounter massive incentive to develop domestic sources of pulp and paper. They import virtually all their supplies, at a cost in 1975 of $2 billion — a severe drain on their meager supplies of foreign exchange and eating up almost two-thirds of their earnings from exports of timber. As a measure of present low-level demand in developing regions, and the amount by which it could expand, total newsprint consumption in fourteen Asian countries, including all the most populous ones except China, is about 600,000 tons per year, or less than Canada's (the United States' is 11.2 million tons).

Demand for paper increases not only as a consequence of growing human numbers, but it expands much more as a consequence of growing human aspirations. In particular, the spread of literacy stimulates a surging hunger for paper. Brazil's consumption doubled during the

1960s, and is likely to have almost doubled again during the 1970s. Within another 10 years there will be another 150 million consumers of print in developing countries. By the year 2000, Southeast Asia could need 5 times as much paper as it accounted for in 1974. Already a lack of paper is causing severe setbacks to education and communication in many developing countries. A number of them have found it difficult to obtain newsprint even at 2 or 3 times the prices of 1972. American consumers objected when, during the 1973-76 newsprint shortages, prices rose from $187 to almost $300 per ton, yet in several parts of Asia still higher prices have not been uncommon. Indonesia, after paying out $92 million for pulp imports in 1977, can hardly be blamed if it wishes to exploit its forest resources at an even faster pace than hitherto, in order to generate its own pulp — at present a mere 15 percent of consumption.

Review of tropical forest trade

Tropical-forest countries earn an appreciable amount of foreign exchange through their wood exports, $4.2 billion in 1976. This is a massive increase from $272 million in 1954, and represents a growth rate far faster than the world's total trade in forest products. In fact, tropical timber is now one of the fastest-growing exports of the developing world, pulling in about as much revenue as sugar, cotton or copper.

Substantial and expanding as these export earnings are, trade in tropical timber nevertheless amounts to only about 15 percent of world trade in forest products. Finland and Congo have land areas and forest estates roughly the same size, yet in 1973 the value of Finland's forest exports was 60 times greater than Congo's. Latin America has more than 5 hectares of forestland per person, compared to a world average of about 1 hectare, yet it imports more forest products by value than it exports.[6]

Thus tropical-forest countries have good reason to believe that exploitation contributes to the welfare of their citizens, and could contribute far more. Given the impoverished state of most of their citizens, it is difficult to argue with this aim — provided that efforts to meet immediate goals do not pre-empt opportunities to accomplish long-term goals of similar sort, and provided that other legitimate interests, such as humanity's heritage in species, are not unduly or unnecessarily diminished.

Damage to forests through logging

It is the tradeoff between immediate development and long-term conservation that raises some major questions. How large are the forest areas affected by logging, and do they represent a sizeable proportion of all tropical moist forests? Does logging leave them in a permanently impoverished state?

Due to the diversity of tree species in tropical forests, coupled with the reluctance of international timber markets to take more than a small proportion of wood types available, a commercial logger is inclined to aim for a highly selective harvest, taking a few choice specimens with disregard for what happens to the rest. In other words, a "creaming" operation. Of Amazonia's many thousands of tree species, only about fifty are widely exploited, even though as many as 400 are known to have commercial value.

So when a patch of tropical forest is exploited, only a few trees, often less than 20 out of 400 per hectare, are taken. Yet the logging operation can leave many of the remaining trees damaged beyond recovery, far more than would be the case in a temperate-zone forest. Trees are strongly linked together with vines, lianas and other climbing plants, as many as 2000 per hectare, some of them 200 m long.[7] Commercial trees are often limited to those that reach to the topmost storey, where, enjoying the sunlight, they develop wide-spreading crowns, as much as 15 m across. When one of these giants is felled, it is likely to cause several others to be broken or pulled down. Furthermore, tropical trees are highly susceptible to attack by pathogens; as a result, a minor-seeming injury, such as a patch of bark torn off, can leave a tree vulnerable to irreparable damage. Logging roads and haulage tracks, sometimes averaging as much as 10 km for each square kilometer of forest exploited, can, together with dumping zones and landings for logs, account for 10-30 percent of the forest area.

Surveys in Southeast Asia reveal that average logging leaves between one-third and two-thirds of residual trees effectively wrecked.[8] On top of this, almost one-third of the ground may be left bare, in many instances with the soil impacted through heavy machinery. With greater care (see Chapter 13), the damage could be reduced by half. But less destructive exploitation would raise timber prices for the consumer — and to that extent, the consumer, who is presumed by the timber corporation to prefer prices as low as possible, is implicitly involved in "mining" of the forest.

As for wildlife, a number of research findings point to the consequences of logging for primates and other better-known creatures.[9] For example, certain monkeys of Southeast Asia can survive well enough in disrupted forests (in secondary forests, too), but the howler monkey disappears as soon as the virgin ecosystem is disturbed, while the orangutan and the proboscis monkey of Borneo could become endangered were their forest habitats to be extensively exploited.[10] In Africa, large-scale timber felling could benefit the black-and-white colobus, but it causes the red colobus and the sooty mangaby to suffer severely.[11]

What is the overall impact of logging on tropical moist forests? It is difficult to arrive at any firm conclusion, due to the huge and dispersed areas involved, and due to the lack of documentation on which to base a solid assessment. Nevertheless, for purposes of coming to grips with trends of disappearing forests, it is appropriate to come up with some kind of answer, even if little better than an "informed guesstimate". During the 10 years 1964-73, the affected area in Africa grew by 33 percent, in Latin America by 46 percent, in Southeast Asia by 144 percent and in the tropics as a whole by 78 percent. The area in question totalled somewhere between 460,000 and 720,000 km².[12] The amount of forest in Southeast Asia that is newly affected each year currently amounts to 10,000-27,000 km²; in Latin America, 8000-25,000 km²; and in Africa (mostly West Africa), 32,000 km². This makes a total for the tropics of 53,000-87,000 km². Moreover, these figures refer only to legal fellings of industrial timber; illegal fellings could swell the totals a good deal more (as in Indonesia where "timber poaching" is a great and growing problem — see Chapter 10) by sometimes twice as much.

Logging impact varies from area to area. In some places the

consequence is only light modification, in other places it amounts to gross degradation of the forest. Where the disruption is marginal, the original forest may restore itself within a decade or so. Where the disruption is extensive, the forest may take many decades to recover and the ensuing ecosystem may remain a good deal different from the original one for a whole century, if not longer. As mentioned, research in Southeast Asia suggests that between one-third and two-thirds of the remaining trees are damaged beyond recovery when a few commercial logs are removed. By contrast, field reports from FAO staffers indicate that, for the tropics as a whole, one-tenth may be a more reasonable estimate. For purposes of present calculations, a figure of one-third is proposed — with the emphatic proviso that this is no more than an interim figure in the absence of anything more substantive, and used only to formulate a "working appraisal" of what is happening to tropical forests. This means that timber exploitation causes the elimination of somewhere between 17,700 and 29,000 km² of tropical moist forests each year.

The slash-and-burn cultivator

The logging impact can be grossly aggravated by what happens after the commercial exploiter leaves his patch of forest. Along the timber tracks come subsistence peasants, able to penetrate deep into forest areas that have hitherto been closed to them. Clearing away more trees in order to plant their crops, they may soon cause far more damage and destruction that the lumber man did. Not only do they arrive in large numbers, but they stay in the locality permanently.

Not that the slash-and-burn cultivator has always been destructive. Before he became so numerous, he could operate as a shifting cultivator. He would fell and burn a patch of forest, raise crops for 2 or 3 years until the soil lost its fertility, or until weeds moved in, then he would move on and repeat the process in another part of the forest. This was a style of agriculture that allowed the cultivator to make sustainable use of the forest environment. As long as there were not more than four or five persons per square kilometer, and a patch of farmed forestland could be left fallow for at least 10 years in order to renew itself, the system worked.[13] Now that cultivators have increased in numbers to a point where there are often 3 times as many people per square kilometer, they find themselves with less space to move around in. The result is that they make intensive as well as extensive demands on the forest, leaving local ecosystems with little chance to recover.

Roughly speaking, it is thought that 50 million cultivators in primary tropical moist forests occupy at least 640,000 km², a Texas-sized area, while another 90 million cultivators in secondary forests occupy twice as much land, altogether accounting for over one-fifth of all tropical forests. According to preliminary reckonings, 100,000 km² of forest are eliminated each year, perhaps much more. The greatest loss occurs in Southeast Asia, where cultivators clear a minimum of 85,000 km² each year, adding to rather more than 1 million km² of formerly forested croplands in the region. Africa south of the Sahara is believed to have lost 1 million km² of moist forest to these cultivators even before modern development trends started after World War II. Africa's current loss is put at 40,000 km² per year, and as much as 400,000 km² of its moist forestlands may now be under this form of agriculture.[14] A similar story applies in Latin America, though fewer details are available. All forms of expanding agriculture in Latin America, of which slash-and-burn cultivation is a major type, are thought to be accounting for 50,000 km² a year.[15]

The figures above represent minimal estimates, prepared through order-of-magnitude reckonings. A further assessment can be arrived at through looking at the consequences of commercial logging, viz. the amount of forest accounted for by cultivators who move into virgin territories after the logger has quit the scene. Field investigations in Ivory Coast indicate that for every 5 m³ of logs removed by the timber exploiter, 1 hectare of forest disappears at the hands of the follow-on cultivator. What happens in Ivory Coast can be said to apply broadly in other parts of West Africa with their high-density populations; it is unlikely to apply in Congo, which, with an area similar to Ivory Coast's but with only one-seventh as many people, is under less pressure from spreading agriculturalists. Similar differentiation holds good for Southeast Asia and Amazonia.

To take a general overview, Africa in 1973 produced 31.2 million m³ of logs, Southeast Asia 81 million, and Latin America 25.5 million. Together with smaller amounts elsewhere, this makes a total for the tropics of 149 million. Using the very rough rule of thumb developed in Ivory Coast, this could mean that, in the areas in question, 62,400, 162,000, 51,000 and 298,000 km² of forest were eliminated by slash-and-burn cultivators. The last figure, almost 300,000 km² for the tropics, compares with a minimal estimate of 165,000 km² through the preceding calculation. Because of differentiated impact, the figure of 300,000 km² is probably way too high, while 165,000 km², being a minimal conservative estimate, could be decidedly too low. For purposes of an overall appraisal of destructive trends, a figure of 200,000 km² is adopted here — albeit an estimate that is rough and ready in the extreme, but one that serves as a "reasonable working figure" for present purposes.

Fuelwood

A further major factor in destruction of tropical moist forests is demand for fuelwood. As mentioned, it is thought that almost half of all wood cut world-wide each year is used as fuel, with over four-fifths of it going to meet the needs of people in the developing world (Table 1).[16] A few household surveys suggest that the amount of fuelwood actually cut could be 2½ times as large as is "officially" estimated.[17] The situation has been grossly aggravated by the increase in oil prices, putting kerosene beyond the means of many households. To this extent, the OPEC countries bear a major though indirect responsibility for part of the exploitation pressures now directed at tropical moist forests.

On the basis of field reports, it is realistically reckoned that one person can obtain a sustainable supply of fuelwood from the equivalent of half a hectare of forest each year. More usually, however, in order to exploit supplies close to hand, as many as fifteen persons may be taking wood from 1 hectare — an excessively concentrated, and so unsustainable, rate of use. In large parts of the tropics, much wood is taken from secondary forests, scrub patches and village woodlots, rather than from virgin forests. For example, in Southeast Asia about one-third of the fuelwood comes from outside forests proper. Since at least 200 million people (out of 1 billion in the tropical moist forest zone) live within or on the fringes of forests, and since a good part of their fuelwood gathering goes to serve commercial markets in far-off urban areas, it is reasonable to suppose that at least one-fifth of fuelwood cut throughout the developing tropics comes from primary forests. This means that fuelwood gathering leaves around 25,000 km² of primary moist forests grossly impoverished, if not destroyed, each year.

Assuming that human populations continue to expand, and that the remaining forests continue to be reduced (not only through exploitation for wood, but to make way for agriculture), residual tracts will become subject to increasing exploitation and over-exploitation. In some areas demand has already grown so great, and pressure on available supplies has become so acute, that it already costs as much to heat the cooking bowl as to fill it.

Cattle raising

A major cause of forest elimination in Latin America is cattle raising. The forest is cleared away entirely, in order to establish man-made grasslands. The pastures remain productive for 6-10 years, then are taken over by scrub growth. The rancher does not usually mind since he can move on to another patch of forest and start again.

An increasing number of ranching enterprises in Latin America are foreign-owned. A U.S. consortium of Brescan-Swift-Armour-King Ranch holds around 720 km² in the eastern part of Brazilian Amazonia, with an investment of $6 million. Other multinational corporations in Brazilian Amazonia include Heublein, Sifco Industries and Twin Agricultural and Industrial Developers from the United States, Mitsui, Tsuzuki Spinning, and Nichimen and Grubo Bradesco from Japan, Liquigas from Italy, and George Markhof from Austria, among many more from industrialized nations. Investment on the part of the twelve largest enterprises totals $21 million, except for Volkswagen with $35 million.[18] Volkswagen believes that although people may come to purchase fewer cars in the wake of the oil price hike, they will hardly be inclined to eat less beef. Volkswagen holds a concession of 1400 km² in the eastern Amazon, of which half is to be converted into pastureland. By mid-1976 the Company had burned about 100 km² of forest, enough for a herd of

10,000 cattle. The eventual aim is to increase the grasslands to 700 km², to support 120,000 cattle.

To date, some 300 ranches have been established, with a cattle population of 6 million. This has entailed the elimination of 66,000 km² of forest. Virtually none of the timber felled has been disposed of as commercial wood, even though the marketable lumber could fetch $35 per cubic meter; the subsidized rancher does not find it worth his while to do other than douse herbicide on to the area to be cleared, then put a match to it. Result: an average of 50 m³ of useable timber per hectare goes up in smoke, representing a total loss to date of $7.7 billion, or about 2½ times as much per year as Amazonia's commercial sales of timber.

The rationale for cattle-raising is two-fold. First, due to Brazil's political desire to assert its political sovereignty over its vast and little-settled sector of Amazonia, the government seeks to develop the forestlands through whatever means may appear appropriate. Secondly, Brazil has an eye to the world's growing beef shortage. According to the U.N. Food and Agriculture Organization, world-wide demand for meat is projected to rise from 1970 to 1990 more rapidly than for other foods except fish. To meet this growing demand with its soaring prices, Brazil is determined to become one of the biggest beef exporters in the world. In 1973 the country possessed 95 million head of cattle, a total surpassed only by the Soviet Union and the United States. By 1980 Brazil hopes to have doubled its 1973 output of meat and to rank as the world's number one beef exporter.

However, raising beef in tropical forestlands is not so straightforward as it might seem. Stocking rates are low, a mere one animal per hectare. Steers take 4 years before they are ready for slaughter, at a weight of 450 kg. Soils quickly become exhausted of nutrients, and pastures feature poorer and poorer grass unless they receive ever-growing amounts of fertilizer. A few ranches have already been abandoned and at least 200 look likely to become unprofitable after only 5 years. Due to a spreading problem of toxic weeds, some ranches have lost one-fifth of their cattle. Yet so compelling are the political considerations underpinning Brazil's urge to open up its sector of Amazonia that exceptional financial incentives are offered to attract cattle-ranching investors.

Ironically, much more beef could be raised, at far lower environmental cost, in those parts of southern Brazil's agricultural lands that are left unused, almost 800,000 km².[19] There is little inducement, however, for the country's largest landowners (a mere 10 percent of all landowners control 80 percent of the land) to aim for intensive management of their present holdings in southern Brazil as long as they encounter powerful financial persuasion to clear new territories in Amazonia. To the wealthy stockman who obtains Amazonian land for next to nothing, it matters little that he needs 10 times as much space to raise his cattle herds than in sub-tropical parts of Brazil where typical pastures lose only 30-40 percent of initial stocking capacity after 20-30 years.

The upshot is that in Brazil, as in many parts of the tropical developing world, stock raising remains one of the most wasteful of all agricultural industries.[20] It has even been suggested that cattle husbandry in Latin America's existing grasslands could probably be made 4 or 5 times more efficient, and meat output increased 10 times, merely through improved breeds of livestock and prophylactic drugs to counter epizootics, plus better management all round. This would enable Brazil to produce all the extra beef it wants without eliminating a single additional rainforest tree. Much of the beef raised in Amazonia is for the local Brazilian market. The average Brazilian citizen now consumes only 16 kg of beef per year, less meat than a domestic cat enjoys in the United States. But a good deal of the beef goes overseas, an export trade now worth $25 million a year.

It is this factor of export that points up once again the relationship between developed-world lifestyles and changes overtaking developing-world environments. As beef produced in Europe and North America grows more expensive, the affluent consumer stimulates the spread of ranching into forest zones of tropical America. He does not do it wittingly, and certainly not with wanton intent. But he does it effectively and increasingly.

As the international beef trade grows, more countries of Latin America, notably Peru and Colombia, aim to convert portions of their Amazonian lowland forests into cattle ranches. Bolivia hopes to open up its sparsely populated eastern region, an area larger than Spain, through an initiative on the part of the Anglo-Bolivian Land

and Cattle Company, which plans to obtain financial support from Britain, the United States, West Germany and France. Bolivia intends to sell off almost 1 million hectares of virgin forest, at a mere $42 per hectare, to 150,000 white settlers whom it hopes to attract from southern Africa.

Between 1962 and 1985 it is expected that at least 325,000 km² of Latin America's tropical forests, or an area the size of Norway or New Mexico, will have been cleared for pasturelands (Brazil, 125,000, and Colombia, 66,000). This works out at an average of just under 13,500 km² per year. Since the rate is likely to be greater at the end of the period than at the start, due to growing population pressures if nothing else, the figure for 1979 could well have reached 20,000 km² — a figure that is accepted for this review of destructive trends in tropical moist forests.

Summary of forest elimination

Elimination of tropical moist forests stems primarily from the commercial logger/follow-on cultivator combination, which is thought to be accounting, as a preliminary and very approximate calculation, for 200,000 km² per year. The fuelwood cutter could well be responsible for 25,000 km² a year, and the ranching entrepreneur (confined to Latin America) for 20,000 km² (Table 9). This makes a total of 245,000 km² per year. These figures do not include other agents of forest destruction, such as the commercial logger who over-exploits a patch of forest without being followed by the slash-and-burn cultivator; the cultivator who clears forest without any pioneering assistance from the logger; the plantation operator who replaces virgin forest with monocultures of tree species such as eucalyptus, pines, rubber trees and oil palms; and others who eliminate the forest for various reasons, but whose destructive impact is not on a scale to match the three main categories.

The total figure of 245,000 km² is way beyond the mean of the best estimate hitherto available, that of FAO, viz. 120,000-170,000 km². The figure of 245,000 km² is considered realistic on two grounds. First, the FAO data derive in many instances from trends documented in the early 1970s, if not before — since which time, exploitation patterns have accelerated markedly. Secondly, FAO calculations generally represent, for the sake of caution, minimal estimates. Of course, there is merit in caution when it is applied for the sake of accuracy. But to help us "get a handle" on the problem of destruction of tropical forests, and thus establish the size of the problem we are grappling with, it is worthwhile to make an estimate of what we believe could be going on as well as what we know is going on. It is in this spirit that the figure of 245,000 km² is advanced.[21]

Until more information is available, then, it is not unreasonable to suppose that the earth is losing around 670 km² of tropical moist forest a day, or an area the size of Wales or Massachusettes each month.

Table 9
Preliminary estimate of amount of tropical moist forest lost each year

Cause	Amount (km²)	
Combination of commercial logger and follow-on cultivator	200,000	(range, 165,000 to 300,000)
Fuelwood cutter	25,000	
Cattle rancher (only in Latin America)	20,000	(323,000 estimated to be cleared during 24-year period 1962-85, or average of 13,458 each year; greatest rate of destruction will occur in latter part of period)
Total	245,000	
	(compare FAO figure of 120,000 -170,000)	

Note: These figures represent preliminary and very approximate estimates of destruction trends. They are presented as no more than an attempt to form a working idea of the size of the problem.

An annual loss of 245,000 km² amounts to 2.6 percent of the tropical moist forest biome of 9,350,000 km². As human populations grow and their aspirations too, the rate of loss can be expected to increase.

Sources: see text.

12 Ways to Relieve Excessive Exploitation

Excessive exploitation of tropical moist forests can be relieved in several ways.

(a) More efficient use of all wood cut

A major way to reduce exploitation of forests everywhere is to make more efficient use of all wood cut. Here we will consider just a single option, greater recycling of paper.

There is much scope for greater recycling, especially on the part of those countries that consume most, the advanced nations. Not only can many fiber-based materials be reprocessed into paper, but many more can be utilized for manufacture of fiberboard, particleboard and moulded products.

Of all paper products used world-wide, less than 40 million out of 160 million are recycled.[1] The United States consumes over 70 million tons of paper and paperboard per year, or 3½ times as much as in 1944. Of this amount, it recycles only a little over 16 million tons, for a re-use rate twice as high as in 1944, but still only around 23 percent, as compared with 40 percent achieved by Switzerland, Holland and Japan (during World War II, Britain recycled 62 percent). Roughly speaking, each American citizen, junking an average of 180 kg of paper each year, is throwing away the equivalent of three conifer trees. So the United States is annually discarding material worth almost one billion trees, or a 5000 km² forest (the size of Delaware). The United States is also wasting 4 times as much paper as is used by all countries of the developing world put together, with their 11 times as many people.

175

To increase recycling requires no new technology. Rather it depends on government measures. The U.S. government could readily offer incentives, provided it believed its citizenry would go along. Without policy shifts of this sort, America's recycling could actually decline. Government initiative would mean not only a reduction of exploitation pressures on forests, but also it would generate benefits of other kinds. Were recycling to rise by 1985 to 26 percent, instead of falling to 17 percent (both of which levels are on the cards), the difference in terms of waste-disposal costs would amount to at least $230 million.[2]

(b) Substitute materials

Demand for forest-derived fiber could also be reduced through greater use of other waste materials. The amount of crop residues available for this purpose each year includes 885 million tons of straw, 55 million tons of bagasse (left-overs from crushed sugarcane), 30 million tons of bamboo and 30 million tons of reeds.[3] Yet to date these alternative supplies of cellulose provide only 5 percent of all pulp used. Around one-third of developing countries' manufacture of pulp is based on these non-wood materials, primarily bagasse and bamboo (China derives almost half its pulp this way). By contrast, North America, finding hitherto that it can derive its pulp from more convenient sources, produces only 1 percent from substitute materials.

A number of other waste materials can be used for manufacture of boards. For example, corn cobs and stalks, peanut shells, sunflower seed hulls, and even coffee grounds left over from the manufacture of instant coffee, are all available in exceptionally large amounts in industrialized countries. Boards made from these agricultural throw-outs are generally at least as good as particleboard manufactured from commercial wood.[4]

Similarly, several wood-industry purposes can be met through a fast-growing plant that substitutes for smaller hardwoods, viz. kenaf. With intensive cultivation, kenaf yields 13-23 tons per hectare. This output compares favorably with some of the faster-growing hardwoods and represents between 5 and 7 times more pulp per hectare than pine trees.[5]

In addition, coconut trees could supply wood for a host of purposes, ranging from pulp and charcoal to low-cost roofing and parquet floors.[6] If dead coconut trees, numbering perhaps 1 billion each year out of an estimated 44 billion in the tropics, were put to use, this would represent a huge amount of supplementary raw material.

Why are these substitute materials not used? The main reason is that loggers tend to believe there is plenty more wood available from their traditional sources. They can best be persuaded otherwise through government intervention, in the form of taxes, subsidies and other financial incentives.

(c)   Plantations

In a few localities of the tropics, primary forests are cleared in order to make land available for plantations. To the extent that these man-made forests supply the quantities and types of wood required by world markets, they reduce the pressure to exploit primary forests. By the year 2000 enough "tree farms" could have been established to meet an appreciable proportion of global demand for timber and pulp from the tropics.

Most tree species utilized are exotics, notably eucalyptus and gmelina for hardwoods, and pines and other conifers for softwoods. So fast-growing are some of these trees that 500 km² of plantation can readily produce 1 million m³ of marketable timber per year — a volume that can be obtained only from 10 times as large an area of virgin forests.[7] As for pulp, an annual output of 150,000 tons can be achieved from a 1100-km² plantation in the northern temperate zone, from a 310-km² plantation of conifers in the tropics, and from a 190-km² plantation of hardwoods in the tropics.[8]

Certain tree species sprout like mushrooms in the tropics. For example, a highly-fertilized eucalyptus seedling can grow at least 30 cm per month, going on to reach 20 m in height and over 25 cm in diameter at breast height after only 8 years, whereupon the plantation produces commercial wood that averages out at 30, and even up to 50 m³ per hectace per year.[9] The Caribbean pine reaches almost 30 m in height after only 12 years, whereupon it yields an aggregate of 300 m³ per hectare, whereas a Douglas fir, by contrast, will have reached only 10 m in that time, and its wood will still not be ready for market.

But tropcial plantations bring problems. As is the case with most monoculture crops, diseases and pests are numerous and varied. When plantation trees are harvested, they take a large stock of nutrients with them. From the standpoint of wildlife and ecological diversity, they are a disaster. Hardly any animal native to Madagascar lives in the island's extensive eucalyptus forests, and lemurs have become endangered far more through plantation projects than through hunting.

Even economic difficulties arise for these fast-cash trees. Since the cost of establishing a tropical plantation runs to around $250 per hectare, and if the plantation then yields, say, 21 m^3 per hectare per year, the cost of the wood, at 10 percent interest after 10 years, is $3.09 per cubic meter. If the rotation period is 20 years, then $4; if 30 years, $6.92; and if 40 years, $13.47. If the interest rate is increased only marginally to 13 percent, the cost at 10 years is little different, $4.04, for a 25 percent increase; but after 40 years it becomes $39.52, for almost a 200 percent increase. Clearly, plantation forestry is very sensitive to changes in interest rates, likewise to inflationary trends.

Furthermore, investment is required on a large scale. A 50,000-hectare plantation costs $12.5-20 million to establish, and a mill capable of handling the plantation's production, viz. a mill with output of 300 tons per day, costs at least $50 million (a major economy-of-scale mill costs 10 times as much). To establish plantations and mills in tropical countries with combined capacity to meet projected demand for timber and paper products requires investment of at least 6 billion dollars.[10]

Further hefty investment is required for a related form of plantation forestry that could contribute much to the future of virgin tropical forests — farm woodlots and local-community tree blocs to supply fuelwood for developing-world households. The aggregate area required, at an annual output of only 10 m^3 per hectare, would amount to 600,000 km^2, and with investment running at $100 per hectare, this means a price tab of $6 billion. Insofar as the OPEC countries have helped to precipitate the crisis of fuelwood demand (through putting alternative fuels such as kerosene beyond the reach of many households), they could make good use of their petro-dollars by subsidizing this development of fresh sources of fuelwood.

Because of the scale of investment required for plantation forestry and associated processing industries, many tropical-forest countries are increasingly looking toward the foreign investor. This explains why half of Latin America's total sales of paper and paperboards have recently been accounted for by affiliates of U.S. timber corporations.[11] It also accounts for Brazil's agreement with eleven Japanese companies for a $1-billion, 4000-km² pulp project. Yet foreign investors are not moving into the field of tropical plantations as fast as they might. They are not sufficiently assured concerning security of prices for their products, or security of tenure for their holdings. Each inflationary upheaval in world currency systems, and each nationalization of a foreign enterprise in a tropical country defers the day when enough plantations will be established to relieve exploitation pressures on remaining virgin forests. Considering that plantations require a lead time of at least 10 years before they start to produce wood in bulk, there is urgency in stabilizing the politico-economic environment for the foreign entrepreneur — with all that entails for ultimate conservation of tropical moist forests (see also Chapter 13).

Tropical plantations now amount to around 85,000 km². Of this total, around 40,000 km² are in Latin America (over half in Brazil), 30,000 in Africa (mostly in West Africa) and 10,000 in Southeast Asia. Another 5000 km² or so are established each year — only one-third as many as will be required if tropical plantations are to supply enough wood to relieve extreme exploitation pressures on virgin forests over the next two decades, let alone the next century.

The greatest expanse of tropical plantations to date is in Brazil. The country illustrates the need for developing regions to exploit their own potential sources of pulp and paper. In 1962 Brazil consumed 0.07 million tons of paper, in 1975, 1.9 million, and is expected to require 4 million tons in 1985[12] — by which time each of Brazil's 135 million citizens is likely to be accounting for at least 27 kg of paper per year, way above the average for the developing world though still only one-twelfth as much as an American citizen now consumes. Between 1968 and 1974 Brazil more than doubled its production of pulp, to place it among the world's ten leading pulp producers. Yet in 1974 the country imported almost 700,000 tons of pulp and paper, worth $349 million. By 1980 Brazil aims to produce enough pulp to meet its own needs and, by the year 2000, to have a surplus of 20 million tons per year for export to other countries of Latin America, worth, at present prices, around $5.5 billion.

This enventual aim will require an additional 40,000 km^2 of plantations. To date, almost all Brazil's 25,000 km^2 of man-made forests are located in the southern sector of the country, way outside Amazonia. But since 1969 the average price of land for reforestation in some of the heavily populated southern areas has increased 11 times, so there is strong incentive to look for opportunity elsewhere — notably in Amazonia, where there is likely to be 10,000 km^2 of plantations by 1985. Nevertheless, even if all additional plantations were located in Amazonia, this need affect little over 1 percent of present virgin forests.

Much the best prospect is to establish tropical plantations in forest territories that have already been exploited, and now amount to poor-quality secondary forest, degraded grasslands and areas that have been over-burdened by slash-and-burn cultivators. Indonesia alone features 440,000^2 of such misused lands, an area larger than the country's production forests. That this strategy is often feasible is demonstrated by plantations on abandoned coffee sites and on impoverished savannah lands in Venezuela and other parts of Latin America. A number of pioneer tree species grow satisfactorily in such areas. Regrettably, an outcome of this sort is, on present showing, unlikely. For one thing, a plantation entrepreneur prefers to locate his venture within an extensive tract of primary forest, so that he can exploit the virgin timber to capitalize his plantation (see Chapter 13). For another thing, already cleared forestlands are generally occupied by human settlements of one kind or another and it is politically difficult to uproot them in order to plant trees.

Moreover, were these difficulties to be overcome, plantations would not necessarily save what remains of primary forests. One cannot preserve the gold in the stream by giving local people a large income. Even with a very large income, some of them might continue to take the gold on the grounds that if they don't somebody else will.

(d) Agro-forestry

As indicated in the preceding chapter, a prime agent in present destruction of tropical moist forests is the shifting cultivator. What to do about this person's traditional way of life, that, due to pressure of human numbers, no longer makes sustainable use of forest environments?

One solution lies in stepping up the productivity of the cultivator's croplands,[13] leaving him with less cause to move into fresh forest areas every few years. There seems little doubt that shifting cultivation can be made much more intensive and productive. Traditional farmers in West African forestlands usually manage no more than 100 kg of maize per hectare, whereas modern farmers in the same region can produce many times more.[14] In Southeast Asia, shifting agriculture produces enough food for only a handful of people per square kilometer, whereas an equal area of irrigated rice can feed as many as 700 persons. Chinese farmers in western Borneo raise a variety of crops — grains, pepper, rubber, a dozen sorts of vegetables — and intersperse them with fish ponds and livestock grazing; this system enables them to make permanent use of impoverished tropical soils, eliminating their need to move on every few years. Lacandon farmers in the Chiapas Forest of southern Mexico grow as many as eighty varieties of food and raw material crops in a single hectare, and exploit the surrounding forest environment for up to 100 species of fruits and other wild foods, 20 varieties of fish, 6 types of turtles, 3 kinds of frogs, 2 types of snails, 2 species of crabs, 2 species of crocodiles and 3 kinds of crayfish.[15]

However, improved agriculture for the shifting cultivator requires modern perquisities such as high-yielding grains, seed varieties that flourish with little or no tilling of the ground (to reduce soil erosion) and plant types that can cope with telescoped fallow periods. Most crops of these sorts prosper only with plenty of insecticides, herbicides and fertilizers, all of which are scarce commodities in developing countries. According to FAO, Indonesia applies only 2.63 kg of fertilizer per square kilometer of arable land, compared with 9.16 kg in the United States, even though Indonesia tries to support 716 of its citizens off each square kilometer, compared to 102 in the United States. Because of high prices, fertilizer remains beyond the reach of

impoverished peasants of the tropics. Prices have been pushed high
due to the oil price hike on the part of OPEC, and are kept high due to
inflated demand on the part of rich countries (North Americans and
Europeans use more fertilizer for their golf courses, gardens and
cemeteries than all shifting cultivators put together). As long as he
encounters problem of this scale, the forest farmer finds it hard to
adapt his traditional style of agriculture.

Fortunately, a new strategy is emerging. It encourages the peasant
farmer to plant trees rather than cut them down. This approach, or
"agro-forestry", depends on offering the cultivator incentives to
establish a plantation of fast-growing trees on a patch of cleared
forestland at the same time as he plants food crops.[16] By the time he is
ready to move on, the plantation trees will be about ready to close
their canopy. The tree plantation can be intercropped with food plants
such as maize and bananas, also with coffee, tea, spices, fruit trees
and many other items. Trial projects now feature tall-growing timber
trees, medium-height cash crops such as coffee, low-growing food
crops such as manioc, and fish and giant snails in water channels — a
regular Dagwood sandwich of products. In this way, growing food
can be combined with restoration of forest cover, instead of leaving
behind degraded scrubland.

Trial projects show that agro-forestry also succeeds financially. In
eastern Nigeria a cultivator can earn $200-300 per year from the trees
he plants, while the Forest Service finds that a plantation established
through agro-forestry costs only $200-350 a hectare, compared with
$800 through direct planting.[17] If the cultivator uses his earnings to
buy fertilizer and pesticides he can grow 4 times as much maize,
cassava, yams and other food crops.

Agro-forestry can also be combined with private commercial
enterprise. The Paper Industry Corporation of the Philippines
embarked in 1974 on a program in conjunction with the World Bank
to encourage forest farmers to rent patches of deforested land on the
Company's 190,000-hectare concession.[18] A typical smallholder is
allocated 10 hectares, 8 of them to be planted with pulpwood trees and
2 to be used for growing foodcrops and raising livestock. The farmer
receives a loan to cover up to 75 percent of the plantation in costs, plus
the first year's food production; his own main contribution is his

labour in planting the trees, then tending them until they become ready to cut. By late 1976, 3849 farmers had planted 12,400 hectares with almost 9 million trees, for eventual sale to the Company's pulpmills. An average smallholder can hope to earn, within 8 years of planting his trees, at least $2600 per hectare.[19] By 1985 the Company expects to obtain about 40 percent of its 650,000 m³ of pulpwood per year from these farmers. Moreover, in view of the fact that the Philippines has been importing paperpulp worth $30 million per year, the project will make a marked contribution to the national economy as well as stemming deforestation and fostering re-forestation.

(e)   "OPEC-ization" of hardwood exports

How about a cartel on the part of timber-exporting countries? An initiative along these lines would enable the countries in question to maintain their export earnings while reducing exploitation pressures on primary forests.[20] True, the consequences need not necessarily work out along those lines; exporting countries might seek not only to earn more in value per unit of wood, but to export more in volume. However, a significant price hike is likely to lead to a damp-down in demand in consumer countries and to a levelling-off of international trade in tropical hardwoods. During the mid-1970s economic recession, Japanese construction builders turned to alternative materials for their housing needs rather than continue to pay the pre-recession prices for Southeast Asian timber. Similar shifts to substitute materials in the United States suggest that as prices rise, demand drops off. At first, of course, a cartel-organized price hike might trigger protests in consumer nations, on the grounds of "unfair monopolistic practices". But consumers could also consider whether they prefer to go on squawking at the inflationary impact of increased prices, or to recognize the conservation benefits of a cartel.

Is a cartel feasible? Almost 80 percent of the world's hardwood exports are now accounted for by only three countries — Philippines, Indonesia and Malaysia. In 1977 these producers exported over 35 million m³ of unprocessed logs, a total projected to reach 43 million by 1985. By contrast, demand on the part of developed-world consumers has been projected to rise way beyond supply. This situation could be exploited by the "big three" nations, which hold a large monopoly of relatively uniform, high-density stocks of hardwoods (alternative sources such as Latin America yield only one-third as much hardwood timber per hectare as a typical forest of the Philippines). If these three countries were to jointly limit their export of logs, they could earn more income per log without jeopardizing their total foreign exchange earnings.

In point of fact, a preliminary cartel has already been established by the Southeast Asian Lumber Producers Association. The Southeast Asia cartel came into effect in February 1975, then was partially suspended when the global economic recession of 1975/76 caused a temporary cutback in developed-world demand for tropical hardwoods. It is now being brought into force once more, with gradual limitations on log exports. Worth $1.7 billion, the Association could soon be in a position to impose its strategy as concerns marketing and pricing. A similar initiative is being developed by the Organization of African Producers and Exporters of Wood, a group of eleven timber-exporting countries that includes the eight which account for almost all of Africa's exports.

The Southeast Asia cartel also envisages increased revenues through greater processing of timber on the part of exporter countries. At present 70 percent of the region's exports are made up of raw logs and the countries derive only a fraction of the final market value of finished products that undergo processing in Japan, Taiwan and South Korea. The value of a log exported raw earns around $70 per cubic meter, but it doubles or triples when it is processed into sawnwood, plywood or veneer. In 1976 the United States imported processed tropical hardwoods from Japan, Taiwan and South Korea worth over $100 million, at prices generally ranging from $120 to $575 per cubic meter (best-quality veneer, after going through several stages of processing, can be worth as much as $4000 per cubic meter in final finished form). This all means that the 46 million m^3 of logs exported by all tropical countries in 1977 could have earned an extra $4 billion in product value. To discourage developing-country processing with the profits it entails, the main timber-importing countries, notably the United States and Japan, apply protective tariffs of 10-20 percent on sawnwood and plywood from developing countries, while allowing raw logs to be imported duty-free.

(f)   Forest industrial complexes

An unusually promising way to achieve sustainable exploitation of tropical forests lies with the many diverse products they could yield for industrial purpose. Of tropical forests' plant biomass, a mere 1-2 percent is generally of use to the conventional logger. The rest could serve many needs, though hitherto it is generally ignored since its value is not recognized. Were the productive diversity of tropical moist forests better understood, there could soon be scope for integrated processing plants that handle a wide variety of products — in short, "forest industrial complexes".

There is a broad range of items immediately available. Generally known as "minor forest products", their aggregate worth, when they are comprehensively exploited, need not be so minor — and they can all be extracted with trifling disruption for forest ecosystems. They include oils, gums, resins, waxes, latex, tannins, alkaloids, drugs and medicines, dyes, edible and oil-bearing nuts, spices, fruit, rattans, bamboos, guanos, bark products, forage, perfumes and other extractives such as citronella oil, insect products such as lac resin (the main ingredient of shellac), insecticides, and honey and beeswax. Among the hundreds of industrial goods whose manufacture depends on these products are leather articles, paints, glues, caulking materials, tennis rackets and cough medicines. The value of these items can be appreciable. Sarawak in 1973 exported 28,000 tons of illipo nuts, worth more than $4 million. Indonesia exports 50,000 tons of rattan a year, worth almost $4 million — rattans being climbing palms used for cane furniture, basketry, fishtraps, hats, matting, brooms, cordage and rope. Indonesia also exports a further 80,000 tons of essential oils (sandalwood oil, palmrose, clove, cinnamon, turpentine, etc.), resins, exudates, bark and other "minor forest products", worth another $27 million a year.

The two main components of wood, viz. lignin and cellulose, can be applied for all manner of innovative purposes.[21] Lignin constitutes 20-30 percent of wood and is available in abundant forms among the

immense diversity of tropical forests. It can be used in the
manufacture of plastics, polyesters, ion-exchange resins, adhesives,
rubber reinforcers, fertilizers, vanillin, emulsions, tanning agents,
solvents, asphalt strengtheners, dispersants for oil-well drilling,
ceramic processors, and soil stabilizers. Cellulose is used in the
manufacture of rayon, plastics, phenols, furfural, and formaldehyde,
and serves as a raw material for hydrolysis to sugar. In addition,
"wood engineering", or synthesis of various wood components
(particles, fibers, strands, flakes) with non-wood components
(plastics, metals, minerals), points the way to entirely new types of
products. For example, the yellow handle of the everyday screwdriver
is made from a mixture of wood and plastic; the same for spectacle
frames. Possible new products along these lines already total 3000.
Even foliage can be used for the manufacture of a variety of chemical
products, including pharmaceuticals such as chlorophyllcarotene
paste that serves to treat skin burns, nervous disorders and rheumatic
pains.

These innovative approaches could encourage the exploiter to make
more efficient and systematic use of tropical forests. This would be a
marked advance beyond present practices, which have been described
by Dr. K.F.S. King, former Director of FAO's Forestry Department,
as "primitive, costly and wasteful". Indeed, when one considers the
spectrum of valuable products available from tropical moist forests,
by contrast with the few that are generally harvested, one can even say
that the forests are over-exploited and under-utilized.

Potentially most important of all, tropical forests could serve as a
major source of energy. Apart from fuelwood, they offer scope to
generate energy of sorts that would benefit many developing
countries. Green plants capture the energy of sunlight and convert it
into food and fuel. It was this process of photosynthesis that
originally gave rise to startpoint materials for geologic formation of
oil, natural gas and coal. How to cut out the one-third of a billion
years that have transformed ancient green plants into petroleum,
and to harvest the stored solar energy of present-day plants?
Photosynthetic plants offer by far the simplest way for man to collect
solar energy, whereupon he can process the biomass to extract its
stored energy in the form of oil, gas and other fuels. Of course the

energy value of wood is lower than that of oil: burning 1 ton of dry wood yields about 4 million kilocalories, while a ton of oil yields 10 million kilocalories. Nevertheless, biomass-derived fuel is a type of energy that makes use of earth's single truly renewable resource: sunlight. Moreover, this would be, by contrast with fossil fuels, a non-polluting way of generating energy.

Utilized in this manner, tropical forests, with their high rates of photosynthesis, could supply appreciable amounts of energy on a sustainable basis.[22] One ton of tropical dry wood can yield 300 kg of a coal-like residue (for use in lime and cement kilns, steel industry and domestic households), 14 liters of methanol (for use as a fuel and as a solvent), 140 m^3 of gas (largely useful through recycling to energise the production process), 76 litres of wood oil and light tar, 53 liters of acetic acid (used as a basis for acetone, and for the manufacture of textiles), 8 liters of esters (used for methyl acetate and ethyl formate), 12 liters of creosote oil (used for timber preservation), and 30 kg of pitch (used for waterproofing, road surfacing and as a caulking material).[23] Some estimates suggest that the total energy available in new growth of tropical forest material each year matches half the world's present consumption of energy of all forms.

Foremost among the techniques for extracting energy from forest material is pyrolysis. This amounts to heating organic material in air-free containers to high temperatures, whereupon a crude light oil is released with around 75 percent calorific value of ordinary oil. Also produced is a mixture of gases, and a flaky char. To date, the process has generally been applied to forestry wastes such as lumbering leftovers and sawdust, and to other plant-material refuse such as rice straw, cocoa pods, ground-nut shells and the like. But pyrolysis need not be confined to waste materials of forestry and agriculture. It can carbonize entire trees. In Ghana, a U.S. AID-supported research project indicates that a 40,000-hectare plantation of fast-growing trees could produce energy equivalent to 500,000 tons of coal per year (together with food crops interplanted among the trees, amounting to 60,000 tons of peanuts and 54,000 tons of corn). A capital-intensive plantation, of the same size but with sophisticated processing facilities, could produce 50,000 tons of methanol, 12,000 tons of pyrolytic oil, 150,000 tons of ammonia fertilizer, 17,000 tons of char and 80,000 kilowatt hours of electricity per year (together with 60,000 tons of peanuts and 50,000 tons of corn).[24]

Of these various products, the one that can most readily substitute for petroleum is methanol, also known as wood alcohol or methylated spirits. Alcohol can be used to drive an ordinary car when mixed with petrol in a ratio of 1:9, while only a few adjustments to the car's engine enable it to run off neat alcohol. Brazil, finding that its imports of oil topping $4 billion a year have been proving an intolerable drain on its foreign exchange reserves, has gone into the business of "growing gasoline", producing around 1 billion liters of biomass-derived alcohol per year. True, Brazil uses ethanol from sugarcane and cassava rather than methanol from wood, but the strategy is virtually the same. Many a car running around Rio de Janeiro is partially fueled with alcohol, and the Volkswagen assembly plant in Brazil utilizes engines that are adapted to a diet of nothing but alcohol. An Alcoholic VW, with exceptionally high octane fuel in its tank, surges along the road with never a knock.

Before the prospects of "petroleum plantations" can become a widespread reality, there is need to track down those tree species that best lend themselves, through genetic breeding, to ultra-rapid production to biomass. Were variations of giant ipilipil, for example, to be found with capacity to produce 100 m^3 of wood per hectare year after year, they could generate 500 barrels of oil per hectare, worth almost $7000. Some tree varieties, like certain tree species, are more efficient than others in photosynthesizing carbon dioxide. By the time research is underway on sufficient scale, the gene pools of potentially useful species and subspecies could be sorely depleted through over-exploitation of virgin forests.

A process akin to pyrolysis, hydrolysis, derives alcohol from plant biomass. But hydrolysis can produce not only fermentable sugars leading to liquid fuels, but it can produce non-fermentable sugars leading to a high-protein feed for livestock. Cellulose, the most abundant and naturally renewable material on earth, is not generally digested by ruminants. When wood chips are cooked in a chemical solution, the cellulose is converted into a sweet-smelling concoction that looks like a mixture of wet sawdust and dirt and proves to be a nutritious digestible material for feedlot livestock.[25] Raising cattle in the moist tropics through sustainable use of the standing forest is preferable to replacing the forest with man-made pasturelands. The day may come when the stockman in Amazonia is advised to take a few trees, dice and cook them at high temperature, then mash and serve cold.

In addition, foliage can tempt jaded cattle appetites. Over 90 percent of foliage is potentially useable as an animal-feed additive or substitute. According to Dr. Joseph A. Tosi of the Tropical Science Center in San Jose, Costa Rica, this approach could enable 1 hectare of tropical rainforest to produce more meat and leather per year, and to do it at lower cost, than through conventional cattle husbandry.

A related process is gree-crop fractionation, producing leaf proteins and other foods for direct consumption by man. Certain plant leaves and stems can be ruptured to release juices and saps that contain a number of proteins, also sugars, salts, lipids and vitamins. This process could allow man to obtain at least as much quality food from a tropical tree as when he clears away the trees to plant conventional crops.[26]

All in all, there is good cause to regard tropical forests as a source of many varied products, beyond the handful of items for which they are currently exploited. In light of these possibilities, plus many more that are not yet identified but are almost certainly on the cards, there is prospect that these forests could eventually feature nodes of industrial development, where manufacturing and processing industries utilize raw materials drawn from a surrounding sea of relatively undisturbed forest.

13 The Role of Multinational Corporations

In all three main tropical regions, much exploitation of forest and forestlands is carried out by multinational corporations. Many of these corporations' activities are beneficial, not only for their own stockholders but for the economies of the countries concerned. Conversely, some of their activities deserve scrutiny. Equally to the point, these corporations represent a vehicle by which industrialized nations intervene deeply in development processes in emergent regions. Forestry corporations amount to a medium through which the developed world expresses its demand for materials from tropical forestlands, notably timber and paperpulp, also beef. By the same token, they represent an important medium by which the developed world can potentially express its interest in conservation of natural resources, including unique forest ecosystems and species.

The principal responsibility for conservation of these resources, being national as well as natural resources, lies with governments of the tropical countries concerned. At the same time, developed world governments, through their attitude towards the giant timber corporations based in North America, Europe and Japan, contribute to survival prospects of tropical forests. Through permitting corporations to pursue exploitation activities that prove unduly disruptive of tropical forests, developed nations encourage the destruction of forest ecosystems and species' habitats. If developed nations were to constrain the corporations into taking account of environmental factors, they could make an outstanding contribution to conservation of species and forest tracts — even if, as a consequence of environmental safeguards, tropical hardwoods and similar products were to cost more.

Size and scope of forestry corporations

Several U.S. forestry corporations are active in tropical regions. Aong the leaders are Weyerhaeuser, Georgia Pacific, Westvaco, International Paper and at least another twenty well-known names. In the forestry sector of Latin America, around fifty U.S. corporations are now involved in almost 100 projects. In Brazilian Amazonia, Georgia Pacific exploits a concession of 4000, and Brumasa, a plywood manufacturer, 2000 km^2, while other corporations operate sizeable areas. In Indonesia, Weyerhaeuser holds a concession of 6000 km^2 with a start-up investment of $32 million, while Georgia Pacific exploits a concession of 3200 km^2 with over $8 million already invested. Many other examples could be cited.

A number of Japanese corporations, including Sumitomo, Nippon, Oji and other leading enterprises, are active in a joint concession of 800 km^2 in East Kalimantan in Indonesia, with a reputed investment of at least $41 million. Mitsubishi is a major stockholder in an enterprise in East Kalimantan, with $2 million invested. In South Kalimantan, Mitsui holds a forest concession of 740 km^2, capitalized to an extent of over $2 million, plus forestry investments worth $3 million in other parts of Indonesia. In Brazilian Amazonia, eleven Japanese companies are investing $600 million (in conjunction with the Brazilian government's $400 million) in a single pulp project, schedules to start with an output of 250,000 tons of pulp per year from 4000 km^2 of eucalyptus plantations — the largest such enterprise in the developing world.

While a good number of European corporations are active in the tropics, notably in Africa, they tend to be smaller in scale. A leading company is Britain-based Unilever, which has acquired a majority shareholding, in conjunction with a Canadian firm, MacMillan Bloedel, in an Indonesian timber enterprise in East Kalimantan. Bruynzeel of Holland and Borregaard of Norway have substantial timber interests in Amazonia, while (as described in Chapter 11) Volkswagen, Liquigas and several other non-timber corporations have gone into large-scale conversion of virgin forests of Amazonia into grasslands for cattle ranching.

Foreign corporations and tropical forestry

Exploitation of natural resources in the tropics requires large amounts of investment plus sophisticated technology. This is exceptionally the case for forestry. In order to exploit their resources, developing countries often find themselves dependent on foreign sources of capital and skills, almost at any cost. As a Nigerian delegate put it at a recent United Nations Hearing on Multinational Corporations:

> "A poor country, starved of foreign exchange, over-burdened with foreign debt, and struggling to implement a modest development programme, will, in the absence of alternatives, readily enter into various agreements with multinational corporations on unequal terms, reflecting its weak bargaining position and its desperate pursuit of a modest rate of investment."

These circumstances often lead to an unbalanced relationship between the overseas investor and the host country, since the country does not wish to impose regulations that might "scare away" the foreigner's funds and expertise. In turn, this allows certain corporations to use their commercial muscle to wield political influence that sometimes surpasses that of governments in all but the largest and most stable countries of the developing world.[1] While this assertion is, in the view of many corporations, a highly arguable point, there are plentiful examples of the degree to which a multinational corporation can sometimes undermine the basic sovereignty of a nation-state. For instance, it is difficult for countries of Southeast Asia to take a tougher stance with regard to foreign investment from Japan;[2] these countries are much more dependent on Japanese trade and investment (not to mention aid) than the other way round. While this does not make Japanese corporations omnipotent, it tends to strengthen their hands in the bargaining process with developing-country governments. A frequent result is that the foreign entrepreneur finds himself with exceptional power to dictate the way he manages his forest concession, with emphasis on his own narrow short-term interests and with scant regard for the host country's long-run needs.[3]

Moreover, forestry, being dependent on rapidly expanding technology and sophisticated machinery, is an exceptionally capital-intensive activity — emphasizing the fact that investment can usually be provided only by mega-corporations with large financial muscle in their home countries. In turn, heavy capital investment tends to foster certain undesirable forms of exploitation. An entrepreneur usually has to build his own roads for his remote forest concession, as much as 4 km for every square kilometer of forest in East Kalimantan, at a cost of $12,500 per km. To offset this large investment, the entrepreneur looks for a high average daily output of timber. So he feels inclined to extract logs at whatever cost to the forest ecosystem. Similarly the unit cost of bringing a log to the sawmill or shipping station is exceptionally sensitive to the volume removed per unit area. This persuades many corporations in Southeast Asia to extract as much as 100 m³ per hectare if not more — a volume of timber that is often way beyond what the forest can regenerate.

Worse still, an exploiter often feels driven to apparently reckless forms of exploitation by virtue of the high investment rates that his investment entails.[4] Being apprehensive about what the future holds for him, he places a high value on money. Finding that he has to pay astronomical rates of interest, he seeks to recover the capital on his project, plus profits, within relatively few years. In times of monetary instability and inflation, he even considers it prudent to extract whatever revenues he can within 10 years at most, instead of the 30 years or more that are required for forest regeneration. Moreover, the investment, being in a foreign land, is subject to appropriation with inadequate compensation at next to no notice.

For a variety of reasons, then, an exploiter often feels impelled to take his harvest from the forest in apparent indifference to the wider needs of the host country. In the process, he may eliminate wildlife species and genetic reservoirs without thought for the natural heritage of the community at large. Yet his actions are not so egotistical and callous as is sometimes suggested. He merely operates within the laws of the commercial game as laid down by society. Within this context, the onus for change is on governments to amend the situation, rather than upon private entrepreneurs to make sacrifices as if they constitute a public charity.

Weyerhaeuser in Indonesia

In order to see how one particular foreign timber corporation has established itself in a tropical forest nation, let us take a lengthy look at Weyerhaeuser's venture in Indonesia. Not that Weyerhaeuser should be considered characteristic of the way many corporations conduct their affairs in tropical-forest zones of the developing world — far from it. Weyerhaeuser's record appears to be a good deal better than most of its competitors'. This point is stressed, based on the author's own experience at Weyerhaeuser's concession in East Kalimantan and at the corporation's headquarters in Washington state, and on reports from other field researchers with direct experience of Weyerhaeuser's activities. Weyerhaeuser staffers are generally ready to discuss their operations and to consider differing viewpoints — a reaction in marked contrast to that of many other corporations approached by the author.

Weyerhaeuser is the largest U.S. timber corporation on earth, as measured by volume and value of its forest holdings.[5] Among U.S. industrial corporations, it ranks about 75th, with world-wide sales in 1977 of $3383 million. It owns 23,200 km² (a New Hampshire-sized area) in the United States, it holds harvesting rights in 35,600 km² (almost twice the size of Massachusetts) in Canada, and it controls around 8400 km² (two-thirds the size of Connecticut) in Southeast Asia — the latter holdings consisting of a sizeable sector of East Kalimantan in Indonesia and a smaller area in Sabah in Malaysia. These Southeast Asia ventures amount to 12 percent of the corporation's total holdings, and represent about 3 percent of total gross capital investment of $1.5 million. Weyerhaeuser is by far the largest foreign investor in the forestry sector in Indonesia, which, as mentioned, is the world's foremost producer of tropical hardwoods. Weyerhaeuser has perhaps more experience and technological skills in forest management than any other timber corporation, plus a first-rate global marketing network, so the corporation can appear an attractive proposition to developing nations.

In 1971 Weyerhaeuser and Indonesia got together. The corporation took a 65 percent interest in a 6000 km² concern in East Kalimantan, P.T. International Timber Corporation (the local partner being a private army-owned holding company, Tri Usaha Phakati, that is involved in at least fourteen timber concessions). Although its Indonesia venture has a legal and operational identity wholly distinct from the parent company in the United States, Weyerhaeuser, as the leading shareholder in ITCI, is the dominant partner. Weyerhaeuser supplied start-up capital of around $32 million from its U.S. headquarters and has been reinvesting around $5 million per year from its Indonesia profits.

For a time, Weyerhaeuser was also sole owner of another concession of 950 km² in East Kalimantan. Weyerhaeuser disposed of this area after thirty-five local sawmillers set up an illegal business on one-sixth of the concession, a government-sponsored resettlement program took over one-seventh as a site for transmigrants from Java and almost one-quarter was lost through boundary conflicts. In addition, Weyerhaeuser formerly operated 1000 km² in southern Philippines, but it withdrew after a company plane was high-jacked, a number of staff were killed by insurgents and an earthquake damaged the veneer mill.

During the first 7 years of operations, ITCI's sales of logs averaged around $37 million per year. In 1976, when the timber industry was recovering from the global economic recession that had sent prices tumbling, the corporation grossed $55 million from export of 1.2 million m³ (almost 7 percent of all Indonesia's log exports). These 1976 export earnings amounted to 29 percent of all Weyerhaeuser-controlled operations outside the United States, derived from only 14 percent of foreign forest holdings. In 1977 ITCI's log sales of 1.47 million m³ pulled in $66 million, out of which it paid royalties, taxes and other dues to the Indonesian government totalling $29 million.

In response to the obvious question, "So how much profit are you making?", ITCI offers the obvious answer that it would rather not say. However, certain statistics from a major corporation, which remains anonymous, indicate something about the profits picture. Total government levies, royalties, taxes and surcharges on each cubic meter of timber exported in 1976 amounted to a total of $13.54. Overall costs of cutting a log and getting it out of the forest to the point of export, plus other variable costs, amounted to around $25. Added to this were various fixed costs, notably overheads, of $15. So total

costs amounted to $53.54. These figures mean that on each cubic
meter of log worth an average in 1976 of $63, the corporation in
question made $9.46. If the Indonesian partners then took 35 percent
(a standard share), the foreign investor was left with $6.17. Certain
corporations exported as much as 500,000 m³ in 1976, which meant
that the foreign (usually American or Japanese) part of the joint
venture derived a net profit of over $3 million. In several instances,
this meant, in turn, that the foreign investor earned a return of at least
25 percent on his original foreign investment in a single year.

The corporations believe that they need a high rate of return on
investment to serve as sufficient incentive in circumstances where they
could lose a good deal. From late 1974 to early 1976, when the global
trading recession and especially the Japanese housing slump brought
export prices tumbling as low as $25, each log exported did little better
than break even — sometimes not even that. During this critical
period, one-fifth of East Kalimantan's forest exploiters went
bankrupt. The larger-scale corporations were in a position to bear a
sizeable setback, as much as $1 million or more in a few cases. Even
so, several foreign enterprises have pulled out of Indonesia. During
the economic recovery of 1977 and 1978, export prices sometimes soar
as high as $85 —whereupon Indonesia doubled its export tax,
reducing the profit margin by $2-3 cubic meter.

To return to Weyerhaeuser, what of its future in Indonesia? ITCI
plans to maintain its 1976-77 level of exports, viz. 1.2-1.5 million m³
per year. In accord with Indonesia's requirements that major forestry
entrepreneurs install processing facilities within a few years of start-
up, ITCI began, in late 1977, to construct a $6-million sawmill —
though the mill will handle only 90,000 m³ of timber annually, a mere
7.5 percent of ITCI's anticipated output. By 1985, and again in
conformity with Indonesia's requirements, Weyerhaeuser will have to
transfer as much stock as is necessary to ensure that local partners
take on a majority holding in ITCI.

Whatever one's reactions to this account of Weyerhaeuser's
activities in Indonesia, the corporation appears to go to greater
lengths than virtually any other foreign entrepreneur to abide by
Indonesia's forestry regulations. (Certain corporations seem to devote
a good deal of ingenuity, not to say money, to cutting every last

corner.) Moreover, Indonesia's policies concerning its forests make plain that the question is not whether the forests should be exploited, but how they will be exploited. A large-scale corporation can afford the technology to utilize trees that a small-scale operator would jetison, e.g. "sinkers" or the one tree in ten that turns out to be too dense to float downstream to the point of export. Were no foreign corporations like Weyerhaeuser at work, the forests would be exploited through fly-by-night operators, who, with limited capital and so with scant incentive to take risks by going for long-term profits, would engage in an even more disruptive and wasteful harvest.

At the same time, Weyerhaeuser faces a number of problems in its Indonesia venture. Like other investors, the corporation is acutely susceptible to market-price fluctuations, which means that from one year to another it either takes a hiding or it makes a killing. Foreign investors are much upset by periodic Indonesian decisions to impose, without warning or consultation, increases in the royalty rate for exported timber. Weyerhaeuser also feels singularly taken aback when timber poachers find they can operate with impunity on the company's concession, occasionally taking 30 m^3 or almost $2000 worth of material a day. In addition, Weyerhaeuser encounters a growing problem with shifting cultivators, who sometimes take over hundreds of hectares of forest in just a few months. Above all, Weyerhaeuser has reason to be hesitant about Indonesia's political instability in general. For these reasons, other U.S. corporations such as Crown Zellerbach and International Paper have looked at Indonesia and turned away.

In sum, many overseas investors are inclined to see sense in a cut-and-run strategy as the only realistic attitude for a foreign entrepreneur with prime responsibility to his company's shareholders. Many foreign corporation executives in Indonesia are candid that they believe it foolhardy to consider forestry operations in terms of more than a few years. After all, Indonesian officials do not look beyond 3 to 5 years at most, the competitive profit-maximizing market-place does the same, and international trade patterns do the same.

A basic question arises. If the investment environment in Indonesia is so discouraging, why has Weyerhaeuser gone in with a parent-company investment of $32 million — which means the corporation is far more committed to the future in Indonesia than are other foreign timber exploiters? The answer lies with plantation forestry. Weyerhaeuser reasons that future wood supplies for the global economy will derive increasingly from tropical zones, and that regions like Southeast Asia, within another 10-15 years and certainly by the end of the century, could generate vast quantities of pulp, lumber and other products through plantations. Weyerhaeuser wants to ensure a large slice of this action for itself. To put it simply, the corporation is undertaking a considerable risk now against the prospect of a major return later. In fact, ITCI is the only corporation in Indonesia to try plantations, even though reforestation is required by all logging contractors under Indonesian law. The corporation invests around $1 million per year in plantations, and has already established 2500 hectares of experimental plots at a cost of $450 per hectare. Its forest nursery can produce 4 million seedlings per year. In order to capitalize its plantation venture, Weyerhaeuser feels some justification is engaging in logging activities that could turn out to be a "mining" operation.

At the same time, the general instability of investment prospects in Indonesia is causing ITCI to slow down its plantation program. In fact, the outlook now seems so uncertain that Weyerhaeuser is wondering whether it will prove good business to stay, or whether it should not pack up. When a corporation with Weyerhaeuser's experience feels impelled to start counting its marbles in that basic sense, the commercial scene must be unpromising indeed.

Weyerhaeuser's logging impact

Meantime, Weyerhaeuser is not sure what ecological impact its logging has on the virgin forest in its concession. Despite a research budget of over $1 million per year, the corporation will not know until 10 years after it began operations whether its harvesting will turn out to be a once-and-for-all harvest or whether it could lead to sustained-yield exploitation. In any case, due to factors that have to do with instability of tenure for its forest holding and insecurity for its investment, the corporation aims to log its entire concession by 1990, when its concession runs out (the Indonesian government, expecting timber corporations to abide by a 35-year cutting cycle, allows them only a 20-year lease). Meantime, Weyerhaeuser has been encouraging some investigations concerning what happens to wildlife in its concession; it gave approval to two University of Washington anthropologists to look at logging's repercussions on apes and monkeys.

As mentioned in Chapter 10, scientists of Southeast Asia have found that logging can leave between one-third and two-thirds of the residual forest trees damaged beyond recovery. In addition, as much as 30 percent of the ground may be left bare, due to logging tracks, feeder reads, dumping grounds and the like. This amounts to substantial impact, and could mean that the surviving forest will grow into a different kind of forest — at least during the many decades, if not centuries, that are required for secondary forest to become primary forest again.

As a result of logging, then, certain ecosystems of the virgin forest could turn out to be fundamentally modified. In turn, this could mean that certain species' life-support systems become grossly disrupted. As described in Chapters 3 and 8, many tropical-forest species are little able to tolerate change. They have evolved in stable conditions for millennia, and they are not adapted to sudden environmental upheavals such as modern technology can inflict. Moreover, a proportion of tropical-forest species, possibly as many as 10 percent, exist in unusually limited areas (sometimes as little as a few dozen square kilometres), or they are highly specialized in their ecological needs and exist at very low densities. In the light of these characteristics that predispose certain species to extinction far more rapidly than is the case for temperate-zone species, what are the prospects for species in Southeast Asia forest tracts that are undergoing logging?

Weyerhaeuser's Indonesia concession amounts to 6000 km², or about 0.064 percent of all tropical moist forests. The number of species believed to exist in the entire biome is variously estimated at between 500,000 and 4 million (see Chapter 2). So the number of localized-distribution or specialized-needs species that might well exist in the Weyerhaeuser concession could be, according to this reckoning, between 32 and 256. True, a calculation of this sort is crude in the extreme, and it is presented merely to make the point that a 6000-km² area in Borneo, one of the richest biological areas on earth, could contain a fair number of species that are found nowhere else and that are especially vulnerable to sudden extinction. If the ecological impact of logging turns out to be as disruptive as scientist observers have repeatedly suggested, it is not unlikely that Weyerhaeuser's operation could cause the extinction of at least a few species. These species would almost certainly be insects and other obscure creatures of the deep forest, as yet unidentified by science and of little ostensible interest to many people. But, as documented in Chapter 5, species already serve many pragmatic purposes of direct utilitarian benefit to humanity. The demise of a few bugs in East Kalimantan would represent an irreversible loss of unique resources, whose potential value to people everywhere, both present and future, is, although undetermined, not to be dismissed.

What measures could Weyerhaeuser reasonably take to ensure that no species are thus driven under? First, prior to felling a tree, the corporation could sever lianas and other climbing plants that would otherwise cause neighboring trees to be broken when the tree in question is brought down. Some lianas grow as long as 200 m. According to studies in Sabah, cutting lianas could reduce logging damage by 20 percent,[6] at a cost of around $2 per tree, and adding $0.25 to the price of each cubic meter of exported log. Secondly, if the corporation were to try to reduce damage further, it could use a helicopter to extract logs by air. This practice would prove very expensive, and no cost estimates are available since it is a technique used only very occasionally in Indonesia. Still, helicopters and balloons are regularly used to extract logs in the northwest timberlands of the United States. Thirdly, a corporation could conduct an ecological reconnaissance of its concession, in order to establish which areas constitute unique ecosystems and thus possibly contain limited-range species. These areas would then need to be set aside from logging, or subject to very light and careful logging. The cost of this approach would not be trifling, but again no estimates are available.

It is significant that no corporation in Indonesia has bothered to do some preliminary arithmetic with regard to measures to look out for environmental values. Presumably this is because there has not been enough pressure from either the host or the home country to take such considerations into account (a deficiency that can readily be remedied — see later in this chapter). On their home turf in the United States, American corporations take various steps to safeguard wildlife. For example, they avoid cutting trees within 400 m of a bald eagle's nest during the nesting season. As for other environmental concerns, timber corporations reckon that measures to reduce pollution from their mills adds about 15 percent to production costs. Clearly the corporations are able to pass on the increased costs to their customers without protests that conservation is overly inflationary. With sufficient pressure on them, the same corporation could perhaps find that they could make their tropical operations sensitive to environmental values without seeing their profits disappearing. Similarly, environmental pollution in Japan has become so bad that Japanese corporations are being obliged by their government to spend $75 billion between 1978 and 1987 to tackle the problem; if Japanese timber corporations were to spend a mere $1 billion in Southeast Asia during the same period, this need add only a very small percentage to the cost of each cubic meter of tropical hardwood, and would go a very long way to leave a healthier forest after the loggers have taken their harvest.

Of course, to enable each corporation to maintain its competitive edge in the market-place, all corporations would have to be obliged to apply the same environmental safeguards. According to some corporation executives, this would make Indonesian logs unable to compete with logs from other Southeast Asia countries. In turn, this would mean that all Southeast Asia countries would have to agree to implement similar logging regulations, and preferably the same for all tropical countries that export hardwood logs. Difficult as these initiatives would be, and inflationary as the whole strategy would prove for the end-product consumer in importer countries of the developed world, the alternative is that the present prospect continues, viz. that the forests at issue undergo extensive disruption with possibly irreversible injury to unique ecosystems and vulnerable species.

In addition to the ecological impact of logging, a question arises with regard to a corporation's social and cultural impact on local peoples. There are divergent views on this complex problem. According to Weyerhaeuser's Senior Vice-President, Charles W. Bingham,

"Any major investment brings major changes in the economic areas, and those changes tend to translate gradually into social change ... I am sure we do disrupt primitive societies ... I believe this is cultural enrichment, however, not deculturalisation. I do not believe disease, poverty and illiteracy are inalienable human rights, or that primitive societies should be forced to remain primitive, simply to provide museum pieces for their more affluent world neighbors' entertainment.[7]

By contrast, anthropologists argue that forest peoples are left with little real choice other than a sudden switch to the brave new world of Western-type development.

Moreover, the indigenous knowledge of forest tribes is rapidly eroded when they are overtaken by the life-style changes they encounter through the arrival of multinational corporations. This indigenous knowledge includes much traditional lore concerning wild food plants, primitive crop cultivars, and forest sources of drugs (see Chapter 8). In the wake of multinational corporations' activities, with their fundamental transformation if not elimination of traditional ways of life, this valuable knowledge is disappearing within just a few years.

The community's role is regulating corporations: the U.N. Code of Conduct

Because of the implications of tropical-forest depletion for the global heritage, the problem deserves to be treated as a matter of concern for the community of nations. To tackle the problem, a number of initiatives could be considered, notably under the umbrella of the Code of Conduct being formulated through the United Nations Commission on Transnational Corporations.[8] The Commission seek primarily to regulate financial areas of conflict, notably corporation practices with regard to taxation, transfer pricing and profit remittances. Despite a number of obvious limitations (must it be merely voluntary?), the Code will serve a vital educational role. To encourage the social responsibility of corporations, governments and citizens need to know what these global enterprises are doing and planning, and how their activities will affect the areas where they operate. To meet this need for information, the Code envisages that corporations will commit themselves to disclose details on many of their operations.

Regrettably, there has been hitherto little attention directed toward environmental factors, though there is little reason why a broad-ranging "environmental component" could not be incorporated into the Code. While the disclosure mechanism in question is currently intended to focus on financial and accountancy matters, the same mechanism could extend to environmental factors. Along these lines, a corporation would agree to inform interested parties about the environmental consequences of its activities. In support of the spirit of this initiative, corporations could further agree to make themselves subject to independent screening, on the presumption that they will wish to be internationally accountable and socially responsible, and be seen to be so.

Forestry corporations and environmental safeguards

How would an "environmental component" in the Code of Conduct affect forestry corporations in the tropics? One obvious possibility is for corporations to accept responsibility, as part of their overall disclosure commitment, to undertake environmental impact assessments of their activities, and to publish the results. In particular, they could be expected to disclose information on which wildlife communities and species pools are being affected, either marginally or conclusively, by their activities, and what reasonable steps they plan to avoid irreparable harm to exceptionally important species such as endemics (see proposals with effect to Weyerhaeuser above).

While a forest exploiter might be reluctant to forego unusual commercial advantage in order to safeguard environmental values, the initiative would at least induce him to take explicit account of the environmental costs of his activities. This in itself would be an advance over the present situation, where a corporation can take its

harvest of timber with implicit indifference to other resources at stake
(such as species) and to a host of environmental factors (such as
ecosystem stability and watershed health). Even more, the measure
would represent a marked shift in "burden of proof" responsibility.
The onus would be on the corporation to watch out for environmental
disruption, without waiting for outside observers to point out the
spillover consequences of its operations. Disputes may well arise,
concerning, for example, the amount of ecological disruption that an
exploiter should "reasonably" avoid in order to safeguard
environmental values. Arbitration and conciliation, through "fact-
finding studies", could be assigned to environmental agencies with
acknowledged expertise, such as the International Union for
Conservation of Nature and Natural Resources, or perhaps a specially
established body such as an "Expert Group on International
Environmental Standards". A precedent lies with the World Bank's
Center for Settlement of Investment Disputes. While the Center's
membership of sixty-five nations is mostly made up of developing
countries, developed countries generally accept its international
arbitration.

Other initiatives to regulate corporations

Apart from the Code of Conduct, other initiatives are available.
The great majority of multinational corporations are based in a
handful of developed countries. These countries could require their
corporations, through the law, to take account of environmental
consequences of their activities overseas. The United States is
considering a measure along these lines, through its Securities and
Exchange Commission. The Commission regulates 10,000 publically
owned corporations, including virtually all major enterprises. In
accord with the provisions of the U.S. National Environmental
Protection Act, the Commission has developed a set of guidelines and
regulations, which, if adopted, will require all corporations under its
jurisdiction to disclose failures to comply with environmental laws.
Eventually this initiative could cover the activities of American
corporations overseas as well as within the United States.
A further initiative open to home governments would be to

encourage conservation precautions on the part of corporations through special taxation measures. Were a forestry enterprise to leave part of its tropical concession in an undisturbed stage, it could be allowed a tax rebate. If, by contrast, it engaged in forms of exploitation that prove unusually harmful to society's interests, it could be required to accept an extra tax burden. This would mean that after-tax revenues could not only reflect the corporation's private output, but its social impact.[9] Certain corporations might even feel inclined, in order to enhance their good name, to accept "self-imposed taxes". For example, the U.S. corporation Sears has proposed that global enterprises could make a "civic contribution" of about 2 percent of net profits toward projects particularly attractive to important public-interest groups, including conservation bodies.

Were a corporation found in breach of legal requirements, various penalties could be devised to fit the circumstances. For example, Pan American Airways was recently caught illegally shipping endangered wildlife, whereupon the court extended the option of paying a fine in the usual manner, or paying a sum twice as large to a conservation body such as the World Wildlife Fund. The same could apply to forestry corporations. Or a corporation at fault could be required to express "positive repentence", along the lines of practices in West Germany where tax violators are obliged to publish their fraud in newspapers. This latter measure would help with the imbalance of information: through a corporation's public relations measures, everybody hears about the positive aspects of a corporation's doings, whereas adverse activities receive little publicity. The imbalance could be further countered through a dispensation similar to the "fairness doctrine" applied to television advertising in the United States, whereby private individuals or groups are allowed opportunity in the media at public expense to indicate where private enterprise may be in conflict with the public's interests.

Suppose legal and taxation provisions, along the lines set out above, were to be enforced widely with regard to tropical forests. As a consequence, forest patches of exceptional significance for the community's natural heritage, such as areas of high species endemism, would be lightly exploited or left untouched altogether. This would mean less tropical timber on the market at a time when world-wide demand is rising steeply. The result would be an increase in prices. But this would be no more than in accord with the pattern of many environmental measures which produce services (e.g. cleaner air and similar amenities) rather than goods (raw materials and manufactured products) and are thus inflationary. The citizen who is a conservationist as well as a consumer would have to decide where his priorities lie.

14 The Role of International Aid Agencies

International aid agencies have contributed, through their development projects, to the present plight of tropical forests. On the one hand, they have not done nearly so much as they could in the way of promoting sensible management and conservation of forests. On the other hand, their activities have disrupted tropical forests, not only through their support for exploitation of virgin ecosystems, but through road building, settlement schemes and so forth. While their negative impact has not remotely matched that of multinational corporations, it is far from trifling.

In the eventual upshot, of course, there should be no intrinsic conflict between development and conservation. Just as there can be no long-term economic advancement without conservation of society's life-support systems, so there can be, in developing nations, little scope for environmental concerns unless there is full-bore attack on the main form of degradation of the human environment, viz. poverty. The head of the World Bank, Robert S. McNamara, hit the nail on the head when he declared, at the 1972 Stockholm Conference on the Human Environment,

> "The question is not whether there should be continued growth. There must be. Nor is the question whether the impact on the environment must be respected. It has to be. Nor — least of all — is it a question of whether these considerations are interlocked. They are. The solution of the dilemma revolves clearly not about whether, but about how."

While far less than it should be, the scale of international aid is not trifling. The United Nations agencies spend almost $2 billion each year on development projects. The World Bank group now commits around $9 billion a year. A number of regional banks — the Inter-

American Development Bank, the Asian Development Bank and up to a dozen others — make substantial loans. In addition to these multilateral agencies, a number of bilateral programs contribute appreciable sums; the leader, the U.S. Agency for International Development, spends almost $3 billion abroad each year. Overall foreign aid now amounts to $27 billion each year. By contrast with this development spending, environmental spending is minuscule. The U.N. Environment Program accounts for only about $35 billion per year, and UNESCO's Man and the Biosphere Program has an annual budget of less than $30 million. All U.N. spending on the environment comes to less than $100 million per year, or 0.37 percent of development spending.

Tropical Forestry

To date, only a small proportion of development aid has been allocated to tropical forestry, whether for exploitation, management or conservation. The U.N. Development Program, which, with its budget of over $500 million, serves as a major channel for U.N. project financing, accords forestry only 6½ percent of its funds. The World Bank has extended forestry loans and credits between 1953 and 1976 worth a mere $440 million, out of total budgets for those years of $65 billion; forestry has accounted for an average of only 1 percent of Bank lending for agricultural and rural development, entailing 17 out of over 1000 projects. Significantly, the Bank, having published a lengthy series of detailed Sector Policy Papers on most major areas of economic development (agriculture, education, health, urbanization, etc.), waited until March 1978 before coming around to forestry, almost a decade after the first Papers appeared. As for bilateral agencies, U.S. AID has been characteristic in giving very low priority to forestry, due to a philosophy that has viewed forestry as somehow significant but hardly a priority item as compared with "truly important" sectors such as food production. A similar story could be told of many other aid agencies. In short, forestry has tended to be regarded by international organizations rather as it has been viewed by developing-nation governments, viz. as a Cinderella-type activity.

This situation is now changing, albeit slowly. The leading innovator is the World Bank, which has tentatively scheduled $500 million for 1979-83, covering a series of projects in the $10-15 million range.[1] At an average rate of seven to ten projects per year, this will amount to 5 times as many projects as in the previous 5 years. More important still, the scope of the Bank's forest projects is to be expanded. Hitherto, the Bank has been inclined to concentrate on fast-growing plantations, pulp-and-paper mills, and other forest-industry activities. This program, with its *ad hoc* approach, has not paid much attention to the potential contribution of forestry to economic development in general. From here on, the focus is to be on broad-scale benefits of forestry for local communities, through reforestation and afforestation projects, plantations for fuelwood as well as for industrial materials, village-level woodlots, and agro-forestry. Best news of all is that the Bank is to engage in "environmental forestry", such as watershed management, shelterbelts, soil stabilization and land rehabilitation. Within this overall strategy, the Bank has decided that, as an operational guideline, "Particular emphasis will be given to development strategies which present a viable alternative to ecologically destructive development patterns".

Among the bilateral agencies, U.S. AID is to beef up its meagre funding for tropical forestry, likewise with emphasis on programmes with wide-ranging components (to date AID has had only one professional forester on its staff). Even so, funding in fiscal year 1979 for research and improved use of tropical moist forests will amount to only $25 million, or around 1.5 percent of AID's budget.

As described in Chapter 11, AID is fostering research into tropical tree species such as the giant ipilipil, to be used for fast-growing timber, for livestock fodder, as a source of fertilizer, and for various environmental benefits. In the Philippines, a $8.7-million AID project is investigating the tree's extraordinary capacity to sprout like a beanstalk, with a view to oil production. In 1977 the Philippines imported 83.4 million barrels of oil worth $1.2 billion (29 percent of all imports). Preliminary results suggest that a plantation of giant ipilipil, producing a sustainable output of wood for boilers, could generate enough steam per hectare to generate electricity equal to 41 barrels of oil. Were the wood to be pyrolysed into oil and other fuels, 1 hectare could theoretically produce the equivalent of 83 barrels. Using a mixture of the two processes, the country's oil imports could be replaced through "petroleum plantations" covering 13,450 km², or less than 20 percent of national territory. Fortunately, the Philippines has plenty of deforested land that is little used for agriculture. Considering that the Philippines' energy consumption is projected to increase at 7 percent throughout the last quarter of this century, and that energy requirements in the year 2000 will therefore be 6 times above the 1974 level, this technological initiative could go some way to relieve pressures to exploit the Philippines' remaining forests for fuelwood.

As a further example of how AID could help safeguard tropical forests, there is urgent need to spread the use of better stoves for the millions of developing-world households that employ fuelwood for cooking and thereby cause a considerable and growing drain on forests. Many stoves use only 10-15 percent of heat generated (and an open fire, 5-10 percent), whereas a 40-65 percent efficient stove, made mostly of mud, can be marketed for as little as $5. Improved stoves in widespread use in a typical developing country can reduce the area needed for fuelwood plantations by at least one-quarter. Better still, a cheap solar-powered stove could eliminate the use of fuelwood altogether, while exploiting the tropics' most abundant natural resource. To date, a solar stove costs $30-50, way beyond the means of many households. Worse, development agencies give little attention to the challenge; at a conference of the International Society for Solar Energy, held in New Delhi in early 1978, only 3 out of 450 papers dealt with solar stoves.

International aid agencies and environmental safeguards

In order to safeguard environmental values of forestry and of other development sectors, international aid agencies could consider a number of measures. For example, and as has been proposed for multinational corporations in the preceeding chapter, aid agencies could incorporate environmental impact statements into their development projects. Insofar as public bodies are not subject to the profit-and-loss considerations which govern private enterprises, it should be no unacceptable burden for these organizations to examine the environmental consequences of their activities. The Jonglei Canal project in southern Sudan is designed to channel water from several thousand square kilometers of Sudd swamp, an exceptionally rich biotic community (see Chapter 3). The project could entail considerable — and hitherto little considered — consequences for species. Principal responsibility for the project's execution lies with international development agencies.

True, an aid agency may sometimes argue that the ecological gain of environmental safeguards appears too limited, or too diffuse, or too long term, to offset an urgent need for, say, greater food output. This is a major reason why environmental impact statements have not always been popular with agencies — or, for that matter, with developing nations themselves. But the mere procedure of environmental assessments at least obliges participant parties to pay explicit attention to potential environmental costs — an advance over the present situation, where a development project can convert a swamp into irrigated cropland, or eliminate a stretch of forest for agricultural settlement, with implicit indifference to other natural resources at stake.

Protection of environmental values, notably species, can often be accomplished at little extra project cost, provided the opportunity is identified in time. During the first 2 years or so after AID began environmental screening of its projects in 1976, it found that 154 out of 572 projects (27 percent) were likely to have environmental repercussions. The cost of making the assessments amounted to $3.18 million, or 0.38 percent of total project costs. Similarly, The World Bank examined 434 projects between mid-1971 and the end of 1973 and found that 159 were likely to have adverse effects. The additional project costs to take environmental safeguards into account ranged from 0 to 3 percent.[2]

In addition, aid agencies could well move beyond their traditional mode for evaluation of development projects, generally some form of cost-benefit analysis. Because of the different analytical tools available for economics and ecology, project evaluation has tended to emphasize the "accuracy" of the economics side, and to play down ecological factors which appear, by comparison, to be "fuzzy" at best. Moreover, economists tend to think within time horizons of 25 years at most, more often as little as 10, sometimes even less.

Ecologists, by contrast, believe that the appropriate time-scale is one that extends into the indefinite future. In addition, economic systems aim to maximize gains that are quantifiable in monetary terms, whereas ecological considerations seek to minimize costs that generally lie beyond the measuring rod of money units.

As an example of how to tackle the trade-offs between economics and ecology, the environmental benefits of forestry projects can be assessed as follows. A recent World Bank appraisal of a community woodlot project in Kenya reveals that a number of "non-wood" benefits, on top of the 5 m³ of fuelwood produced per hectare per year, can be legitimately included in a cost-benefit analysis: per cubic metre of fuelwood, a saving of cattle dung, formerly burnt as fuel and now available as fertilizer, $1 per year; per cubic meter of fuelwood, a saving of 2.5 man-days per year that would otherwise be spent in roaming far and wide in search of alternative sources of fuelwood, and that can now be spent in growing food; per hectare of plantation, a saving of 1.5 man-days per year that would otherwise be spent in collecting water from distant sources after local streams and rivers have become silted up through deforestation of watersheds; plus additional environmental "goods and services" supplied by tree plantations, e.g. windbreaks and shade for livestock. The economic value of these indirect benefits is reckoned to offset as much as one-half the cost of establishing the Kenya woodlot and make it much more competitive as an economic proposition.

Recent progress with environmental safeguards

Among development banks, the greatest progress with environmental safeguards seems to have been accomplished by the World Bank. According to a comparative survey by the International Institute for Environment and Development (1977),[3] the Bank's position is now "more sophisticated and comprehensive than that of any of the other development banks ... and it is continuously evolving in a positive direction". In principle, the Bank is committed to a review, and where necessary to a restructuring, of every project that has a significant environmental component. This screening process begins with an environmental reconnaissance when a project is first conceived, moves on to environmental monitoring during the phase of on-the-ground activity and winds up with an environmental post-audit.

By contrast, some other development banks have not yet articulated their environmental awareness. Some have not even recognized the nature of the challenge. In several instances, there remains uncertainty about how to ask the right questions, let alone how to supply the best answers. For example, the European Development Bank does not consider environment in its constitution, nor does it undertake any sort of environmental assessments. The Asian Development Bank has appeared unwilling to accept any in-house environmental expertise that could review projects, although, to its credit, it has incorporated measures for watershed reforestation into a recent loan to Indonesia for a water project. In the main, regional development banks have done little to foster conservation. This reluctance to consider environmental factors is all the more regrettable in that these lending agencies are in a fine position to promote conservation, by, for example, offering low-interest loans or outright grants for development projects with an "environmental component".

As for bilateral agencies, only U.S. AID has made much of an effort. AID has had an Environment Assessment Guidelines Manual since 1974, and now conducts systematic evaluation of its projects. It aims to produce environmental-impact statements that cover a whole string of factors — overview description and analysis of proposed project; probable significant environmental effects, both beneficial and negative; the relationship of the activity to land-use policies, plans and controls for the affected area; description and evaluation of the environmental effects of reasonable alternatives, particularly those that might enhance environmental qualities or avoid some or all of the adverse effects; significant adverse effects which cannot be avoided; and other interests of the United States and the host country that relate to environmental concerns. A notable feature of this AID strategy is that environmental factors are taken into account at the pre-feasibility and feasibility stages of project planning. This encourages an analysis of alternative approaches to achieve the same objectives of the project. Experience shows that it is more efficient in environmental senses, and generally less costly in economic terms, to aim to present, rather than to compensate for, adverse environmental consequences.

Other U.S. agencies come into the picture. The Export/Import Bank annually advances loans and financial guarantees for U.S. development projects overseas worth more than $6 billion. Many of these activities entail significant environmental repercussions. For example, the Bank has recently loaned Indonesia $1.7 million to buy dredges to drain and fill 8800 km² of tidal wetlands, with additional loans envisaged. The proposed project will result in the destruction not only of healthy fisheries, but of important mangrove swamps that constitute habitats for the endangered gibbon and hawksbill turtle, plus whole communities of other species. The Bank is also funding construction of a railroad through Gabon's rainforest, with unknown consequences for myriad species that exist in this sector of one of Africa's "Pleistocene refuges" (for an account of these refuges, with their concentrations of endemic species, see Chapter 9). To date, Export/Import Bank has not considered the environmental consequences of its projects.

A further U.S. organization is responsible for financial underpinning of many American investments abroad. This is the Overseas Private Investors Corporation, that annually insures, against expropriation and other risks, more than $1 billion of business investments, including many projects with significant environmental effects. For example, in 1971 OPIC extended to the U.S. timber corporation, Georgia Pacific, a guarantee worth $1.5 million to cover its Indonesian forestry operations; and in 1975 it extended further insurance worth $1.2 million for Georgia Pacific's veneer plywood plant in Indonesia. Between 1971 and 1975 OPIC extended a $9 million guarantee to Weyerhaeuser's wholly owned subsidiary in East Kalimantan, and between 1972 and 1977 it extended two insurance policies for Weyerhaeuser's much larger operation through the International Timber Corporation Indonesia — these forms of insurance safeguarding the U.S. company against expropriation, currency inconvertibility, and war, revolution and insurrection. Despite the major support that this insurance offers to U.S. timber corporations for their ventures in tropical forests, OPIC to date has not engaged in environmental impact assessments.

The United States is not the only advanced nation to offer government support for private overseas investment. The Japanese Ministry of Finance lends funds to Japanese corporations through its Export/Import Bank. In addition, the Japanese Overseas Economic Cooperation Fund fully covers any future losses that private investors might incur through fluctuation in currency markets. Currently, OECF is extending credit to Japanese timber enterprises in Indonesia.

In summary, then, international aid agencies present a mixed picture as concerns their approach to environmental responsibility. Yet these bodies could make a strong contribution to the conservation scene. Not only could they ensure environmental evaluation of the projects that they choose to fund for reasons of economic development, but they could look out for projects that offer unusual scope to enhance environmental interests, and thereby stimulate environmental awareness among developing nations.

Part III

A COMPREHENSIVE STRATEGY FOR CONSERVATION OF SPECIES

15 Zoos, Parks and other Protection Measures: How Many Make Enough?

A range of immediate measures is available to protect species and genetic resources, namely zoos and botanical gardens, and parks and reserves. This chapter considers how many are needed to do a sufficient job.

(a) Zoos and botanical gardens

Zoos and botanical gardens, plus related strategies such as gene banks, cater for both animals and plants, keeping samples of species alive under varying degrees of captivity. Generally speaking, plants are more readily maintained than are animals, yet zoos have recorded a string of successes with captive breeding of animals.[1] For example, the Pere David's Deer and the European Bison, having lost their wildland habitats many decades ago, have been kept alive solely through zoos and similar facilities.

However, the varying genetic attributes of animal species affect their prospects in zoos and other artificial environments.

Breeding animals in captivity often results in breeding them for captivity. By way of illustration, the Nene goose, frequently cited as a success story, was rescued from its native Hawaii (where it had been reduced from about 25,000 in the year 1700 to only 43 by 1940) and the survivors were bred up at the Wildfowl Trust in England until a sufficient number could be released into the wild to establish a new population. The wild stock of over 3000 individuals now shows a high level of infertility among males, apparently associated with in-breeding. This problem bears out the rule of thumb that a vertebrate breeding stock with fewer than 50 individuals is liable to carry on built-in potential for its own destruction, since in-breeding brings together the harmful genes that larger pools can accommodate. While some species are much better adapted than others to captive breeding, scientists have almost none of the necessary background information for virtually all species that are threatened or rare.

Furthermore, many species seem disinclined to breed in captivity. Cheetah, penguins and humming-birds are notoriously difficult. There has been very limited reproduction on the part of whales in captivity and virtually none for bats. Only about 10 percent of reptile species in zoos have propagated themselves.

In any case, zoos as a "last-ditch strategy" for conservation do not always produce the best return per dollar. The cost of maintaining, say, a 100-plus herd of certain herbivores could range from $75,000 to $250,000 per year, much more than is generally the cost of maintaining a similar number in the wild — and even then, the stock could well lose half its genetic variability. Similarly, while it is true that genes may shortly be synthesized on a sizeable scale, opening the way to eventual development of whole new organisms, this procedure would prove far more costly than conserving gene pools already available in natural form.

By contrast with animals, plants present a rather different challenge. It can be a relatively simple matter to maintain a genetic stock of plants in an artificial environment far removed from its natural habitat.[2] This *ex situ* mode of conservation allows hundreds of plant species to be protected in a small area such as a botanical garden. Regrettably, of the world's 458 botanical gardens, only 82 are located in developing countries with their rich assemblies of tropical species.

Plants lend themselves to a yet more concentrated approach: gene banks. Seeds of many plant species, especially those with dry, small seeds, can be stored dormant for long periods without suffering, at a humidity level of about 5 percent and a temperature of $-20°C$, without suffering physical damage or loss of genetic integrity. Within a small space, a single center can protect many thousands of species. For example, the National Seed Storage Laboratory of the U.S. Department of Agriculture at Fort Collins, Colorado, contains materials of 1310 plant species.

There is considerable risk, however, in supposing that gene banks can represent any absolute answer for plants. First, the technique simply does not apply to many seed plants, and to most vegetatively propagated plants; for example, members of the orchid family and tree species such as oaks and poplars. In particular, the reservation applies to many tropical plant species; for example, the cacao tree's seeds can be conserved outside the wild only with great difficulty. Moreover, for the huge majority of species, botanists simply do not have enough information to say whether seed-bank storage could work.

Secondly, gene banks cannot permanently preserve the vast numbers of races of plants that need to be maintained for future breeding, due to the technical difficulties involved. These difficulties include low storage tolerance of many seeds, mutability of strains, inevitable accidents in storage facilities (power failures, blown fuses) and unwitting or deliberate disposal of strains (a far from uncommon occurrence in storage facilities — plus vulnerability to damage and guerilla action).

Thirdly, and most important of all, there is the risk of reduced adaptiveness. When a plant is preserved in refrigerated conditions, its evolution is effectively frozen until such time as the genetic material can be grown afresh. Meantime, various threats to which it is subject in natural environments — insects, pathogens and the like — continue to evolve, producing new forms of attack to which the host plant will not have co-evolved adequate defenses during its term of refrigerated protection.

In sum, seed collections, whether cultivated or frozen, tend to become genetic ghettoes. Gene banks, like botanical gardens, can serve as no more than a stratagem to supplement preservation of genetic variability in the wild, i.e. *in situ*, especially if the purpose is to safeguard genotypic variability of species over periods of many decades, if not centuries. At the same time, to preserve a species in natural surroundings means that man safeguards not only a single genetic system, viz. that of the species itself, but of several interlocking genetic systems that form part of the ecosystem of the species in question. In this way, man not only preserves a species known to science and recognized as threatened, but he also preserves many other species, some of which may not even have become known to science.

(b)   Parks and other protected areas

So the best way to safeguard species and genetic resources is in the wild, i.e. through parks and reserves. Of the world's 149 million km² of land, around 1.6 million, or just over 1 percent, have been set aside as parks and equivalent reserves that merit inclusion in the United Nation's List of such areas.

This network is far too small. Worse, it is not representative of earth's terrestrial ecosystems. Almost half the total area is located in North America, notably in Greenland and the Arctic zone of Canada. Of almost 200 biogeographic provinces in the world, around one-eighth are represented by no parks and reserves, and another one-seventh by only one or two such areas.[3] Especially poorly protected are grasslands and Mediterranean-type zones — areas that have been subject to intensive human impact for long periods. Tropical moist forests are exceptionally badly placed with only around 150,000 km² of parks and reserves; almost half the unrepresented or under-represented biogeographic provinces are in this one biome. In South America's tropical moist forests, protected areas comprise less than 1 percent of the forest expanse, in Southeast Asia less than 2 percent and in Africa less than 3 percent (almost all in one country, Zaire). By contrast, preliminary estimates suggest that at least 10 percent and perhaps as much as 20 percent of tropical moist forests need to be preserved, in select localities covering distinct ecosystems, in order to ensure preservation of sample biotic communities with their endemic components. Moreover, since many species in this highly differentiated biome are characterized by localized distribution, a few large parks and reserves will not suffice to protect the range of biotic diversity. An extensive and strategically sited network is needed.

In order to appreciate the problems of setting up a network of this scope, let us look at an aspect of theoretical ecology that reflects on protected areas, the theory of island biogeography.

Theory of island biogeography

Man's disruptive activities aside, natural processes cause habitats to become fragmented. They split up and split again, until one area is isolated from others of its kind. The result is a patchwork pattern of island-like enclaves. Man's activities compound this process, reducing the fragments in size and increasing their degree of isolation. In these islands, communities of species can exist in equilibrium with the carrying capacity of the life-support system in question; the larger the area and the less it is isolated, the larger the number of species "at equilibrium".[4]

This has critical implications for parks and reserves. When a protected area is set aside, it is almost certainly destined to become an island of undisturbed nature in a sea of man-dominated, and hence alien, environments. In accord with a protected area's size and its distance from other undisturbed natural environments, its number of species will decline from the number supported by the area when it was part of a "continent", to the number it can support as an island. Eventually the number of species will fall until it reaches a new equilibrium. The question is, how great will the decline be? Are some species more susceptible to elimination than others? What can be done to amend the process? And how can we make protected areas as efficient as possible for their task of conserving species and habitats?

In accord with an island's size and its distance from other undisturbed natural environments, its number of species will decline from the number supported by the area when it was part of a "continent" to the number it can support as an island. Eventually the number of species will fall until it reaches a new "steady state". The question is, how great will the decline be? Are some species more susceptible to elimination than others? What can be done to amend the process? Above all, what does the theory of island biogeography tell us about the size, shape, design and location of protected areas?

It is possible to arrive at an estimate of likely losses in "park islands" by looking at what has happened when geographical islands have appeared in nature, generally after a continental area has become submerged and has left behind a series of islands. The highest extinction rates have occurred on small islands with rare species — a finding that augurs ill for parks and reserves unless they exceed a critical minimum size.

Ten thousand years ago, rising sea levels inundated low-lying coastal regions of the New Guinea Shelf region, leaving a series of "land-bridge" islands. At the time when the islands were isolated, they were presumably "super-saturated" with species; that is to say, they must have initially supported wildlife communities with a richness and a diversity of species in line with what continental areas could support.[5] Thereafter, their species totals would steadily decline to levels appropriate for their areas at equilibrium. Islands that are now smaller than about 250 km[2] have the same number of bird species as similar-sized oceanic islands that never had a land-bridge. In other words, they have lost their entire "excess species" during the 10,000 years since their connecting links to the mainland became submerged. Larger land-bridge islands, covering 1000 to several thousand square kilometers (equivalent in size to a number of present parks and reserves in the tropics), have proportionately more bird species, though considerably fewer than large islands the size of New Guinea or of equivalent land areas on New Guinea. An island of 7500 km[2] has typically lost 51 percent of its excess species during the past 10,000 years and about 72 percent of the survivors are species of secondary forests.

Similar studies have been conducted in islands of the Malay Archipelago, in the Caribbean, in the Adriatic and off the coast of California. While most of these studies tend to support the findings set out above, an investigation in the West Indies suggests that larger islands, by virtue of a greater variety of habitats, are ecologically richer in general, and may thus tend to support more bird species than smaller islands.[6]

In terms of practical consequences for conservation, these findings of island biogeography suggest that if 90 percent of an original habitat is grossly disrupted through the hand of man, and the remaining 10 percent is protected as a park or reserve, we can expect to save no more than about half of the species restricted to the particular area. During the early period after the preserve is established, "equilibration" (the extinction process) will occur at a higher rate than later on. Conversely, if the size of a protected area can be increased 10 times, the number of species with prospect of long-term survival will be roughly doubled. If the 10 percent of original habitat is split up between two protected areas, the total number of species saved could well be smaller than if the 10 percent were set aside as a single conservation bloc; and each of the two areas will retain fewer species if they are distant from each other than if close. (At the same time, a number of small preserves may offer a better chance for some species to survive in at least one area or another.) As a rough rule of thumb, arithmetic loss of space leads to geometric decline in the value of the remaining space.[7]

All in all, then, it is reasonable to anticipate that if the extent of a natural area is reduced for whatever reason, this will almost certainly lead to a decline in its array of species. The biotic impoverishment will still proceed even if a carefully planned network of preserves is established, and even if these protected areas are managed in ideal fashion indefinitely. True, the process is likely to take place slowly, and the fallout may well amount on average to only a relatively small number of species per decade. But the hurricane of change that is now overtaking most natural environments will leave a trail of disruption that will surely persist for at least a century, in some areas far longer. So we need to think in terms of ecological trends that will extend throughout the foreseeable future, and we should certainly not formulate conservation plans with an eye to just the next few decades.

Susceptible species

Certain species, when confined to protected areas, are more susceptible to extinction than others. Some are good at colonizing new refuges, some are hopeless. Of 513 bird species on New Guinea, 302 are not found on any oceanic island more than a few kilometers away. Just because a bird can fly 50 km over land does not mean that it will fly 5 km over water — an attribute that is especially characteristic of tropical birds, and in particular of tropical forest birds. Even a highway can present an insurmountable barrier to certain species (also mammals), notably those that are adapted to the darkness of the forest depths and cannot stand even a brief period in open sunlight. If a road bisects a park, effectively splitting the park into two refuges for certain categories of birds and mammals, as many as one-sixth of such species can be considered to be doomed. This factor is especially important for road-building projects such as the Transamazon Highway system in Brazil's sector of Amazonia. By virtue of encouraging settlement in a broad-flanking swathe on either side of the Highway, the project is likely to have serious long-range consequences for wildlife populations that are left split into two.

Ecologists suggest that the settlement swathes could be intersected at intervals with corridors of undisturbed habitat, to assist migration of forest species across the Highway. So far, Brazil has not made any moves in that direction.

Even in protected areas covering several thousand square kilometers, some species have negligible prospects of eventual survival because of other traits that stack the odds against them. This is particularly true of three categories of species. The first includes those individuals which require large territories, so that even an extensive area includes only low numbers, as is the case with many carnivores such as the cheetah. The second category includes those species whose members have specialized habitat needs, with the result that, as in the first category, initial populations total few individuals. An example is, or more probably was, the ivory-billed woodpecker. The third category includes species which are dependent on seasonal and patchy food sources and are inclined to undergo drastic fluctuations in population numbers, as is the case with flower-feeding and fruit-eating birds. In fact, it is probable that some species will be eventually doomed even in parks as large as 10,000 km², and they will be still more likely to go under if they are protected in a network of many small reserves even if the aggregate area of these preserves is several times larger than 10,000 km².

By way of illustration, New Hanover Island, a little to the east of New Guinea, covers about 1150 km². During the late Pleistocene, it was connected by a land bridge to the larger island of New Ireland, and must have shared most of New Ireland's species. Today, New Hanover has lost about 22 percent of New Ireland's species. While this fractional fallout may not sound serious, nineteen of the lost species belong to a group of twenty-six species confined to the larger Bismarck Island, including every endemic Bismarck species in this category. In other words, New Hanover has differentially lost those species most in need of protection.[5]

Size and design of protected areas

Now that ecologists can make rough estimates of extinction rates for the most vulnerable categories of species, notably birds and mammals, they can determine what minimal areas are required to keep extinction rates "reasonably low". For example, if the aim is to keep the extinction rate of a community of bird species at less than 1 percent per century, then, generally speaking, there is need to establish a preserve of at least 2500 km².[8] Most of the world's parks and reserves are smaller than this, even though the area in question is not unduly large, i.e. a square of 50 km each side. Moreover, small patches of tropical moist forest cannot safeguard the organic diversity of forest ecosystems. This is not merely because of the low densities of many species. Certain forest animals must move long distances through the forest to find the food they need. For example, a number of butterflies depend on aminoacids from pollen in certain kinds of plants in order to sustain their egg production, and they sometimes have to travel several kilometers to find pollen. Thus for these butterflies, an area of less than 100 km² is not likely to be enough. When one considers the needs of all forest species, it is plain that 2500 km² should be considered a working minimum, at least until such time as we achieve better understanding of forest ecosystems.

An alternative approach lies in determining minimal areas for gene pools. To consider a few examples, wild fruit trees in Malaysia's lowland rainforest occur at low densities and a sample survey of 676 hectares has revealed few species with more than 24 individual trees per 100 hectares, while 11 out of 18 species have fewer than 13 trees per hectare. So if, as is likely, each species requires 10,000 trees to provide an adequate gene pool, considerable areas will have to be set aside to cater for these species.[9] In the same region, hornbills that possibly require minimal populations of 5000 individuals to ensure adequate gene pools will need between 2000 and 10,000 km² and monkeys with similar-sized populations anywhere from 250 to over 3000 km².[10] If a tiger population could survive with as few as 400 individuals, the area required to support them may need to be as big as 40,000 km².

Protected areas in Amazonia

Considering the importance of Amazonia for species conservation, it is worth considering its prospects in some detail. In view of the region's diversity, a representative network of protected areas will be needed to safeguard a considerable number of ecosystems.

According to island biogeography, saving 1 percent of Amazonia's moist forests might correspond, very roughly, to saving 25 percent of the region's species, and 10 percent could correspond to saving 50 percent. So 20 percent might make a sound job of safeguarding pretty well the entire spectrum of species in Amazonia, except for those with a highly localized distribution that lies right in the track of the Transamazon Highway or some other major development. However crude these calculations, they provide an informed first guess about the challenge facing conservationists in Amazonia.

Recent research has identified eight phytogeographic zones in Amazonia.[11] These "plant regions" have their characteristic floral communities, and hence their distinctive faunal communities too. Clearly, these zones require representative protection. Moreover, and as indicated in Chapter 9, the climatic changes of the Pleistocene, with their periodic drying-out of the forest zone, caused a series of sixteen "refuges" for surviving species to emerge in Amazonia. These refuges feature exceptional concentrations of species, with large numbers of endemisms. So conservation should focus also on these priority areas.

Translating these research findings into conservation programs works out somewhat as follows.[12] Suppose each of the eight subdivisions merits three protected areas, each area measuring 2590 km² (1000 mi²). This would amount to 62,160 km². In addition, a number of smaller parks and reserves would be required, in order to protect, for example, species of highly limited range, unique micro-habitats, and exceptional localities such as turtle or bird-nesting areas. Three such additional areas in each subdivision, measuring 1000 km² each, would amount to 24,000 km². The protected areas would need buffer zones around their perimeters to hold off man-derived disturbances from outside. If each such strip were 10 km wide the total area involved would be 98,460 km². This makes the overall total just under 185,000 km² — an area four fifths the size of Great Britain, though only 3.5 percent of Amazonia's 5.2 million km².

To date, Brazil has established one major park, the Amazonas National Park, approximately 10,000 km². Another has been proposed, the 50,000-km² Rio Negro National Park. Regrettably, neither of these two giant parks contains any of the vegetation formations or the Pleistocene refuges that have been designated as priorities for conservation. But President Jaoa Baptista Figueiredo, speaking of future development of Amazonia, has stressed the need for "preservation of ecological equilibrium", to which protected areas of forest are "indispensible". In fact, Brazil plans to create a total of 175,000 km² of parks and reserves in Amazonia by 1980, virtually the total area recommended by the ecologist planners (above). Meantime, four of the Pleistocene refuges fall entirely within those parts of Brazilian Amazonia that have been designated as growth poles for intensive development through cattle ranching and smallholder cultivation, while major parts of other high-priority conservation foci overlap with development areas. If any one of the refuges was to be eliminated, a large number of species would go with it.

As for other parts of Amazonia, Peru has established two parks in its sector, the Manu Park, 15,000 km², and the Pacaya-Samiria Park, almost 14,000 km². Venezuela's Canaima Park has been expanded to 30,000 km². Colombia plans to establish as many as twenty new parks.

Protected areas under threat

Whatever the needs of the future, protected areas already in being often fare badly in the face of economic pressures to put them to more useful-seeming purposes.

In Southeast Asia, and especially in the lowland forests, parks and reserves come under attack of many kinds. In Sumatra, two parks have been violated by logging operations, a nature reserve has been given out for timber concessions, a sawmill has been built on the edge of the Gunung Leuser Reserve and forests supposedly protected as hydrological reserves are being exploited for various purposes. In East Kalimantan, one third of the 2000-km² reserve has been taken by logging. In Malaysia the 5000-km² Taman Nagara Park is threatened by logging interests that eye the $1.8 billion worth of timber within its borders, and the same for the 2000-km² Endau Rompin Park. In the Philippines, there is much hunting and haphazard collecting of fuelwood in parks and reserves, shifting cultivators seem to operate with impunity, and certain areas even feature townships; the 73,000-

hectare Mount Apo National Park in Mindanao, southern Philippines, contains several endemic species, plus a concentration of the extremely endangered monkey-eating eagle, yet the park may well be reduced to 13,790 hectares, with the rest given over to logging and settlement. Brazil's Xingu Park in Amazonia has been reduced by one-quarter through highway construction, while another park in Brazil, the Serra do Cipo Park of Minas Gerais, an area rich with endemics, is grazed by appreciable numbers of cattle, is burnt every few years and features a truck road.

Many other instances could be cited to indicate how protected areas often fail to withstand economic pressures. The process seems likely to grow critical for wildland conservation in the years ahead unless protection policies and practices can better integrate parks with their socioeconomic environments.

New parks and reserves

At the same time, several countries have recently set aside an impressive array of parks and reserves — impressive, that is, as compared with previous situations, marginally significant compared with what is required. Regrettably, some of these areas are no more than "paper parks", since their purpose is little understood by officialdom, and they are subject to various forms of disruption by local citizenry. Still, many of the initiatives are to be applauded. Peru hopes to protect almost 55,000 km² of its 650,000 km² of tropical moist forest by 1980; several areas are to be established after the pattern of the Manu National Park, that incorporates the drainage of an entire tributary river system. As mentioned, Brazil hopes to set aside 175,000 km² of its sector of Amazonia. Indonesia plans to expand its parks and reserves from 36,000 to 100,000 km² by 1983. Zaire intends to increase its network from 78,130 km² to 351,000 km² or 15 percent of the country by 1980.

If the latter "big three" countries of the tropical moist forest zone follow through with their plans, their protected areas will amount altogether to 626,000 km² (an area almost the size of Spain and Portugal, or Texas) or 6.7 percent of the entire biome. This will be highly encouraging, even if well short of the minimum 10-20 percent of the biome postulated by the theory of island biogeography. To ask a country to set aside one-tenth of its national territory is equivalent to asking the United States to set aside an area twice the size of California.

16 Economic Factors: Problems and Opportunities

As this book has indicated, conservation tends to tackle symptoms rather than causes of destructive processes. In effect, it waits until a habitat is severely disrupted through man's exploitation, then it tries to save the species occupying the habitat through a last-ditch rescue effort. In essence, a fire-brigade response. True, the situation has recently improved in certain countries, but world-wide the tendency remains much the same.

Given the broad-scale disruption that is likely to threaten habitats in virtually every last corner of the earth during the next few decades, more attention needs to be directed at the nature of economic activities that cause the problem. This is no new challenge. As was stated by an anonymous writer in England almost 300 years ago: "We arrest the man or woman who steals the goose from off the common, but we let the person loose who steals the commons from under the goose."

If the problem has been recognized for centuries, why have we been slow to devise solutions? Answer: we have found the problem, and it is us. Any person who, as a consumer, stimulates economic activities, makes his contribution. Yet it is not easy to see what the well-intentioned individual can do about it. If, being mindful of all the trees that are converted into paperpulp each year, he decides to boycott the Sunday issue of the *New York Times,* his gesture will have no effect. If he spends 5 minutes each week in persuading one friend to follow his example, he still achieves nothing worthwhile. If, however, he and sufficient friends write to their political representatives, they may get somewhere. This, then, is the name of the game: initiatives at the level of the community.

Something the same applies to the individual who is engaged in economic activities as a private entrepreneur. His honest attempts to make a living may disrupt the habitat of scores of species. Yet, however well intentioned he may be, he will not be persuaded to operate his enterprise in an uncompetitive manner merely to safeguard the interests of the community, unless the community makes it worth his while: again, the need for community-level action. By the same token, a tropical-forest country of the developing world is unlikely to refrain from exploitation of its forests in order to serve the greater good of humankind, unless humankind recognizes the sacrifice and tries to compensate it. Although these economic factors are crucially important for measures to protect species, conservationist strategies generally take little account of them.

Little wonder, then, that there has been limited mileage in educational campaigns to make individual citizens more aware of the species problem. A citizen is left bewildered, if not discouraged, by his inability to do much as a single citizen. A citizen is a consumer, and even a saint likes to read newspapers. Similarly, a better-informed exploiter will still go ahead with what he regards as his legitimate interests, even though it may mean the depletion of a species' habitats. So educational campaigns are hardly pertinent to the purpose for which they are often proposed, viz. the persuasion of individual persons toward an attitude which makes them more caring about wild creatures. They are likely to serve a valid purpose only when they stimulate public support for community-level initiatives — and it is changes of this scale that are the focus of this chapter.

Collective goods

To restate a basic principle, species deserve to be protected for society by society. Similar collective needs are frequently met through collective action. Within the context of an individual nation, examples of "collective goods" include public education, national defense and other major government programs. At international level, collective goods are exemplified by the United Nations agencies and by a variety of intergovernmental organizations such as the European Common

Market. These collective goods are provided at collective initiatives through the collective purse.[1]

It is in this spirit that species should be safeguarded as common heritage resources of unique and indivisible value. Like other collective goods, the protection of species generally does not offer incentive to the market-place system to supply the public support that species deserve. Unless the community acts through collective decision to assume responsibility, species are likely to receive less than a socially optimal amount of protection. There is little reason in principle why species should not receive support of this kind and scope; public investment, at both national and international levels, already serves many efforts to conserve environmental resources, for example, through clean-up measures for the atmosphere and water bodies. Moreover, collective authority is active at national level to protect species through national parks and other measures — but, while species merit expanded protection by national bodies everywhere, this chapter argues that a major responsibility lies at international level in recognition of species' value to the community of nations. In other words, the species problem postulates comprehensive measures on the part of global society.

An expanded approach of this sort would go far beyond the present fragmentary efforts by isolated groups of private individuals which, by virtue of their restricted resources, prove all too limited as compared to the needs at issue and as compared to the resources of the community at large. The World Wildlife Fund, together with a number of similar private organizations, achieve a good deal for threatened species within their limited means. But since its start up in 1961, the World Wildlife Fund has raised only around $30 million through private contributions — a mere fraction of sums expended by the public on books, magazines, films and other expressions of interest in wildlife. Over 5 times as much money is spent by the U.S. public alone, in a single year, on seed for wild birds. This suggests that the public senses far more interest in wildlife and species than is reflected through donations to private organizations.

This is not to imply, of course, that an enlarged community-level approach on behalf of species would leave no role for private organizations. The World Wildlife Fund and other groups could still play a valuable role as "pace setters", identifying new needs, catalysing fresh initiatives, coordinating conservation efforts within different sectors of the community at large, etc. In short, they could continue to serve as an "advance guard," in the overall conservation campaign.

Community action in support of species

There is urgent need, then, for the community at large to recognize its responsibility to exercise collective authority on behalf of the community's heritage in species. To consider some specific initiatives, society-level measures can be categorized as follows.

1. *Acknowledgement of deficiences and failures of the market-place system*

As indicated in Chapter 6, much decline of species is due to the deficiencies and failures of the market-place system, which sometimes favors the here-and-now needs of private individuals to the detriment of long-term needs of the community in general. Moreover, the market-place tends to ignore the value of resources without a price tag. So serious are these shortcomings of the market-place that, in January 1976, twenty-seven leading economists, including three Nobel Prize winners, stated that

"The wastefulness of Western economies — in energy, in food, and in the despoiling of the environment — is not an oversight but an inherent trend in a system which still produces primarily for corporate profit. . . . we believe that Western societies (need) to explore and develop new modes of resources allocation and new ways of establishing human societal priorities for national economies, (together with) the necessity for a new international allocation of resources."

Apart from these conventional shortcomings of the market-place, species constitute an unusually "disadvantaged" category of natural resources. Whenever natural resources are degraded, such as the atmosphere and large water bodies, the public soon becomes aware of what is happening: people can see, day by day, how their environments are becoming degraded. By contrast, when species are in danger, little is heard of the way that society's heritage is being steadily depleted (except, of course, for a few dozen better-known instances such as the tiger and the gorilla). And whereas pollution is almost always a reversible problem, extinction of species is not.

To see how the market-place contributes to the decline of species, let us look at the cheetah in Africa. The cheetah comes into conflict with ranching interests in its savannah grasslands when, finding its usual wild prey squeezed out through expanding herds of livestock, it takes to killing calves and sheep. The value of ranching products, such as meat and wool, are sensitively registered through the market-place, whereas the value of the cheetah, having no market for the "goods and services" represented by the creature's ultimate survival, is effectively set at nil. The problem is compounded by the fact that the potential value of the price-less cheetah is becoming increasingly recognized. Being an animal that can suddenly launch into a 100-km-per-hour sprint and maintain the speed for at least a kilometer, the cheetah can clearly sustain a high oxygen debt at next to no notice. This capacity may hold clues for treatment of respiratory and circulatory disorders in humans — provided the cheetah survives long enough to be available for research.

Thus arises the multiple asymmetry of evaluation of species "worth" as compared with conventional products of the market-place economy. The conservation cause could hardly be given a bigger boost than through acknowledgement, on the part of governments, the private sector, conservation organizations and other parties involved, that this asymmetry of evaluation lies at the heart of the problem. In order to remedy market-place defects and failures, there is need for "compensatory adjustment" on the part of collective authority. Governments should step in to take account of the fact that the open market-place does not cater for all economic needs of society, and especially that the market-place ignores and even depletes the common heritage species. A shift in attitude along these lines would represent a major advance, since species have hitherto received grotesquely little attention in proportion to their potential value and the irreversible injury to which they are susceptible.

So much for the principles involved. Now for some practical steps.

2. *Adjustment of discount rates*

The exploitation of natural resources is greatly affected by discount rates. A rate commonly adopted for private investment, and generally established by Western-world governments as a standard by which to assess the profitability of public investments, is 10 percent. This rate is considered appropriate for two reasons. First, it is thought to reflect the internal rate of return on marginal foregone projects in the private sector. Secondly, it is believed to reflect the rate at which individuals are willing to borrow and lend in the market-place, and thus represents the citizenry's view of what the future is worth. However, it means in practice that an investor looks to recover his capital and to take his profits within 5-7 years or so, and to pay no heed to what may happen after that. So long-term considerations are ruled out. An international timber corporation cannot concern itself with forest harvesting cycles that extend over 30 years and still less can it give thought to conservation implications, such as survival of species, that extend into the indefinite future.

So there is a case for a variable system of discount rates, in order to attribute proper weight to the costs of future generations that suffer loss through the elimination of a unique forest ecosystem or the extinction of a species. Instead of rates set by the market-place, we could devise a set of discount rates for "projects with a conservation dimension" that explicitly allow for factors not adequately covered by market-place mechanisms. In the case of tropical moist forests, for example, it would safeguard certain ecosystems for the future, keeping open options for succeeding generations.

In operational terms, a "social rate of discount" would, in order to emphasize future needs and responsibilities, offer a lower rate of discount than that of the market-place. It would reflect not only private economic factors, but issues of public policy and social ethics. It is reasonable to assume that a forest ecosystem with endemic species will be of at least as much interest to society in 100 years time as it is now. In order to promote preservation of these exceptional resources, it would be appropriate to apply a very low discount rate, conceivably as low as 1 percent. True, a reduced discount rate would tend to generate many additional opportunities for investment, and some mechanism would have to be devised to achieve an appropriate allocation of capital.[2]

3.   *A tax on non-renewable resources*

A related strategy could lie with a tax on the exploitation of tropical hardwoods and other raw materials that serve to advance the lifestyles of affluent nations.[3] Since an "international tax" would raise the price of timber and other raw materials to manufacturers in developed countries, it would help to direct the attention of the community to long-term considerations. In operational terms, it would induce industry in developed nations to make more intensive use of their timber supplies, and to expand recycling processes; in turn this would lead to more efficient exploitation of the raw resources. At the same time, the initiative would enable citizens in affluent, resource-hungry nations to act with a clearer recognition of their role in exploitation of resources of unique value. For example, a 0.1 percent value-added tax on developed-nation imports of tropical timber would yield $5 million per year, much more than the amount allocated to forestry annually by the U.N. agency principally responsible for forestry, the Food and Agriculture Organization

This proposal, like the idea for a two-tier discount rate, implies that responsibility for the initiative would be accepted by community authority, i.e. by governments and intergovernmental organizations. This need not entail an arbitrary or authoritarian response. Governments already make many judgments on behalf of their citizens: for instance, they override current preferences of individuals by instituting compulsory pension schemes, thereby restricting citizens' predilection for immediate consumption. In accord with this spirit, governments could assume responsibility for high-value and unique resources, and conserve them until such time as individual citizens perceive the value of these resources and adapt their preferences accordingly.

Public reaction to these proposals would enable governments to form a clearer picture of their citizens commitment to safeguarding future interests. With refinements through experience, then institutional devices could even serve as some sort of proxy pricing system to express people's minimal evaluation of the resources in question. If citizens began to object to the financial strains involved, on the grounds that they would be unduly deprived of immediate returns from exploitation, the initiatives would have to be amended or even terminated. But citizens would thereby act with some explicit understanding of the prospects which face their descendants. This would be a marked contrast to the present situation, where citizens have scant opportunity to appraise their role in the situation. In fact, the exercise could eventually serve as a measure of the readiness of citizens to pay for their commitment to their descendants: it would permit them to "put up or shut up".

4. *The indivisible value of species*

A species saved for one sector of society is automatically saved for the whole of society. Similarly, the elimination of a species represents a unique and irreversible loss not only for the country or countries concerned but for the community at large. This indivisible value argues that the community should play a greater role in species conservation. If all nations have a responsibility to the rest of the global community to safeguard species within their borders, all nations have a responsibility to share the costs of safeguard measures. Just as the benefits cannot generally be restricted to a few, so the costs of assuring them should not fall heavily on a few or on those least able to bear them.

To illustrate this dimension of the situation, medical application of species' genetic resources assist communities far and wide. A tropical-forest plant with anti-fertility properties could help the family-planning campaign way beyond the borders of the country or countries where it is located. So all potential benficiaries should share the burden of costs of ensuring the plant's survival.

5. *Countering externality effects*

As has been detailed in Chapter 6, much of the present depletion of species' habitats in the tropics is due to externality effects of international trade relations. The unplanned and uncoordinated relationships which give rise to these externalities are often small in scope, difficult to comprehend in their cumulative impact, and do not stimulate much in the way of corrective response by private initiatives. As the economist Keynes once remarked, "There is nothing worse than a moderate evil, because it does not prompt us to do much about it". By the time the externality effects grow so pronounced that nobody can miss them (for example, the silent spring), their "overshoot" impact may make remedies expensive or even impossible.

The classic answer to externalities is to "internalize" them. This is usually achieved in two ways. The law can be invoked to constrain the process that gives rise to an externality, although, as indicated in Chapter 15, this would be difficult in the case of species because of the international dimensions of the situation. Alternatively, or in addition, those individuals and groups who engage in activities that are destructive to species can be persuaded to desist through compensatory payments. Examples could include tax rebates for commercial enterprises that adopt conservationist practices (see Chapter 14). The initiative could even be extended to governments of tropical-forest countries, in order to persuade them to consider the interests of the global community as well as their own citizens (see Chapter 19).

True, measures of this sort amount to "bribes". Yet inducements along these lines are becoming an accepted method of regulating economic activities of the part of one sector of the community in order to safeguard interests of the entire community.[4] In the cases of species, the financial inducement would have to be on a scale large enough to offset the economic activities that undermine species' survival. Sufficient funds could be raised only through some form of tax on those sectors of society that are affluent enough not only to pay but to register an interest in conservation of species and that bear some indirect responsibility for the decline of species in developing regions.

6. *A safety-first attitude toward the future*

Society includes not only people now alive, but future generations. Longer-term considerations are generally reckoned to lie beyond the perception of most present citizens and traditionally have become the responsibility of community agency. The only thing we know for sure about the future is that it will be radically different from the past. In face of this enormous uncertainty, the least we can do for future generations is to pass on to them as many of the planet's resources possible, provided that does not burden us with undue sacrifices. This approach applies especially to unique resources such as species, whose potential value remains largely undetermined — except that it could be very great. Were large numbers of species to be eliminated, the impoverishment for society would fall much more on future generations than on the present community.

While this approach to uncertainty is ultra-conservative, the practical costs are likely to be small both absolutely and as compared with expenditures in other areas where society faces considerable uncertainty, such as public health and national defense. In short, it pays to be vaguely right rather than precisely wrong.[5] The situation argues for a safety-first response through collective authority, which alone has the capacity to pay an "insurance premium" on sufficient scale against future disaster.

These six factors amount to a comprehensive rationale for society to intervene through society-level measures to safeguard society's heritage in species. As economic systems among society become more complex and technologically advanced, the rationale is likely to gain greater cogency.

17 Some Legal and Political Options

As indicated in Chapter 7, a number of conservation measures are available through legal and political initiatives. This chapter reviews several front-runners. Since the chapter is primarily concerned with ways for the global community to assert itself in defense of its global heritage in species, the analysis focuses on options at international level.

Doctrine of "public trust"

The community at large could move to safeguard its common heritage through an international adaptation of the doctrine of "public trust". This legal concept, hitherto practised only at national level, has thrown up many innovative and flexible mechanisms in the field of environmental law. Under the doctrine certain natural resources are considered to be held by the government in trust for the public,[1] these resources including wildlife and outstanding natural areas. The doctrine, together with the legal mechanisms that stem from it, have been extensively articulated in a number of developed countries, where community concern for community values is increasingly acknowledged. By contrast, developing countries have not perceived an urgent need to formulate legal procedures along these lines. Still less has the international community developed legal constrains to regulate the use of unique natural resources.[2]

The public trust doctrine incorporates two basic requirements that allow it to function as an institutional mechanism. First, it embodies the concept of the community's legal interest. Secondly, it is enforceable. These two requirements present no problem within the context of an individual nation. At international level, the first requirement is starting to be met through the adaption of multinational conventions, together with resolutions and declarations of the United Nations and regional bodies, that recognize the concept of the community's legitimate interest in environmental assets of universal value (for some examples, see below).

With respect to the second requirement, however, international society lacks powers of enforcement. This deficiency could be met through a process of international opinion, support and pressure that could promote "enforcement of a sort".

Cynical commentators to the contrary, international law without powers of enforcement is still worthwhile law. All effective laws depend upon the willing support of the general public. Without that support, enforcement is of little use, as witness the 12-year effort to establish prohibition of liquor sales in the United States. The other side of the coin is that strong support for a public objective does not necessarily need formal sanctions to back up legal expression of that objective. If enough individuals proclaim the rightness of what they are aiming for, they can generally get the rest of the community to go along. In fact, persuasion is almost more effective than compulsion in the long run.

Were enough nations to acknowledge the public trust doctrine at international level, this would provide an authoritative basis for promoting a wider acceptance of a basic principle of collective living in the global village — that nations are responsible not only to themselves but to all other nations for what they do. This applies increasingly to the exploitation and conservation of high-value resources, such as the earth's air mantle, the oceans and international waterways, exceptional ecosystems, species and genetic reservoirs, and many other environmental resources. If a sufficient consensus could be established along these lines, select categories of resources, such as species, could be recognized as "resources to be maintained in trust for the global community now and forever". Such acknowledgement could be promulgated through a United Nations Declaration adopted by the General Assembly, followed by international conventions for different types of resources.

While an approach along these lines may sound inconsistent with a central precept of international law, viz. that nations are presumed to exercise complete sovereignty over their natural resources, there need be no intrinsic conflict in practice. After all, collective responsibility for the common heritage does not necessarily mean collective rights in particular resources. An individual nation would no longer be left to rely on its own isolated efforts to protect precious resources such as species. It could receive assistance from the community of nations. The nation in question would continue its own on-the-ground conservation of species and their habitats, while the international community would offer help in support of its common heritage. In essence, the strategy would depend on incentives rather than coercion as a means to induce individual nations to align their individual rights with the interests of the broader community. In addition, the strategy would not down-place sovereignty; on the contrary, it would emphasize it as a functional, rather than an idealized concept. Indeed, management of the planetary ecosystem will depend in large measure on decentralized planning: what better institution to accomplish this than the individual nation which exercises competence in its own bailiwick without forgetting its broader responsibilities among the community at large?

An approach of this sort has already been tentatively established through a precedent on the part of Iran. This country has offered an area of 1300 km^2, constituting "an ecosystem of global importance", to be placed in joint trust between Iran and the community of nations. An international agency is to advise Iran on how to conserve and administer the area for the benefit of all humankind.

Tentative steps towards collective responsibility

Approaching the challenge from the other direction, i.e. through initiatives on the part of society at large, the situation is already marked — albeit in very limited fashion — by emergent concepts of collective responsibility for environmental resources of international significance. A number of treaties have been established among groups of nations to protect migratory species, such as birds that travel from temperate zones to the tropics and back again each year, and oceanic fish species that return to territorial waters of individual nations to spawn. Further initiatives along these lines could help the whitethroat in Britain, whose numbers have "crashed" as a result of the Sahel drought, and the Kirtland's warbler, which, despite rigorous protection of its nesting grounds in Michigan state, is declining because of habitat destruction in the Bahamas.

In addition to treaties for migratory species, there are now more than forty multilateral conventions dealing with natural resources. Most of them are regional arrangements, tackling, for example, joint management of the Baltic and Red Seas, and various inland waters. There are also many bilateral agreements on shared resources, transfrontier pollution and other two-nation issues. Together with related declarations, recommendations, and standard-setting procedures on the part of groups of nations, these various initiatives amount to a solid step toward establishment of a body of international environmental law. Especially in the field of shared resources, there is an urgent need for "an accepted way of doing things", in view of the fact that over 200 important watersheds are divided between two or more nations. The distance to be covered by international law is vast and the amount of ground covered is, in comparison, grotesquely small. Still, a start has been made. The question is, can new agreements be achieved fast enough to keep up with the ever-growing deterioration of environmental resources?

All the more encouraging, in this context, is the recent trend towards agreements at global level. They include the World Heritage Trust, the Convention on Wetlands of International Importance, the Convention on International Trade in Endangered Wildlife and Wildlife Products, the Convention for the Prevention of Marine Pollution from Land-based Sources and the Convention on Conservation of Islands for Science. These legal devices serve as a measure of efforts on the part of the international community to take a few cautious steps towards communal responsibility for unique resources of exceptional value to humankind.

At the same time, a number of other initiatives have become stalled. A proposal to clean up the Mediterranean has run into difficulty. The coastal nations of the Mediterranean, while aware that their polluting activities threaten to turn this major water body into a cesspool, cannot reconcile themselves to yielding up a degree of their sovereignty on behalf of the common cause. Equally troubled is the

Law of the Sea Conference, which has been trying to tackle the problem of exploitation and conservation of resources in one of the most extensive of earth's "environmental commons". Far from expanding the concept of humankind's heritage, the Conference has reinforced the notion of national sovereignty as the ultimate good, through extending territorial and other national rights far out into the high seas. At the same time, however, the Conference has managed to establish an International Seabed Authority, which will share in exploitation of a major common heritage resource, the ocean-floor minerals worth \$3 trillion.

All in all, the few initiatives mentioned add up to some initial progress. Of these, the most important, from the standpoint of issues discussed in this chapter, is the World Heritage Trust. It is worth considering in some detail.

World Heritage Trust

The World Heritage Trust was established through UNESCO's 1973 Convention for the Protection of the World Cultural and Natural Heritage. Under the Convention, "Natural Heritage" includes "National features ... and areas ... which are of outstanding universal value ... and ... habitats of certain species of outstanding value". The institution provides international financial support to those countries unable to ensure protection on their own for unique items of humanity's natural and cultural heritage within their national territories. Present provision is for each of UNESCO's 141 members to contribute an additional 1 percent of its customary subvention, plus such further funds as it wishes to offer in support of the Trust.

As the statement above indicates, however, the Trust is severely limited from the start. Its Convention addresses itself only to those few parts of the natural heritage which are "truly of international significance". This means it does not concern itself with all proposed areas and species under threat, even though any species, being unique, could be construed as possessing truly universal value. Which species are to be considered more important than others, and why, is not indicated. But, due to limited funds, and in order not to "dilute" the idea of the initiative, the Trust is to assist only a few outstanding species and areas.

Furthermore, the idea has been slow to get off the ground. Several years went by before a minimum number of states ratified the Convention and brought it into effect among participants. This delay was due largely to the tendency of governments to see little urgency in the problem of humanity's heritage. In turn, this lack of urgency reflected an uninformed view of the value of the heritage and the rate at which it is being eroded. In addition, certain developing countries, recalling how their art treasures have been looted in the past by foreigners, are reluctant to agree that any part of their heritage, whether cultural or natural, is anybody's business but their own.

In addition to these shortcomings, the Trust concept works best in certain limited circumstances. The notion of the Trust was triggered in the mid-1960s by the emergency of the Abu Simbel Temples on the River Nile, which were threatened by inundation through the Aswan Dam. A UNESCO fund-raising campaign for the Temples raised $36 million in short order, and saved the 5000-year old monuments as a significant part of the world's cultural heritage. By contrast, a year-after-year campaign for funds, such as the Trust envisages, for a variety of areas and species, could prove difficult to maintain. A further problem lies in the fact that the site where the Temples have been relocated amounts to only a few hectares, whereas the natural areas and species' habitats to be protected under the Trust will require that many thousands of square kilometers of potentially productive land be withheld from other use. It is ironic that the creature to which the Temples were originally dedicated, the Nile crocodile, is now under great and growing threat. This is due not so much to over-exploitation of crocodiles for their hides, but to loss of crocodile habitat as human communities occupy the banks and shores of every last stretch of water in Africa.

It is also ironic that Indonesia, a major tropical forest country, is receiving international support to save a ninth-century temple, Borobudur. This temple, constituting the world's largest ensemble of Buddhist reliefs, amounts to one of the glories of humankind's cultural heritage. But rehabilitation of the 123-m square, 35-m high temple, with its one million stones, is likely to cost at least $12 million. UNESCO has raised $5 million from its members, and is trying to put up more; the Indonesian government will cover the rest. This prompts the question whether similar measures, on the part of the international community in conjunction with the Indonesian government, could not safeguard far more valuable resources of Indonesia's patrimony, viz. the unique sectors of its tropical forests. Of course, a significant difference lies in the fact that, were Borobudur allowed to decline further, its decay would entail virtually no economic loss for Indonesia (apart from a few tourist dollars), whereas preservation of extensive patches of virgin forest will entail large "opportunity costs" insofar as Indonesia will not be able to derive exploitational revenues. Moreover, the plan to save Borobudur involves a once-and-for-all outlay of funds, whereas an initiative to meet Indonesia's opportunity costs would entail compensatory payments year after year.

Other types of Trust

So how about other types of Trust to conserve humanity's heritage? An obvious candidate would be a Trust for Species. Such a Trust could establish the need to protect through an international fund in support of conservation efforts by individual nations. In essence, a Trust for Species would represent a large step beyond the initial point of departure expressed through the World Heritage Trust, whose core concept represents a fine pioneering initiative but whose operational workings are far too limited to make more than a marginal dent on the problem of disappearing species.

Something of the same spirit and approach could apply to a broad-scale effort on behalf of tropical forests. A first step might be a U.N. Declaration adopted by the General Assembly, in recognition of the twin facts that tropical forests are declining and that they represent a legitimate concern of the community of nations. A two-thirds majority endorsement by the General Assembly should ensure wide participation on the part of tropical nations, and would encourage appropriate measures for exceptional forest ecosystems within their national jurisdictions. In other words, a General Assembly initiative of this order would minimize resistance to collective initiative. The

Declaration would hopefully lead to an international Convention, establishing a Trust Fund in support of significant sectors of the tropical-forest biome.

Of course, these two proposals are highly speculative. The practical difficulties they would throw up are numerous and all too apparent. The proposals are raised here only as exploratory probings, to indicate the scale of measures necessary for the international community to protect its natural heritage. Impractical as they may sound, they should be considered in light of alternatives available. Present steps amount to fragmentary efforts that are far from equal to the task. They also amount to an implicit decision by the community to see its natural heritage slide down the plug.

A third option might offer more realistic prospects. It would be far more limited than the other two in terms of comprehensive measures on behalf of species and tropical forests. In fact, it would not deal with species and forests at all as such, rather with certain environmental questions of general scope. But it could have important spinoff benefits for species and forests. It would amount to a Treaty on environmental impact assessments, to be undertaken by individual nations for projects that may have environmental repercussions in other nations. This idea has already been given an airing in international forums, and has led to some progress in principle. For example, Senator Pell in the United States has introduced a bill into Congress, with the support of President Carter, urging that

> "The United States government should seek the agreement of other governments to the proposed Treaty requiring the preparation of an International Environmental Assessment for any major project, action or continuing activity which may be reasonably expected to have a significant adverse effect on the physical environment or an environmental interest of another nation or a global commons area. . . . The Assessment shall be prepared and submitted by the government of the initiating State to the affected Party or Parties and to the United Nations Environment Program, with a view toward preventing or minimising any potential adverse environmental consequences beyond its territory which might result from the proposed activity."

The Treaty would notably apply to dams and other major water projects that effect "downstream territories", also industrial plants whose pollutant emissions spill over on to neighboring nations. In case of dispute among the nations in question, the statement could be referred to an independent body with acknowledged scientific expertise, which would serve as a sort of "international ombudsman" to arbitrate conflicts between exclusive and inclusive rights and interest.[3]

Eventually the spirit of this proposal could be expanded to tackle environmental questions that go beyond water engineering works and polluting industries. It could reach out to consider development activities that impinge not only upon the territories of neighboring nations, but upon the rights and interests of all nations. Were a particular nation to undertake a project that would endanger, say, a bird species, the activity could be construed as affecting an integral part of the planetary ecosystem. Of course, in terms of simple physicobiotic environments, this might seem to be stretching the concept of ecological relationships. But, insofar as the activity would affect the global community, the community should be consulted by virtue of its "stake" in the bird species as part of the common natural heritage. However much this might appear a long step beyond the limited scope of a Treaty on environmental assessments, it could ultimately be viewed as a consistent extension of the spirit of the Treaty. It would thereby engender a sense of responsibility among nations to adapt or abandon projects that would undercut humankind's patrimony in species. (A precedent for this kind of spirit has been established by the Netherlands, which has decided to re-route a proposed canal in the Dollard area of the Wadden Sea in order to protect a unique waterfowl habitat of international importance.) As a "worst case" consequence, extinction of a species through human activity would arise only as a result of informed public discussion, and through a clear decision that the costs of conserving the species are too high.

Something the same could apply to tropical moist forests. Over-exploitation of forests may not only have direct and easily recognizable consequences for neighboring nations, through repercussions on watersheds and international river systems, but it can lead to further effects which are not so apparent in practice and more difficult to nail down in principle; for example, disruption of climatic patterns in regions far afield, and depletion of the earth's single main repository of species. Due to an accident of geography, Brazil exercises sovereignty over most of a vital global resource, the Amazonia rainforest. The role of this forest in the natural economy of the planet makes it reasonable for other nations to take a strong interest in what happens to the forest. Despite its traditional powers as an independent nation, Brazil can scarcely consider itself in a position to disregard the ultimate needs of human beings way outside its own borders — notably of farmers in the grainbelt of North America who could suffer from reduced rainfall were the forest to disappear, plus the people around the world who benefit from the surplus grain produced by those farmers. Of course, the same constraints apply to the other seven nations whose borders embrace Amazonia. For purposes of their own regional needs, the eight nations signed a pact in late 1977, with the general aim of ensuring that development of Amazonia shall maintain harmony between economic growth and environmental conversation, and with the particular aim of ensuring that use of Amazonia's waters by any participant nation shall not cause any harm to other nations. A Venezuelan delegate expressed the common intention as follows: "The Amazon Basin Pact reaffirms before the world that, as we have exclusive jurisdiction over this immense region, so also, do we accept and fulfill the responsibilities of initiating its development without destroying its ecological balance and of using its immense potential riches in a rational way."

Of course, far-reaching initiatives along these lines depend upon political will. In turn, this depends upon perception of common needs and opportunities. As this perception grows stronger, so nations will come to acknowledge reciprocal responsibilities. They will then become more inclined to take broader-ranging measures to meet new challenges of collective life within the global village. In short, perception is all.

Perception of common interests

Perception of common interests still has a good way to go. As long as individual nations do not recognize that their common good diverges from, and is greater than the sum of, national interests, they are unlikely to commit themselves to initiatives in support of the common cause. However, a nation's conviction concerning its sovereignty has to do with its sense of wealth of natural resources. In some circumstances, feeling wealthy can be as significant as actually being wealthy. By virtue of their rich diversity of species, many developing nations of the tropics are the equivalent of "biological millionaires" as compared with the ecologically impoverished nations of the rest of the world. If this fortunate endowment were to be better recognized, it might help developing countries to feel open to international initiatives that would enhance their international image in terms of status and responsibility.

The failure of international law to take steps toward a conservation strategy for species is not due to a missing legal theory. It is due to a missing consensus about common interests at issue. So there is need to establish a consensus, however loose, about conservation of species as a worthy objective of society at large. Using this consensus as a basis on which to build a structure of international agreements, the community of nations could then move on to interpret the concept of common heritage through an institutional framework that embodies specific conservation measures. The greater the consensus established, the better the prospect of articulating a conservation strategy as an authoritative expectation of the community of nations. In response to this expectation, individual nations would be more ready to conform to communally perceived needs and opportunities. Rather than feeling pressured in a manner that they feel offends their sovereignty, they would find that their prestige and political authority within the global community would be reinforced.

18 What Developing Countries can do for the Global Heritage

Developing countries can do much to safeguard the global heritage in species. At least two-thirds, and possibly three-quarters, of all species on earth exist in the tropics, a zone that is pretty well made up of developing countries. Yet, while the tropics merit exceptional efforts at conservation, they have hitherto received exceptionally meager measures. Moreover, pressures of growing human numbers with growing aspirations are causing natural environments to be degraded at ever-more rapid rates.

So what can developing countries do to turn around the adverse trend? A long list of possibilities is available. They can set aside more wildland territories in order to protect representative ecosystems. They can clamp down on illegal hunting and trade in wildlife products. They can reduce conflict between wild creatures and domestic livestock. They can boost tourism as a support for parks and reserves. Above all, they can stem the wholesale conversion of virgin landscapes to croplands and the like by making sure that development projects are the right ones at the right time and right place. They can pursue all these initiatives, plus a good many more. The fact that many developing countries do not pull the levers for these measures is not generally due to lack of awareness, or obtuseness, or worse. It is due more to deep-seated problems in the workings of developing countries — problems that often stem from the "common heritage/common property" conflict. The nature of these problems, and ways to tackle them, are the subject of this chapter.

To be sure, a number of developing countries have already taken sizeable steps towards conservation of their species. Tanzania, with a government budget about as much as New Yorkers spend on ice cream each year, allocates a larger share of this impoverished national kitty to conservation of its wildlife than the United States spends by proportion on its bald eagle, mountain lion and other wild creatures. Tanzania's parks and reserves amount to 9 percent of the country, the equivalent of the United States setting aside California, Oregon and Washington states. When Peru received its first donations from the World Wildlife Fund and other outside organizations in the mid-1960s, these contributions almost equalled the entire funding allocated by the country to its conservation efforts. By 1975, however, Peru had invested sums of its own that totalled 50 times more than the total financial aid extended from outside during Peru's entire conservation history. Something the same holds true for several other developing nations, notably Iran, Costa Rica and Zambia, and their achievements may soon be matched by Venezuela, Zaire and Gabon, among other countries — all are establishing extensive networks of parks.

Conservation of tropical moist forests

Apart from these various options to advance conservation, certain developing countries can, at a single stroke, safeguard a far greater segment of earth's species than can be accomplished through any other single conservation initiative anywhere. They can achieve this by doing a better job with their tropical moist forests. Of course, several other countries can also do much to safeguard their savannah grasslands, their arid zones, their montane territories and their coral-reef ecosystems, all of which, generally speaking, are not receiving a fraction of the protection they deserve. But no biome is being destroyed more rapidly, and no biome offers a better return per conservation dollar, than tropical moist forests.

True, developing countries are unlikely to look out for their forests merely in order to preserve 40-50 percent of humanity's heritage in species. However valid this motivation might be, it is not going to appear so pressing to developing countries' leaders as the urgent need to enhance their citizens' lifestyles. Fortunately, there are many ways to boost people's living levels through improved forestry, with the important spin-off benefits that this will achieve for the survival prospects of millions of species.

So, in order to sharpen the focus of this chapter, the analysis will be confined to this one biome. It will serve to point up the many ways in which developing countries can mesh conservation with economic advancement — a key factor, considering the apparently conflicting claims of the two. Bio-ecological needs are not the only absolutes at issue; the subsistence peasant has more immediate concerns than the ultimate welfare of natural environments. Unless he takes care of his short-term needs, he may not be around to see how long-term considerations work out. And when he engages in land-use practices that are wasteful of natural resources — resources which sometimes appertain to humanity's heritage — he is not usually acting in blind disregard of his own ultimate interests. Rather he is acting with rational regard for tonight's supper.

This conflict is particularly acute in the case of tropical moist forests. The countries in question derive appreciable revenues from their timber exports, and they can use these foreign-exchange earnings to improve their citizens' living levels right across the board. Understandably, then, they are reluctant to forfeit large and immediate revenues in order to safeguard their countries' heritage in species (let alone the global community's heritage). Were these countries to consider setting aside huge blocs of forestland as protected areas, they would face "opportunity costs" of exploitation foregone — costs that would already be high, and will go rapidly higher as the urge for economic advancement generates pressure to put every last square meter of land to productive use.

Traditional attitude to tropical moist forests

On top of these various conflicts, there is a further factor at the core of the problem of tropical moist forests. These forests have not always been viewed by developing countries as resources that can permanently contribute to economic development. On the contrary, they have often been considered to be obstacles in the path of expanding civilization. As a result, Forestry Departments have been inclined, by tradition, to be Cinderella agencies, overshadowed by more powerful bureaucracies such as Ministries of Agriculture. In fact, Forestry has often evolved as a sub-agency under the Ministry of

Agriculture. In order to achieve political clout, Forestry departments try to play the development game according to the old-established rules, which means that the sector must produce as many cash revenues as possible, fast. This fosters an attitude of once-and-for-all exploitation of forests, in disregard of broader needs.

Even less are Forestry Departments inclined to look at the many benefits which forests confer on society through their "environmental services". Forests protect watersheds, releasing moisture in a steady year-round flow rather than in seasonal flash-floods — an especially important function in mountainous regions such as Southeast Asia and Central America. Forests form new soils as well as reducing the erosion of existing soils. Forests temper local climates. Forests harbour wild creatures, with their genetic reservoirs. Forests offer the finest sites on earth for basic ecological research into patterns of evolution. Forests supply opportunity for education, recreation and tourism.

Yet these many services are generally ignored. This is due largely to the fact that the pay-off does not arrive in the form of quick cash through the market-place. No consumer can use his "dollar vote" to express his appreciation of watershed health, survival of species, and environmental amenity of a dozen kinds. Nor does the market-place register long-term values. The individual customer is concerned, as an individual, with immediate considerations: he wants a piece of furniture, or a newspaper, now, even though he may, as a member of the community, be equally concerned with the survival of forests into the next century. The market-place reflects the first of his desires in exceptionally sensitive fashion, and it pretty well ignores the second.[1]

The upshot is that, even though forests' overall benefits to society often exceed the benefits they confer on private exploiters, the market-place does not offer an informed and balanced evaluation of goods and services at issue. So private commercial interests, urged on by the clamourous demand of the market-place, and with few restraints on their activities, over-exploit forests. Meanwhile, society-level interests are allowed to disappear down the drain. Thus the institutional milieu serves to promote rather than impede the destruction of forests.

For various reasons, then, the environmental benefits of forests tend to lie beyond the ken of economists, politicians and others who prefer to deal with more recognizable concerns such as timber revenues and elections. Being taken for granted, environmental services do not appear in the economic arithmetic when costs and benefits are calculated for different types of forestland use. In Peninsular Malaysia, for example, it is reckoned that the financial return from the fastest-growing dipterocarp forest is only one-third or less of what is available were the same area to be converted into rubber or oil-palm plantations — but the environmental benefits are not included in the calculus.

Still more do environmental benefits escape the notice of the many people whose preoccupation is tonight's supper. Huge throngs of impoverished peasantry tend to regard forests as "free goods": shifting cultivators and fuelwood gatherers have to pay nobody for their exploitation of forests. They, like others who make a living by chopping down trees, derive something of immediate value. By contrast, the people who suffer from deforestation, while many times more numerous, suffer only in slow and not readily noticeable fashion — so they are little likely to agitate on behalf of Forestry departments.

It is this divergence between forestry's impact on the individual and on the community that lies at the heart of the problem. Despite what certain conservationists sometimes suggest, foresters' fingers are not constantly a-twitch to seize hold of an axe. Rather, foresters are traditionally denied the political support they deserve within the councils of power. Regrettable and perverse as may be the reasons behind this sorry situation, they are powerful reasons. Those conservationists who would like to see a new situation would do well to recognize that the fault lies less with wayward foresters, more with the way the community chooses to run its affairs.

If this conflict of purpose characterizes the community's attitude towards tropical moist forests within developing nations, something the same applies at the level of the global community. However much outsiders might decry the prodigal-seeming approach of developing nations toward their forests, the developed world displays, in practice, a scarcely more rational spirit. As has been documented in Chapters 9-11, there are many instances of tropical moist forests being over-exploited in order to supply developed-world appetites for specialist timber and cheap beef. Moreover, this misuse of tropical moist forests is frequently conducted by developed-world organizations such as multinational corporations. Though increasingly aware that everyone will suffer, and suffer long and hard, if tropical moist forests disappear, the developed-world continues to connive at their destruction.

The upshot is that tropical moist forests, even though they constitute a potentially renewable resource, may be depleted to exhaustion within the foreseeable future, even ahead of major non-renewable resources such as oil reservoirs. It is worth speculating on which would have the greater consequences for the global community, were either of these resources to give out in another or three decades. While economic arguments about oil concern the rate at which the deposits should be depleted (and some economists contend that if the resources were exploited faster, they could contribute more effectively to long-term buildup of "social capital"), the argument concerning tropical moist forests is of an altogether different order: the resource is potentially renewable. Despite this, however, the community at large — both within the countries concerned and outside — generally finds it impossible to establish sustainable use as standard practice.

A new attitude

Fortunately, a new attitude is emerging. Forestry is no longer seen as something confined to chainsaws, lumber and pine seedlings. It is increasingly viewed as an activity that contributes to a broad range of needs and not just for people in the vicinity of forests but for communities much further afield.[2]

This new spirit is coming to life as a consequence of harsh experience with watershed degradation. Deforestation is the main factor that undermines the ecological health of watersheds. Forty percent of developing-world people live in valleylands, hence are highly dependent for their water supplies on the "sponge effect" of forests in surrounding catchment areas. When forests disappear, rainy-season supplies of water tend to be released in floods, followed by months of drought. In parts of the Philippines and Indonesia, the Green Revolution is losing momentum: rice paddies that have been producing three crops of bumper-harvest rice per year can no longer depend on regular supplies of river water for year-round irrigation. In one-third of the rice-growing areas of Southeast and Southern Asia, it is now common for floodwaters to flow deeper than 0.5 m at some stage of the growing season, an amount of water that overwhelms the new high-yielding varieties of rice with their short stems.

Forests affect agriculture in a further indirect manner. When fuelwood supplies give out, peasants often burn dung to cook their supper. According to estimates of the Food and Agriculture Organization, 1 ton of dung used as fuel instead of as fertilizer may mean a loss of 50 kg of food grain; and 400 million tons of dung used in this manner in parts of Asia and Africa each year could be costing 20 million tons of grain, enough to supply the protein needs of around 60,000 people.

In addition to adverse repercussions for agriculturalists, deforestation affects water engineers. Reservoirs and hydropower installations lose efficiency through siltation from erosion. One of the Philippines' major rivers carries an annual load of eroded soil totalling 44.6 tons per hectare of watershed, to be compared with only half a ton for the Mississippi.[3] The Philippines' Ambubkao Dam is expected to have a life span only half as long as planned. During the past 25 years, Haiti's forests have declined from 80 percent of the country to 9 percent; in 1977 the country received only two-thirds of average rainfall, since when there has been a severe drought; the country's single hydroelectric dam, supplying 99 percent of energy needs, now receives so little water that cities are routinely blacked out for half of every day. All Colombia's major cities suffer electricity and water rationing due to massive destruction of forests, while two-fifths of the country's farmers are enduring an unprecedently protracted drought. Panama City fears for the health of its citizenry, due to lack of adequate supplies of good-quality household water.

A miscellany of other problems arise through deforestation. The Panama Canal is becoming so silted up that it will soon be unable to handle outside cargo ships. Typhoon damage in Philippines amounts to $20 million a year, through floods and landslips whose impact is made much worse through deforestation — hence President Marcos' declaration that the decline of the country's forests amounts to a "national emergency". In Thailand, waterways that once provided energy-efficient transportation have become so choked with silt debris as to become unnavigable. Now that additional deforestation-caused troubles, notably disaster floods, are spreading to broad sectors of Thailand, the government has decided that it will use extraordinary powers of summary judgement, even execution, to punish un-authorized cutting in natural forests. Following deforestation along the lower reaches of the Himalayas, a number of river courses along the Nepal-India border are dry for the greater part of the year, but become 1½ km wide during the rainy season; the 1978 monsoon caused the River Ganges to grow 40 times wider, causing damage worth $2 billion.

There is a still wider dimension to the deforestation/water supplies problem. At the beginning of this century, agriculture and industry world-wide used about 350 km³ of freshwater per year. By 1975 the amount had risen to 2730, and by the year 2015 it is projected to reach 7450. Together with other uses such as domestic household needs, the world in the year 2015 could be consuming 8500 km³ of freshwater.[4] This would amount to almost one-fifth of all rainfall running off land into rivers and lakes. Due to seasonal changes in river levels and to limited reservoir storage, only about one-half of all rainfall becomes available for human use. As developing countries modernize and urbanize, their per capita consumption of water increases rapidly, which means that many millions of people are going to become increasingly dependent on developing-world forests. Unless the forests in question are exceptionally well conserved, instead of increasingly chopped down, water supplies could fall far short of demand in many regions by the end of this century at the latest.

The consequences could be severe. Four-fifths of all illnesses in developing countries are caused by poor-quality water, which triggers typhoid and cholera, and encourages insects that carry malaria, yellow fever and filariasis. From 1981 the United Nations is to launch an International Drinking Water Supply and Sanitation Decade, with the aim of bringing adequate facilities to the entire developing world by 1990 at an annual cost of $8.9 billion. The funds are intended primarily for reservoirs, piping and similar installations that deliver water to communities and households. Additional attention might be given to the catchment areas that are to ensure sufficient water supplies in the first place.

It is plain, then, that forestry is not just something of concern to foresters. Campaigns to protect forests, and to reforest cleared forest lands, are being promoted in Malaysia, Philippines, Thailand, Peru and Venezuela, among other countries. The proponents are not only foresters, but agriculturalists, livestock experts, engineers, public health officials and technocrats from economic sectors right across the board. In fact, forestry is now starting to be perceived as a key factor in the cardinal development strategy to "meet basic human needs". In the countries in question, forestry is no longer viewed as a development activity that operates in conflict with, say, agriculture, on the grounds that one dollar allocated to forestry means one dollar less for a "real priority" such as food production. Throughout the biome as a whole, however, there is still a long way to go. The Indonesia government derives from its timber trade over $320 million per year in royalties, levies and taxes, yet devotes only $92 million to forestry funding. Indonesia also spends around $1 billion a year on food imports, an outlay that could be reduced through increased investment on improved forestry for watersheds and thereby for irrigation systems.

Prospects for the future

This chapter has indicated some reasons for over-exploitation of tropical moist forests. Some of these reasons have much in common with the causes of deforestation in Europe and eastern North America when those regions were going through early development and their forests were looked upon as barriers to human expansion. Within this perspective, it is important for outside conservationists to recognize that developing-country leaders are not always irresponsible or worse when they allow their forests to be over-exploited. Those same conservationists would help their cause if they were to understand more of the overall problem as seen by developing-country leaders.

A Malaysian politician recently described how he was taken to task by an American conservationist over the logging threat to his country's Endau Rompin Park. Each hectare of the Park's forest contains around 60 m³ of commercial timber, worth an average of $60 per m³, which means that each square kilometer contains timber worth

$360,000. Since one-quarter of the Parks's 5000 km² are threatened by logging, this means that the Park's survival in undisturbed form will deny the Malaysian economy $450 million in timber revenues. (True, there would be economic benefits to the country through tourism in the park, through healthy watersheds in the park's hinterland, and so forth, but it would not be easy to prove that these other benefits are worth at least $450 million.) The sum in question is roughly the same as the amount that it costs American taxpayers to preserve one of the United States' most scenic forests, through extending the Redwood National Park from 80 to 310 km², i.e. at a rate of $2 million per square kilometer (the funds being paid to local California loggers as compensation). The United States is rich enough to afford such outlays on behalf of one of its parks, whereas Malaysia's emergent economy will find it hard to stand the strain. Moreover, a redwood forest, though an exceptional spectacle, is, ecologically speaking, three-quarters on the way to a desert as compared with a patch of Malaysian rainforest, one of the richest ecosystems on earth. Funds for conservation can achieve many times more in developing countries of the tropics than in affluent lands of the temperate zones. All the more, then, can developing-country leaders do without some of the finger-wagging they encounter from foreign conservationists.

19 What Developed Countries can do for the Global Heritage

Developed countries can likewise do much to safeguard the global heritage in species.

First of all, they can do much more for species within their own borders. They can establish better networks of protected areas. They can reduce the spreading degradation of their environments on every side. They can pursue a host of similar measures. The shopping list of initiatives is well known, and there is no need to go into them all here.

For some countries, the shopping list is shorter than for others. The United States has established an admirable record in recent years. It has greatly increased its parks and reserves, and it is currently planning to set aside a huge chunk of Alaska, an area of around 660,000 km^2, or as much as all of Britain and France. It has reduced pesticidal poisoning of carnivorous birds such as the brown pelican and the peregrine falcon. Through its federal Endangered Species Office alone, it spends $30 million a year on the wolf, the whooping crane and other species under threat. These are only a few of the more notable measures.

What can developed countries do for wildlife elsewhere on earth? What of that sector of the global heritage in species, the millions of mammals, birds, plants and so forth that exist in developing countries? Insofar as all species form part of the common patrimony of humankind, the gorilla, the cheetah and the vicuna belong not only to the countries where they have their habitats, but in some senses they "belong" to Americans and British and Japanese. How can developed-world citizens express their interest in the majority of earth's species that exist in "have-not" countries? To the extent that they feel a sense of responsibility for species in other lands, how can they translate this feeling into action?

As we have seen in the previous chapter, several developing countries are making exceptional efforts to look after their declining wildlife. Taken overall, however, they are making no more than a moderate dent in the problem. Even were all of them to become convinced of the need to preserve species, they generally lack the muscle to do a minimal job: they simply do not have the money and the expertise to get to grips with the challenge. Above all, many of them are running out of space for their human populations, so they are understandably reluctant to set aside extensive territories as parks, and thereby declare these areas as "off limits" to development.

Benefits and costs of safeguarding species

Looking at the challenge on a global scale raises a fundamental question of benefits and costs. Who gains from conservation of earth's species and who pays for it?

In principle, everyone gains from survival of species. If Indonesia, Zaire and Brazil take steps to protect their threatened wildlife, the entire global community stands to benefit from the pragmatic purposes (modern agriculture, medicine and so forth) served by the genetic resources at stake. This argues that the entire global community should be prepared to share in the benefits. Equally to the point, it is developed nations, with their technological expertise, that currently make most use of genetic resources around the world and especially from the tropics, as underpinning for their agriculture, as sources of new drugs and as raw materials for industry. Were Brazil to maintain the forest habitat of its golden lion marmoset, and were this monkey to offer assistance to the anti-cancer campaign after the manner of the cotton-topped marmoset, the communities who would benefit most in the foreseeable future are those of developed countries where cancer is a scourge. People in Brazil, in common with the rest of the developing world, generally do not live long enough to contract cancer. To this extent, the benefits of saving the marmoset would be unequally distributed — and Brazil's efforts to safeguard part of the natural heritage of all nations amount, like the conservation activities of other developing nations, to a "resource handout" from developing nations to developed nations.

Equally to the point, it is developed nations, through their expanding appetites for hardwood timber, beef and other forestland products, and through the technological muscle of their giant corporations, that are unwittingly contributing to the destruction of tropical moist forests. Their hand is also on the chainsaw.[1]

This all argues, then, that the developed nations might well assume a disproportionate share of the costs of conserving the global heritage species. In practice this means that developed nations should subsidize conservation efforts in developing nations of the tropics in order to protect the majority of earth's species.

Compensatory payments for developing-world conservation

Looking at the problem this way, then, developed nations might wish to consider compensatory payments to developing nations in order to offset some of the opportunity costs involved in conservation programs, notably in establishing parks and reserves. When Indonesia or Zaire or Brazil sets aside a sizeable patch of territory in order to preserve virgin ecosystems with their concentrations of species, the country denies itself the chance to exploit these wild lands for timber or beef or whatever. The opportunity costs are already large and are growing larger with every tick of the clock. It would be no more than fair for developed nations to pick up the tab for some of the costs entailed in saving the global heritage.

However "far out" this idea may sound, it makes sense from many economic and political standpoints. In fact, and as many economists, including three Nobel Prize Winners, have pointed out, compensation payments are becoming an increasingly common way for society to regulate its affairs efficiently and equitably. The theory of "grants economics", or the economics of one-way transfer of funds (as opposed to the more usual market-place exchange of funds), postulates that compensation and other grants are not to be regarded as something exotic outside the economic system proper. Rather, they constitute an essential contribution to the functioning of an increasingly integrated society.[2]

Some observers might object that the idea makes only theoretical sense, on the grounds that, practically speaking, the world just does not work that way. To this, the conservationist can reply that the world is going to work a different way from the past anyway, whether through choice or through force of circumstances. As long as nations continue on their present independent tracks, with disregard for the implications of interdependence, the world will steadily work less well. If nations recognize that it is in their own individual self-interest to pool part of their independence in the greater good of the larger community, the world will go round more smoothly. Among all the uncertainties of the shifting international order, one thing is certain: change there will be, in whatever way it comes.

How would a compensation program work out in practice? Let us look at a single aspect of the overall problem, crop genetic resources, and with respect to a single developed country, the United States. As indicated in Chapter 5, the extraordinary productivity of the United States' farm crops is dependent on constant infusion of fresh germ plasm from wild stocks and from primitive cultivars, almost all from outside the country. In fact, America's agriculture may be as dependent on foreign sources of germ plasm as is the country's overall economy on foreign sources of oil. What if U.S. wheat or maize fell victim to disease as virulent as that which has destroyed the Dutch elm and the chestnut? The economic benefits of genetic improvement for U.S. farm crops is roughly estimated by the U.S. Department of Agriculture at over $500 million per year. On the other side of the balance are the costs of maintaining wild and primitive forms of crop plant strains, most of them in developing countries. Were a systematic and comprehensive program to be launched with the aim of preserving these sources of germ plasm, the costs would not be very large by comparison with the benefits — but they would almost entirely fall on the relatively localized communities. They would prove especially burdensome to the individual peasants who would be denied opportunity to break new land in wilderness area, or would be required to persist with primitive cultivars instead of Green Revolution monocultures.

True, an international effort has been organized to safeguard crop genetic resources. The International Board for Plant Genetic Resources coordinates initiatives on the part of individual countries. Despite the size of the task, however, the Board's annual budget is only around $1½ million, a sum grotesquely disproportionate to the economic benefits derived from reservoirs of crop germ plasm, and hopelessly inadequate to cater for a situation that agricultural experts declare is grim and growing rapidly worse. This sorry state of affairs postulates conservation measures of far broader scope.

Due to the fact that it is generally regarded as a "free good", germ plasm is traded internationally at nominal charge. The cost does not fractionally reflect the benefits derived by large numbers of better-fed people. So how about a levy raised on commercial seed companies that sell genetically improved seeds? A U.S. company that produces, for example, 2 million bushels of hybrid corn seed at $20 per bushel could contribute perhaps 1 percent of its $40 million revenues, or $400,000, toward preservation of corn strains in foreign territories. (Were all commercial seed companies to contribute a levy of this order, the revenues would total a sum several times larger than the annual budget of the International Board for Plant Genetic Resources.) The seed companies would doubtless pass on the costs to their consumers, which, while inflationary, would be no more than fair. Were disease to repeat the 1971 débâcle of a 20 percent loss in the American corn crop, a deficit that was valued at $2 billion, the increased charges for dearer corn products would similarly be passed on to customers.

The revenues raised through this levy could be used to subsidize farmers in, say, Mexico, who would thereby be enabled to continue to farm with primitive strains of corn, or who would be required to abstain from digging up patches of land with wild forms of corn. While a Green Revolution farmer in Mexico can grow large amounts of high-yielding corn, another farmer, using a less productive but genetically unique type of native corn, might produce only one-fifth as much. Thus the latter farmer, supposing he can be persuaded to continue with the old race, would need to be subsidized to an extent of

5 times the national corn price for his crop.

Measures that are parallel in spirit and principle to this proposed are not uncommon within certain countries. In the United States public funds are used to compensate landholders who are denied exploitation opportunity because of the need to safeguard the public interest. One example is the Soil Conservation Program. Another is the "easement" subsidy undertaken by the U.S. Fish and Wildlife Service to protect one of the most endangered mammals in the world, the black-footed ferret (see Chapter 6).

So a compensation program to underpin "genetic resource banks" at international level would not be different in principle from well-established procedures within individual countries. The problem would lie with practical difficulties of implementing the program across national frontiers. Even so, the situation is not without precedents. Occasions have arisen when a high-income country finds it is in its interest to extend a subsidy to a low-income country with the aim of modifying a production process with adverse environmental impact. The United States has supplied appreciable financial assistance to Mexico to enable it to eradicate hoof-and-mouth disease in cattle, with a view to safeguarding the U.S. livestock industry. This measure helps both countries. The United States has also undertaken a measure that will benefit Mexico alone, on the grounds that it is a "fair and reasonable thing to do". Irrigation practices in southwestern U.S.A. have greatly boosted crop production, but only at the cost of increased concentrations of salts and other chemicals flowing down the Colorado River into Mexico. To counter this pollution, the United States is building a $115-million desalinization plant, merely to improve the quality of water flowing into Mexico.

The rationale for compensation measures in support of conservation has been given an airing on repeated occasions, notably through the "additionality principle" enunciated at the 1972 Stockholm Conference on the Human Environment.[3] This principle proposes that compensation payments on appreciable scale be made by the community of nations (meaning principally those that can afford it) to the developing world, in order to offset adverse repercussions on emergent economies from measures for environmental conservation. Developing countries consider that funds for environmental action at international level should be independent of those provided for economic development, that is, they should be *additional* to funds already supplied. Still more important, the assistance should not be made available as another form of foreign aid dispensed out of a spirit of charity. Rather it should reflect a recognition of joint responsibility for deteriorating assets of the common heritage.

Subsidy payments for tropical-forest countries

International subsidy would be particularly pertinent to offset the opportunity costs of tropical countries that set aside large forest territories as parks and reserves. In practice, however, implementative mechanisms would not be easy to devise. For one thing, there would be many more nations involved than just two, as has been the case with the United States' initiatives, cited above, with respect to Mexico. In fact, there could be as many as twenty nations on either side.

How far should subsidies go? In order to qualify for some degree of subsidy, a tropical-forest country would presumably have to demonstrate specific loss. Could a country then receive subsidy for all economic loss entailed in setting aside forest areas, or should it accept some measure of responsibility for such loss on the grounds that it should be ready to bear certain "unprofitable consequences" of establishing protected areas in order to safeguard its own natural heritage as well as that of the global community? In addition, there could be a problem with "extortionist threats to exploit" on the part of tropical-forest countries that seek to prise compensation funds from rich countries — a maneuver that would obviously offend the basic spirit of the proposal. To meet this problem, subsidy payments should perhaps be made available only to tropical-forest countries that put up significant funds of their own for the purpose.

Many other operational difficulties would doubtless arise. But these should not prove insurmountable as long as the overall objective of the initiative is kept firmly in view. If the rich nations make substantial subsidies available to tropical-forest countries, there could be many more forests left at the end of the century than now seems likely — with benefit for the entire community of nations.

Conservation measures and "willingness to pay"

Were the subsidy proposal for tropical-forest countries to be implemented, it would need to be subject to periodic appraisal. If citizens in donor countries began to object to the financial strain, the scheme would have to be abandoned. Citizens of donor countries would thereby act in explicit recognition of what prospects face tropical forests. The entire exercise would enable them to gain a clearer grasp of their responsibility in the overall situation. This would be in marked distinction from the present position, where people in advanced nations have little chance to appraise their responsibility in clear-cut terms. Conversely, if, after a few years, public opinion seemed to favor an extension of the initiative, support could be made available for other biomes beside tropical forests, notably grasslands and other major ecological zones that support appreciable portions of the earth's stock of species.

In essence, the process would serve as a measure of the public's willingness to pay for the amount of conservation that it sometimes suggests it would like to see. Eventually it could develop into a framework which reflects costs and benefits as perceived by participant parties. The basic question is how many wildland areas, containing how many concentrations of species, should be protected? and for what period of time, and at how much cost to whose pocket? A pay-for-what-you-want approach would permit a graduated response to these questions. The community at large could express its financial support for those parts of the global heritage which it believes merit the gesture in comparison with other goods and services. This would relieve the "either/or" type of situation where the conflicting issues are seen only in terms of absolute values.

To summarize the overall challenge, the subsidy proposal is advanced as an initial exploration of opportunities for broad-scale measures to meet the problem of disappearing species. Whatever the problems both in principle and in practice, the proposal should be considered in the light of options available. Difficult as community action on this scale would be, the alternative is the present prospect, where support for threatened species amounts to a few tentative pokes at the problem. This limited response represents an implicit decision by society to allow large numbers of species to disappear, even though the costs of protecting them need often not be exceptional in comparison with benefits to be derived.

Sources of funding

Funding for species would probably have to be considered as part of a comprehensive effort to protect the global environment. Whatever the merits of a strategy geared to serving species alone, it could hardly be practical to pursue it in isolation from a broad-front campaign that covers conservation needs for the entire human environment, including safeguard measures to halt the spread of deserts and so forth. It is not realistic at this stage to try to put a figure on the costs of a total campaign. However, it is worthwhile to consider potential sources of funding and to compare them with figures for certain sectors of a global conservation plan.

As already suggested, there are strong arguments to support the idea that funding should come primarily from affluent nations. While the entire global community would hopefully contribute in support of its global heritage, it is reasonable that the main burden of the funding should be borne by those who stand to derive most immediate benefit through utilitarian application of genetic resources, and who disproportionately contribute to depletion of the earth's natural resources through their over-consumerist lifestyles. And when all else is said, the affluent nations are the only ones with sufficient wealth to pick up the price tab.

Two approaches for funding are considered here, the first dealing with taxes on exploitation of resources of the "global commons" and the second dealing with conventional taxation systems within individual nations.

(a)   Global taxes

In support of common heritage funding, there is scope to raise taxes and other levies on economic exploitation of certain forms of common property. For example, the oceans, being part of the community's natural heritage themselves, could serve as a substantial source of revenue. A rough estimate suggests that by 1985 a tax on mining of deep-ocean manganese modules could yield at least $230-800 million.[4] The main exploiters of the oceans, and thus the main candidates for these global taxes, are developed nations. Revenues of this order could cover an anti-desertification campaign, estimated by the Desertification Conference at $400 million a year. Such a campaign would relieve destructive pressures on several ecological zones that border existing deserts, notably the Mediterranean-type areas with their exceptional concentrations of endemic species, and it would help the prospects of 600 million people living in these vulnerable territories.

Further taxes could be raised on production and trade of energy materials. While these materials are handled through sectorial interests (individual nations, corporations, etc.), they can be regarded as constituting part of the planetary resource base on which the welfare of all peoples ultimately depends. By way of example, an *ad valorem* tax of a mere 0.1 percent on internationally traded oil would yield $100 million per year.[5] UNESCO believes that, as a minimum requirement, each of the planet's biotic provinces, almost 200 of them, should feature at least one Biosphere Reserve. To date, less than one-quarter of these provinces features such a reserve. To establish a typical reserve costs around $100,000, and to maintain it another $50,000 per year. So a program to set up another 150 reserves, and to run them until the end of the century, would cost $165 million on oil-tax revenues for only 20 months.

There could even be a case for taxes on international trade in all resources and products. This would impinge most directly on those sectors of the international community that benefit most from exploitation of the earth's stock of resources, viz. the developed nations. These nations, with one-fifth of the world's population, account for four-fifths of all materials traded through the international economy. A 0.1 percent *ad valorem* tax would yield $1 billion per year.

This review of options for global taxes accords with the spirit of a number of proposals advanced for Reshaping the International Order. One of the contributors to the RIO strategy, Professor Jan Tinbergen, a Nobel Prize Winner in economics, not only considers the possibility of taxes along the lines reviewed above,[6] but he goes further, by advocating a number of international institutions to articulate and formalize the established phenomenon of interdependency relationships among the global community; for example, a World Treasury to fund collective activities, together with a World Authority to regulate the use of "international resources".

(b) National taxes for international purposes

A second option for raising funds lies with taxes levied by national government on their citizens. In view of the significant scale of funding required to safeguard species among other environmental activities, these taxes could prove to be no trifling item. Would they prove to be a real burden on taxpayers? When a taxpayer asks, in effect, "Can I afford it?", he should also ask "Afford it in relation to what?" Since we are talking primarily about the rich-world taxpayer, we might well ask what this taxpayer currently spends his "discretionary income" on, viz. his income after meeting essentials.

In the case of the richest nation on earth, many Americans express their interest in animals through owning dogs, around 40 million of them. A good number of these dogs run stray. The expense of capturing and killing these dogs, of medical treatment for 1-1½ million dog bites, of maintaining animal shelters, and of related services, costs almost $500 million per year.[7] Steps to eliminate these negligence-caused expenses, through, for example, punitive taxes and fines to deter defaulters, would not amount to a "sacrifice" in quality of living for all Americans, merely a cut-back in wasteful spending on the part of a minority of them. Were the American public to support stringent deterrent measures, this would result in a significant saving of wasted wealth, plus revenues from taxes and fines. This is not to say, of course, that the funds in question, arising through more efficient ownership of a single animal species in a single country, could then be directed toward saving many thousands of animal species under threat in many other parts of the world. The point is raised to indicate the scale of comparative expenditures; the sum in question, $500 million per year, is almost 14 times greater than the amount raised in all countries by the World Wildlife Fund from its beginnings in 1961 to the end of 1978.

The same point can be made with reference to other aspects of American lifestyles. According to a minimum estimate, at least one-sixth of the 25 million medical operations performed in the United States each year are unnecessary, at a cost of over $5 billion. Hospital beds that are occupied too long, or that should not be occupied at all, account for a waste of another $8 billion. Between 1962 and 1976 the number of alcoholics, i.e. those who consumed liquor to excess, almost doubled; the economic costs associated with misuse of alcohol, through employment and productivity losses, accidents, medical care and other problems, are now estimated, by the U.S. Department of Health, Education and Welfare, in a report of late 1978, at $43 billion per year. One-fifth of all food products for human consumption in the United States each year is wasted, worth $50 billion, while another one-fifth of all food is accounted for through over-eating on the part of the 28 million citizens who are severely overweight, giving rise to a $10 billion slimming industry.

These total funds, well over of $100 billion per year, would transform the challenge of safeguard species, tropical forests and many other resources that constitute the global natural heritage. Thus there is plenty of "slack" that could be taken up without any deprivation of American levels of living. On the contrary, Americans would live better. Moreover, according to a 1977 Harris Poll, four out of five Americans prefer to find ways to live better with basic essentials than to become still more consumerist, and almost as many wish to derive more pleasure from non-material experiences than from satisfying needs for more goods and services.

True, the American economy already spends a lot on environmental conservation, approxiamtely $50 billion per year. But almost the entire effort is devoted to combating pollution and to devising resource-saving technologies within the United States. A proportionately trifling sum is contributed to international conservation, e.g. a few million dollars to the United Nations agencies that cover environmental affairs (to which , true, the United States is generally the largest contributor). The interests of Americans at the start of the twenety-first century might be better safeguarded if they allocated a good deal more funds to sustaining the earth's life-support systems, of which their own habitat forms an integral part.

Of course, the United States is far from being the only nation to engage in over-consumerist lifestyles. Similar figures for wasteful spending could be cited for all affluent nations. In fact, when all forms of unproductive consumerism are considered, the total amount of waste on the part of all advanced nations each year certainly amounts to many hundreds of billions of dollars. So, were the affluent sector of the global community to be asked to pick up the main part of the tab to safeguard humanity's natural heritage, there need be little question of "sacrifices". Rather it would be a case of cutting back on some of the more excessive forms of excess.

Furthermore, affluent nations now include not only advanced nations, but include certain of the oil-producing countries, whose average GNP per citizen now surpasses that of the super-rich Western world. Saudi Arabia has offered to levy 1 cent on each barrel of oil it produces to create a fund of $200-300 million per year for the United Nations Environment Program. A similar degree of "belt tightening" on the part of all super-affluent nations could go a long way to help with many environmental problems, including the problem of disappearing species.

If we now move on to look at a still larger form of "irrational" spending, world armament expenditures, the contrast becomes still more striking. The global bill runs close to $400 billion per year, a total greater than the entire income of the poorest half of humanity.[8] Might not all nations feel more secure about their long-term survival prospects if military expenditures were to be cut by one-quarter, and the released funds spent on protecting humanity's life-support systems? True, environmental degradation is not readily perceived as a threat to national security, certainly not as compared with a threat of military attack. But the time has arrived when political leaders might well consider what disruptions could occur within the community of nations as growing numbers of people with growing aspirations find that the earth's stock of natural resources is being eroded to an extent that it is increasingly incapable of supporting them.[9] Leaders of nations threatened with military invasion rant about not ceding one square meter of soil, while allowing hundreds of square kilometers of soil to be washed away through deforestation. They might achieve a better understanding of the ultimate value of their forests — the least understood of all vegetation formations — if 1 percent, or $200 million, of funding for military research and development each year (absorbing two-fifths of all public and private research and development expenditures and occupying almost half of the world's scientific and technological manpower) were to be spent on those areas of the earth that are less understood by science than certain portions of the moon's surface.

The United States now devotes almost $700 per citizen each year to military expenditure. If the country were to allocate $100 per citizen, or a total sum of around $12 billion, to safeguarding the global heritage, which outlay would offer the greatest ultimate security? Americans are clearly ready to contribute handsomely to what they recognize as worthy causes, since they contribute roughly the same sum to charity each year. As with so many aspects of environmental conservation, the issue hangs on perception of priorities. Conservation funding of this order would greatly increase the United States' prospects into the next century of continued productivity for its food crops, of drugs to combat medical scourges, of raw materials for untold new needs of industry and advancing technology. For an American couple to bring up a child until the end of college now costs around $80,000 — a large financial investment in the future, as well as a tremendous gesture of faith. A small fraction of that amount spent on global conservation would help to ensure for each child a worthwhile patch of the earth-home to spend the rest of his or her life in.

In short, the question is not whether we can afford to support conservation of the natural heritage. Rather the question is, can we afford not to support it. Perhaps we should try not only to be altruistic but realistic, since the two now often mean the same.

20 Conservation of Species and the New World Order

As this final part of the book makes clear, the problem of disappearing species calls for collective measures on the part of both the developing and the developed worlds. The two sectors of the global community need to attempt a joint commitment on a scale that reflects the increasingly interdependent character and needs of the global community. Whether the global community perceives itself as a community or not, it functions as such in many of its ecological relationships and economic interactions. The community will sooner or later be obliged to respond to the problem of disappearing species: either sooner, through protective measures of sufficient scope, or later, when it finds that the disappearance of large numbers of species represents a loss through which the community is indivisibly impoverished for ever.

This approach to the problem accords with a newly emergent spirit that characterizes certain relationships of world society as it heads into the final stage of the twentieth century. In fact, it is not going too far to say that the challenge of conservation of species is a microcosm of broader problems that arise from integrated living in the global village. It is closely tied in with other problems of deteriorating resources — forests, water, land, ecological systems in general. In turn, these problems reflect pressures from expanding population numbers and growing scarcity of food, energy and raw materials. In turn again, these shortages are inter-linked with still other problems of one-earth living, such as sovereignty, international trade and quantity of consumption *vis-à-vis* quality of living. Hardly any other problem, however, receives as little attention as that of disappearing species.

A comprehensive strategy to conserve species will require a marked degree of cooperation between the developing and developed worlds. Most species exist in the developing world and the developed world can exercise only indirect influence over their survival prospects; so for the developed world the benefits of a cooperative endeavour will be all the greater. At the same time, the readiness of developing nations to participate in a joint attack on the problem may depend in part on the response they receive from developed nations with respect to their principal concern, economic advancement. In other words, developing nations may be little inclined to safeguard their disproportionate share of the world's wealth in species, as long as they feel they get less than a fair deal from developed nations concerning international markets, trade liberalization, commodity prices, monetary reform, investments, technology transfer and the like.

New International Economic Order

So it helps to look at the problem of disappearing species within the context of the North-South dialogue between the developed and the developing worlds. In particular, a conservation strategy for species needs to be considered as part of a new broad-front effort to achieve a realistic share-out of all the planet's resources. This effort is known as the New International Economic Order.

There is a parallel reason why the North-South dialogue is the only proper framework for tackling the problem of disappearing species. Twenty years ago there were still plenty of undisturbed environments on earth. Today, it is all too obvious what is happening to them. In another 20 years they could well be changed beyond recognition, unless significant sectors can be protected. In turn, conservation campaigns will be set at naught unless pressures to convert every last virgin environment into human living space can be relieved through alternative opportunities for economic advancement. The largest throngs of people spreading into undisturbed territories are the poorest of the poor, those who feel driven to encroach ever further into wildlands in order to find a patch of ground where they can sink a digging hoe. At present they total 800 million, or almost 1 in 5 of all people of earth. According to the World Bank, their number could decline slightly, to 600 million, by the end of the century if the New International Economic Order can achieve its aims. If things do not turn out well, their number could rise to as many as 1700 million. Considering the amount of disruption of species' habitats caused by the present millions, it is difficult to visualize how any natural environments could emerge unscathed from the impact of over twice as many impoverished people.

The best way to relieve the spreading pressure from all these people is to give them opportunity to locate in concentrated human settlements; in other words, to become urbanized as fast as possible. But urbanization is not likely to work out, except at unimaginable cost in squalid living conditions, unless the towns and cities of developing countries can develop as modernized settlements — and this is unlikely to happen except as part of a modernization process for developing-country economies. In turn, this means opportunity for manufacturing industries, which, in turn again, means access to the big-money export markets; namely, the fat-cat nations of the world. Yet it is precisely at this point in the chain of circumstances that the biggest snags arise, since developing-nations' goods encounter tariffs, quotas and a range of other trade restrictions on the part of developed nations.

Hardly any other factor would help developing-world species more, and probably nothing less will adequately work, than speedy economic modernization of the Third World within a framework of "eco-development". Yet, given the protectionist trade policies of developed nations, hardly any other prospect seems less likely. Not surprisingly, developing-world leaders respond to outside suggestions that they do a better job of safeguarding their wildlife by asking how one can wave the flag for the International Union for Conservation of Nature and Natural Resources, without expressing equal support for the New International Economic Order.

Trade

The New International Economic Order seeks to make a systematic and comprehensive attack on the major characteristics of developing nations — malnutrition, illiteracy, disease, high infant mortality, low life expectancy, joblessness, next to no housing and, much the worst of all, little prospect of a change for the better. In order to tackle this plethora of troubles, the developing world has produced a shopping list of remedies — namely, trade liberalization, stabilized prices for commodities, indexation, debt relief and a greater say in how the global community runs its affairs.

Let us take a look at the central factor of trade. The value of exports from the developed world to the developing world is almost 5 times as great as the other way round. This is not because the developing world cannot produce goods of sufficient quantity and quality. Brazil sells clocks to Switzerland, furniture to Scandinavia, refrigerators to the United States, fashions to Italy and photo-cells to the Netherlands. A similar story can be told of many other developing nations, whose enterprise and capability has allowed them to expand economically at growth rates twice as high as North America and Western Europe achieved during their developing phases. Nor is this achievement restricted to a successful few: the achievement of Taiwan and Hongkong in the 1950s and 1960s are being surpassed in the 1970s by Thailand, Malaysia, Ivory Coast and a host of other countries. Were these countries to maintain their 1970s growth rate of around 6 percent throughout the 1980s they could reach "economic takeoff", thus enabling them to modernize and allow their largely rural populations to earn a living through activities other than extensive agriculture.

Yet the developing countries' record would be a great deal better if the outcome depended on their own efforts alone. The main problem is that they cannot export sufficient of their high-calibre manufactures to the main markets of the global economy, the developed nations.[1] In order to protect their own allegedly fragile industries, developed nations impose trade restrictions of every kind: tariffs, import dues, variable levies, quotas, licensing and outright embargoes. Tariffs across the board work out at an average of almost 12 percent — by contrast with manufactures trade among developed nations, which attracts an average duty of only half as much.

Were the United States to double its imports from developing countries, this would cause, according to the International Labour Organization and the United Nations Conference on Trade and Development, a loss of almost 250,000 jobs. Large as it sounds, this employment upset would not be a fraction as large as is normally caused by job turnover and rising labor productivity. According to the World Bank,[2] West Germany found that, in its manufacturing sector, growth of productivity during the period 1962-75 displaced 48 workers for every one displaced by cheap imports from developing countries; and even in the clothing and textile industries, where imports from developing countries grew rapidly, the ratio was still 3:1. In addition, a shift of production that displaces one worker in a developed nation will directly create jobs for more than two workers in one of the more successful developing countries and up to five workers in one of the poorer countries. If, in order to compensate its own labor force, the U.S. government were to sponsor a job-retraining program, this need cost no more than one-sixth of what the government now spends on unemployment benefits each year, In any case, U.S. employment preserved by trade protectionism is far more than offset by loss of employment in U.S. industries that export to developing countries, and that could export much more if developing-country economies were to grow faster.

So there is no basic conflict between the economic interests of developing countries and those of developed countries. In fact, a radical reappraisal of the international system would respond not only to the miserable fact that annual increases in earnings for the "have-nots" over the past 20 years have averaged only $2 per year, but it would reflect the enlightened self-interest of developed nations, which deceive themselves if they think they can do without the poor nations. As a measure of the extent to which the economic fortunes of the two blocs are interlinked, the poor countries take more than one-quarter of rich countries' exports, worth around $150 billion per year; in return, they are permitted to sell only $30 billion worth of goods. During the recent recession, the developing countries offered the most buoyant markets; between 1970 and 1977, the United States increased its sales to developing countries by 22 percent a year, compared with only 15 percent for sales to developed countries. According to the Overseas Development Council in Washington D.C., an increase of 3 percent in economic growth for developing countries could lead to an extra 1 percent of growth in developed nations, worth $45 billion in their GNP per year.

Furthermore, were rich-world governments to support, rather than impede, the export trade of the Third World, they would give a boost to the household budgets of their own citizens. Cheap imports from developing countries, such as footwear, textiles, clothes and electronic sub-assemblies, would allow the average American shopper to save at least $250 each year. (In fact, there is scarcely a more inflationary practice than trade protectionism.) Moreover, an end to trade restrictions would enable developing nations to earn an extra $24 billion per year — roughly the amount they now receive in foreign aid from developed nations.

So trade liberalization could eliminate the need for foreign aid altogether. Without an open economy for the community of nations, however, there would continue to be a role for aid — again, in the interests of both parties. In order to meet "basic human needs" for the one-fifth of mankind that subsist in absolute poverty, the average annual cost between 1980 and 2000 is projected by the World Bank at an additional $15 billion per year on top of present aid. Not, in point of fact, any great burden for affluent nations: it would amount to between one-tenth and one-twentieth of the amount by which the rich expect to grow richer each year in the foreseeable future.

Ironically, the time when the global economy is slowly climbing out of a protracted recession could be a first-rate time to make some fundamental shifts in the way the global community goes about its business. During "normal" times, public opinion tends to be resistant to new ways of doing things, political attitudes get set in concrete, and an innovative spirit is set aside on the grounds that there is no ostensible need for it. But, as the Chinese say, a time of crisis can be a time of opportunity. The late 1970s could offer a chance to rethink and remodel the taken-for-granted relationships between the haves and have-nots, between the different sectors of the global labor force, between human communities and their resource base.

In essence, then, we can look at the challenge of disappearing species in a new light. In order to conserve wildlife and tropical forests, job retraining in the developed world can achieve as much as can parks and reserves in tropical countries. A 0.1 percent increase in foreign aid can count for far more than a thousand animal-rescue projects. Transfer of appropriate technology can prove far more effective than anti-poaching equipment. An end to trade restrictions can do much more to safeguard many more threatened species than an end to international trade in spotted-cat furs and alligator hides.

The United States as a developing country

To enable us to get a realistic grasp of what the alternative means, let us visualize how the United States would fare were it to be a developing country in the last quarter of the twentieth century. Instead of 70 percent of the populace occupying only 2 percent of national territory, at least as many would be living off the land. Most farmers, with a cash income of $300 per year, would be unable to afford the perquisites of high-productivity agriculture, such as mechanization and sophisticated technology. So their farming practices would be pretty wasteful in their use of the main arable areas, causing huge numbers of subsistence cultivators to spread into drier grassland zones, where each farmer would require a still larger plot to sustain his family. His family, responding to the sudden and narrow-focus infusion of medical aid from foreign sources during recent decades, would number eight to ten persons, and his offsprings' hopes for a steadily improving lifestyle would generate still further pressures for more land on which to support themselves. Indeed, demographers would point out that in view of the fact that over 50 percent of the populace was aged 15 or less (by contrast with around 20 percent in advanced nations), the parents of the future had already been born; and so even if the average American family were to come down to two children forthwith, the present total of 225 million Americans would grow to almost twice as many by the end of the century, with no prospects of zero population growth until well beyond the 500 million mark in another two generations' time.

Not that Americans would listlessly accept their lot. On the contrary, showing exceptional enterprise and willingness to work, they could well achieve economic growth rates to put them on a virtual par with "economic miracle" countries such as Japan and West Germany. Regrettably, these efforts would achieve little so long as America's access to the world's main markets was severely restricted at best. Result: America's citizenry would mostly remain countryside dwellers, and the over-loading of natural environments on every side would increase year by year. Indeed, the broad-scale disruption of virgin ecosystems would be plain for anyone to see, as the western forests made way for agriculture and new settlements, or were exploited for fuel, with the exception of the redwoods which were exported to cater for specialist and insatiable appetites in affluent communities overseas. One by one, the country's notable parks would fall to the hordes of land-hungry peasants, first the better-watered areas such as the Everglades, then the drier wildlands. Eventually, only Death Valley would remain. The only time the advanced world would pay much attention would be when it would wag a finger over the demise of the black-footed ferret and the california condor.

Conclusion

To end on a brighter note, a whole-hearted decision to accept the challenge of disappearing species could have an important spin-off benefit. The effort could help to articulate the common interests of nations. After all, conservation of species can be presented as a less likely source of political friction than many other international problems. A strategy to conserve species might even encourage governments to adopt a more collective approach to other collective issues that confront their global community.

In sum, efforts to conserve species could, by promoting a consciousness of humankind's unity, prove a solid step toward a new world order.

References

Chapter 1   Introduction
1. Anon., 1974, Scientists talk of the need for conservation and an ethic of biotic diversity to slow species extinction, *Science* **184:** 646-647.

Chapter 2   How Many Species?
1. Isaacs, J.D. and Schwartzlose, R.A., 1975, Active animals of the deep-sea floor, *Scientific American* **233** (4): 84-91.
2. Anon., 1974, Scientists talk of the need for conservation and an ethic of biotic diversity to slow species extinction, *Science* **184:** 646-647; Dobzhansky, T., 1970, *Genetics Of The Evolutionary Process,* Columbia University Press, New York; Hocking, B., 1971, *Six-legged Science,* Schenkman Publishing Company Inc., Cambridge, Massachusetts, and 1972 *Biology — The Ultimate Science,* Schenkman Publishing Company Inc., Cambridge, Massachusetts; Mayr, E., 1976, *Evolution and The Diversity of Life,* Harvard University Press, Cambridge, Massachusetts; Raven, P.H., 1974, Trends, priorities and needs in systematic and evolutionary biology, *Systematic Zoology* **23:** 416-439; Raven, P.H., Berlin, B. and Breedlove, D.E., 1971, The origins of taxonomy, *Science* **174:** 1210-1213; and Wilson, E.O., 1975, *Sociobiology,* Harvard University Press, Cambridge, Massachusetts.
3. Janzen, D.H. and Pond, C.M., 1975, A comparison, by sweep sampling of the arthropod fauna of secondary vegetation in Michigan, England and Costa Rica, *Transactions of Royal Entomological Society of London* **127** (1): 33-50; Owen, D.F. and Owen, J., 1974, Species diversity in temperate and tropical ichneumonidae, *Nature* **249:** 583-584; and Rathcke, B.J. and Price, P.W., 1976, Anomalous diversity of tropical ichneumonid parasitoids: a predation hypothesis, *American Naturalist* **110:** 889-902.
4. Raven, P.H., 1976, Ethics and attitudes, in: J.B. Simmons, R.I. Bayer, P.E. Branham, G. Ll. Lucas and W.T.H. Parry (editors), *Conservation of Threatened Plants:* 155-179, Plenum, New York.
5. Borror, D.J. and DeLong, D.M., 1971, *An Introduction to the Study of Insects* (third edition), Holt, Rinehart & Winston, New York; Pyle, R.M., 1978, *IUCN World Conservation Strategy: Invertebrate Animals,* Lepidoptera Specialist Group, Survival Service Commission, International Union for Conservation of Nature and Natural Resources, Morges, Switzerland.
6. Sabrosky, C.W., 1953, How many insects are there?, *Systematic Zoology* **2:** 31-36.
7. Hocking, B., 1971, *Six-legged Science,* Schenkman Publishing Company Inc., Cambridge, Massachusetts; Sabrosky, C.W., 1953, How many insects are there?, *Systematic Zoology* **2:** 31-36.

8. Hocking, B., 1971, *Six-legged Science,* Schenkman Publishing Company, Cambridge, Massachusetts.
9. Elton, C.W., 1973, The structure of invertebrate populations inside tropical rainforest, *Journal of Animal Ecology* **42**: 55-104; Pyle, R.M., 1978, *IUCN World Conservation Strategy: Invertebrate Animals,* Lepidoptera Specialist Group, Survival Service Commission, International Union for Conservation of Nature and Natural Resources, Morges, Switzerland.
10. Murphy, D.H., 1973, Animals in the forest ecosystems, in: *Animal Life and Nature in Singapore,* Singapore University Press, Singapore.
11. Personal letter of 23rd June 1977.
12. Casey, T.L.C. and Jacobi, J.D., 1974, A new genus and species of bird from the Island of Maui, Hawaii, *Occasional Paper of Bishop Museum* **24**: 215-216.
13. Wetzel, R.M., Dubos, R.E., Martin, R.L. and Myers, P., 1975, *Catagonus,* an "extinct" peccary alive in Paraguay, *Science* **189**: 378-381.
14. Gentry, A.H., 1977, Endangered plant species and habitats of Ecuador and Amazonian Peru, in: G.T. Prance and T.S. Elias (editors), *Extinction Is Forever:* 136-149, New York Botanical Gardens, Bronx, New York.
15. Baker, H.G., 1970, Evolution in the tropics, *Biotropica* **2** (2): 101-111; Farnworth, F.G. and Golley, F.B. (editors), 1974, *Fragile Ecosystems,* Springer Verlag, New York; Golley, F.B. and Medina E. (editors), 1975, *Tropical Ecological Systems,* Springer Verlag, New York; and Lowe-McConnel, R.H. (editor), 1969, *Speciation in Tropical Environments,* Academic Press, New York.
16. Prance, G.T., 1977, Floristic inventory of the tropics: where do we stand?, *Annals of the Missouri Botanical Garden* **64**: 659-684; Prance, G.T. and Elias, T.S. (editors), *Extinction Is Forever:* 136-149, New York Botanical Gardens, Bronx, New York; Raven, P.H., Evert, R.F. and Curtis, H., 1978, *Biology of Plants* (second edition), Worth Publishers Inc., New York.
17. Welty, J.C., 1964, *The Life of Birds,* Constable Publishers, London.
18. Slud, P., 1960, The birds of Finca La Selva, Costa Rica, a tropical wet forest locality, *Bulletin of American Museum of Natural History* **121** (2): 49-148.
19. Lowe-McConnel, R.H. (editor), 1969, *Speciation in Tropical Environments,* Academic Press, New York; and 1975, *Fish Communities in Tropical Freshwaters,* Longman Publishers, London.
20. Owen, D.F., 1971, *Tropical Butterflies,* Clarendon Press, Oxford, England.
21. Richards, P.W., 1973, The tropical rainforest, *Scientific American* **229** (6): 58-68.
22. Prance, G.T., 1977, Floristic inventory of the tropics: where do we stand?, *Annals of the Missouri Botanical Garden* **64**: 659-684.
23. Farnworth, F.G. and Golley, F.B. (editors), 1974, *Fragile Ecosystems,* Springer Verlag, New York; Golley, F.B. and Medina E. (editors), 1975, *Tropical Ecological Systems,* Springer Verlag, New York; Lowe-McConnel, R.H. (editor), 1969, *Speciation in Tropical Environments,* Academic Press, New York; Meggers, B.J., Ayensu, E.S. and Duckworth, W.D. (editors), 1973, *Tropical Forest Ecosystems in Africa and South America: A Comparative Review;* Raven, P.H., 1976, Ethics and attitudes, in: J.B. Simmons, R.I. Bayer, P.E. Brandham, G.Ll. Lucas and W.T.H. Parry (editors), *Conservation of Threatened Plants:* 155-179, Plenum, New York.
24. Hamilton, L.S., 1976, *Tropical Rainforest Use and Preservation: A Study of Problems and Practices in Venezuela,* Sierra Club Office of International Environment Affairs, New York.

25. Raven, P.H., 1976, Ethics and attitudes, in: J.B. Simmons, R.I. Bayer, P.E. Brandham, G.L. Lucas and W.T.H. Parry (editors), *Conservation of Threatened Plants:* 155-179, Plenum, New York.

26. Hall, A.V., 1976, *Research in Endangered Plant Species,* Bolus Herbarium, Cape Town, South Africa.

27. Stern, W.L. (editor), 1971, *Adaptive Aspects of Insular Evolution,* Washington State University Press, Pullman, Washington.

28. Carson, H.L. and Kaneshiro, K.Y., 1976, Drosophilia of Hawaii: Systematics and ecological genetics, *Annual Review of Ecology and Systematics* 7: 311-345.

29. Fosberg, F.R., 1975, The deflowering of Hawaii, *National Parks and Conversation Magazine* 49 (10): 4-10.

30. Fryer, G. and Iles, T.D., 1972, *The Cichlid Fishes of the Great Lakes of Africa,* Oliver & Boyd, Edinburgh, Scotland; and Lowe-McConnel, R.H., 1975, *Fish Communities in Tropical Freshwaters,* Longman Publishers, London.

31. Haffer, J., 1974, *Avian Speciation in Tropical South America,* Harvard University Press, Cambridge, Massachusetts; Prance, G.T., 1977, The phytogeographic subdivisions of Amazonia and their influence on the selection of biological reserves, in: G.T. Prance and T.S. Elias (editors), *Extinction is Forever:* 195-213, New York Botanical Gardens, Bronx, New York; Simpson, B., 1971, Pleistocene changes in the fauna and flora of South America, *Science* 173: 771-780; Van der Hammen, T., 1974, The Pleistocene changes of vegetation and climate in Tropical South America, *Journal of Biogeography* 1: 3-26.

32. Brodkorb, B.P., 1971, Origin and evolution of birds, *Avian Biology* 1: 19-55.

33. Gould, S.J., 1975, Diversity through time, *Natural History* 84 (8): 24-32; Stebbins, G.L., 1971, *Processes of Organic Evolution,* Prentice Hall, Englewood Cliffs, New Jersey.

34. Fisher, J. and Peterson, R.J., 1964, *The World of Birds,* Macdonald Publishers, London.

35. Moreau, R.E., 1966, *The Bird Faunas of Africa and its Islands,* Academic Press, New York.

36. Johnstone, R.F. and Selander, R.K., 1971, Evolution in the house sparrow, *Evolution* 25: 1-28.

37. Huxley, A., 1974, *Plant and Planet,* Allen Lane Publisher, London.

38. Martin, P.S. and Wright, H.E. (editors), 1967, *Pleistocene Extinctions: The Search for a Cause,* Yale University Press, New Haven, Connecticut.

Chapter 3 Species Under threat

1. Fisher, J., Simon, N. and Vincent J., 1969, *Wildlife In Danger,* Viking Press, New York; Greenway, J.C., 1967, *Extinct and Vanishing Birds of the World* (second edition), Dover Press, New York; Ziswiler, V., 1967, *Extinct and Vanishing Animals,* Springer Verlag, New York.

2. Drury, W.H., 1974, Rare species, *Biological Conservation* 6 (3): 162-169.

3. Geist, V., 1971, *The Mountain Sheep,* University of Chicago Press, Chicago.

4. Chancellor, R.D. (editor), 1977, *Report of Proceedings of World Congress on Birds of Prey,* International Council for Bird Preservation, London.

5. Pyle, R.M., 1978, *IUCN World Conservation Strategy: Invertebrate Animals,* Lepidoptera Specialist Group, Survival Service Commission International Union for Conservation of Nature and Natural Resources, Morges, Switzerland.

6. Terborgh, J., 1979, Distribution of endemic bird species in Colombia and

Ecuador, in: G.T. Prance (editor), *The Biological Model of Diversification in the Tropics* (in press).

7. Cody, M.L. and Diamond, J.M. (editors), 1975, *Ecology and Evolution of Communities,* Harvard University Press, Cambridge, Massachusetts; Lovejoy, T.E., 1974, Bird diversity and abundance in Amazon forest communities, *Living Birds* **13**: 127-191.

8. Aron, W.I. and Smith, S.H., 1971, Ship canals and aquatic ecosystems, *Science* **174**: 13-20.

Chapter 4   What are Species Good For?

1. Regan, T. and Singer, P., 1976, *Animal Rights and Human Obligation,* Prentice Hall, Englewood Cliffs, New Jersey; Shepard, P., 1978, *Thinking Animals,* Viking Press, New York.

2. Goodman, D., 1975, The theory of diversity-stability relationships in ecology, *Quarterly Review of Biology* **50** (3): 237-266; Usher, M.B. and Williamson, M.H. (editors), 1974, *Ecological Stability,* Halstead Press, New York; Van Dobben, W.H. and Lowe-McConnel, R.H. (editors), 1975, Unifying concepts in ecology, W. Junk, The Hague, Holland.

3. May, R.M., 1974, *Stability and Complexity in Model Ecosystems,* Princeton University Press, Princeton, New Jersey.

4. Gomez-Pompa, A., Vazquez-Waynes, C. and Guevara, S., 1972, The tropical rainforest, a non-renewable resource, *Science* **177**: 762-765; Farnworth, F.G. and Golley, F.B. (editors), 1974, *Fragile Ecosystems,* Springer Verlag, New York; Golley, F.B. and Medina, E. (editors), 1975, *Tropical Ecological Systems,* Springer Verlag, New York.

5. Myers, N., 1976, The cheetah in Africa under threat, *Environmental Affairs* **5** (4): 617-647.

6. Ayala, F.J. (editor), 1976, *Molecular Evolution,* Sinauer Associates, Sunderland, Massachusetts; Lewontin, R.C., 1974, *The Genetic Basis of Evolutionary Change,* Columbia University Press, New York.

7. Dobzhansky, T., 1970, *Genetics of the Evolutionary Process,* Columbia University Press, New York.

Chapter 5   Utilitarian Benefits of Species Preservation

1. Wittwer, S.H., 1975, Food production: technology and the resource base, *Science* **188**: 579-584.

2. Baker, H.G., 1970, *Plants and Civilisation* (second edition), Wadsworth Publishing Company, Belmont, California; Harlan, J.R., 1975, *Crops and Man,* American Society of Agronomy, Madison, Wisconsin.

3. National Academy of Sciences, 1975, *Underexploited Tropical Plants With Promising Economic Value,* National Academy of Sciences, Washington, D.C.

4. McKell, C.M., 1975, Shrubs — a neglected resource of arid lands, *Science* **187**: 803-809.

5. Vaughan, J.G., 1977, A multidisciplinary study of the taxonomy and origin of *Brassica* crops, *BioScience* **27** (1): 35-38.

6. Getahun, A., 1974, The role of wild plants in the native diet in Ethiopia, *Agro-Ecosystems* **1**: 45-56; Williams, J.T., Lamoureux, C.H. and Wlijarni-Soetjipto, N. (editors), 1975, *South-East Asian Plant Genetic Resources,* Regional Center for Tropical Biology/BIOTROP, Bogor, Indonesia.

7. Carlson, P.S. and Polacco, J.C., 1975, Plant cell cultures: genetic aspects of crop improvement, *Science* **188**: 622-625; Day, P.R., 1977, Plant genetics: increase in crop yield, *Science* **197**: 1334-1339; Frankel, O.H. and Hawkes, J.G. (editors), 1974, *Plant Genetic Resources for Today and Tomorrow,* Cambridge University Press, London; Hawkes, J.G. (editor), 1978, *Conservation and Agriculture,* Duckworth, London.

8. Shapley, D., 1973, Sorghum: "miracle" grain for the world protein shortage?, *Science* **182**: 147-148.

9. Epstein, E. and Norlyn, J.D., 1977, Seawater-based crop production: a feasibility study, *Science* **197**: 249-251.

10. Miller, J., 1973, Genetic erosion: crop plants threatened by government neglect, *Science* **182**: 1231-1233; U.S. Department of Agriculture, 1973, *Recommended Actions and Policies for Minimizing the Genetic Vulnerability of Our Major Crops,* U.S. Department of Agriculture, Washington, D.C.

11. Wilkes, H.G., 1972, Maize and its wild relatives, *Science* **177**: 1071-1077.

12. Data from Food and Agriculture Organization, Rome.

13. Bryson, R.A. and Murray, T.J., 1977, *Climates of Hunger,* University of Wisconsin Press, Madison, Wisconsin.

14. Child, J.J., 1976, New development in nitrogen fixation research, *BioScience* **26** (10): 614-617; Stewart, W.D.P., 1977, Present-day nitrogen fixing plants, *Ambio* **6** (2-3): 166-173.

15. Zelitch, I., 1975, Improving the efficiency of photosynthesis, *Science* **188**: 626-633.

16. Wittwer, S.H., 1975, Food production: technology and the resource base, *Science* **188**: 579-584.

17. Harlan, J.R., 1975, *Crops and Man,* American Society of Agronomy, Madison, Wisconsin; Heady, E.O., 1976, The agriculture of the United States, *Scientific American* **235** (3): 106-127; U.S. Department of Agriculture, 1973, *Recommended Actions and Policies for Minimizing the Genetic Vulnerability of Our Major Crops,* U.S. Department of Agriculture, Washington, D.C.

18. Tatum, L.A., 1971, The southern corn leaf blight epidemic, *Science* **171**: 1113-1116.

19. National Academy of Sciences, 1976, *Pest Control: An Assessment of Present and Alternative Technologies,* National Academy of Sciences, Washington, D.C.

20. DeBach, P., 1974, *Biological Control of Insect Pests and Weeds,* Reinhold, New York; Van den Bosch, R., 1978, *The Pesticide Conspiracy,* Doubleday & Company, Garden City, New York.

21. Chirappa, L., Chiang, H.C. and Smith, R.F., 1972, Plant pests and diseases: assessment of crop losses, *Science* **176**: 769-772.

22. Alderson, L., 1978, *The Chance to Survive: Rare Breeds in a Changing World,* David and Charles, Newton Abbot, Devon, England; Bereskin, B., 1976, *Preservation of Germ Plasm — An Overview,* Agriculture Research Center, U.S. Department of Agriculture, Beltsville, Maryland; Lauvergne, J.J., 1975, *Conservation of Animal Genetic Resources,* Food and Agriculture Organization, Rome; National Academy of Sciences, 1978, *Conservation of Germ Plasm Resources: An Imperative,* National Academy of Sciences, Washington, D.C.; Rendel, J., 1975, The utilization and conservation of the world's animal genetic resources, *Agriculture and Environment* **2**: 101-119.

23. Olney, P.J. (editor), 1976, *International Zoo Yearbook,* Volume 16.

24. Beart, S., 1977, Genetic peril in cattle, *Environment* **19** (2): 2-3.
25. Mason, I.L., 1975, Beefalo: much ado about nothing?, *World Review of Animal Production* **11** (4): 19-23.
26. Short, R.V., 1976, The introduction of new species of animals for the purpose of domestication, *Symposium of Zoological Society of London* **40**: 1-13.
27. Myers, N., 1972, *The Long African Day,* Macmillan, New York.
28. Wetterberg, G.B., Ferreira, M., Brito, W.L. dos S. and Araujo, V.C. de, 1976, *Amazon Fauna Preferred as Food,* Food and Agriculture Organization, Brasilia, Brazil.
29. Taylor, R.L., 1975, *Butterflies in my Stomach: Insects in Human Nutrition,* Woodbridge Press, Santa Barbara, California.
30. Conconi, J.R.E. de, 1976, *Insects as a Source of Protein in the Future,* Secretariat of Public Education, National Autonomous University of Mexico, Mexico.
31. Starr, T.B., 1977, The role of climate in American agriculture, *The Ecologist* **7** (7): 262-267.
32. Jennings, P.R., 1976, The amplification of agricultural production, *Scientific American* **235** (3): 180-195; Scobie, G.M. and Posada, R.T., 1977, *The Impact of High-yielding Rice Varieties in America, with Special Reference to Colombia,* International Center for Tropical Agriculture, Cali, Colombia.
33. Altschul, S. von R., 1977, Exploring the herbarium, *Scientific America* **236** (5): 96-104; Lewis, W.H. and Elvin-Lewis, M.P.F., 1977, *Medical Botany,* John Wiley, New York; Morton, J.F., 1977, *Major Medicinal Plants,* Charles C. Thomas, Springfield, Illinois; Wagner, H. and Wolff, P., 1977, *New Natural Products and Plant Drugs,* Springer Verlag, New York.
34. Farnsworth, N.R., 1976, The sleeping giant of the American drug industry, *American Journal of Pharmacy* **148**: 46-52.
35. Neill, W.T., 1974, *Reptiles and Amphibians in the Service of Man,* Pegasus Press, London.
36. Wilson, A.C. *et al.,* 1963, Functions of the two forms of lactic dehydrogenase in the breast muscle of birds, *Nature* **197**: 331-334.
37. Sikes, S.K., 1968, Observations on the ecology of arterial diseases in the African elephant in Kenya and Uganda, *Symposium of Zoological Society of London* 21.
38. Laufs, R. and Steinke, H., 1975, Vaccination of non-primates against malignant lymphoma, *Nature* **253**: 71-72.
39. Nelson, R.A., 1977, *Urea Metabolism in the Hibernating Black Bear,* Mayo Clinic, Rochester, Minnesota.
40. Lemma, A. and Yau, P., 1974, Studies on the molluscicidal properties of endod, *Ethiopian Medical Journal* **13**: 115-124.
41. Levin, D.A., 1976, Alkaloid bearing plants: an ecogeographic perspective, *American Naturalist* **110**: 261-284.
42. Kupchen, S.M., Uchida, I., Branfnan, A.R., Dailey, R.G. and Fei, B.Y., 1976, Antileukemic principles isolated from euphorbiaceae plants, *Science* **191**: 571-572.
43. Lewis, W.H. and Elvin-Lewis, M.P.F., 1977, *Medical Botany,* John Wiley, New York.
44. Schultes, R.E., 1976, *Hallucinogenic Plants,* Golden Press, Racine, Wisconsin.
45. National Academy of Sciences, 1975, *Products from Jojoba: A Promising New Crop for Arid Lands,* National Academy of Sciences, Washington, D.C.
46. National Academy of Sciences, 1977, *Guayule: An Alternative Source of Natural Rubber,* National Academy of Sciences, Washington, D.C.

47. National Academy of Sciences, 1977, *Leucaena: Promising Forage and Tree Crop for the Tropics,* National Academy of Science, Washington, D.C.
48. Calvin, M., 1978, Green factories, *Chemical and Engineering News* 56: 30-36.
49. Wilcox, H.A., 1976, *The Ocean Food and Energy Farm Project,* Naval Undersea Center, San Diego, California.
50. Spurgeon, D., 1974, Sea cows eat their way to domestication, *New Scientist* 1st August: 238-239.
51. National Academy of Sciences, 1976, *Making Aquatic Weeds Useful,* National Academy of Sciences, Washington, D.C.
52. Wolverton, B.C. and McKown, M.M., 1976, Water hyacinths for removal of phenols from polluted waters, *Aquatic Botany* 2: 191-201; Tourbier, J. and Pierson, R.W. (editors), 1976, *Biological Control of Water Pollution,* University of Pennsylvania Press, Philadelphia.
53. Hillman, W.S. and Culley, D.D., 1978, The uses of duckweed, *American Scientist* 66 (4): 442-451.
54. Hawksworth, D.L. and Rose, F., 1976, Lichens as pollution monitors, *Studies in Biology* No. 66, Edward Arnold, London.
55. Thomas, W.A. (editor), 1972, *Indicators of Environmental Quality,* Plenum, New York.
56. Bauerle, B., Spencer, D.L. and Wheeler, W., 1975, The use of snakes as pollution indicator species, *Copeia:* 366-368.
57. Hillaby, J., 1975, Deformed froglets and walking catfish, *New Scientist* 67: 32-33.
58. Degens, E.T., Khoo, F. and Michaelis, W., 1977, Uranium anomaly in Black Sea sediments, *Nature* 269: 566-569.
59. Farnsworth, N.R., 1969, Drugs from the sea, *Tile and Till* 55; Ruggieri, C.D., 1976, Drugs from the Sea, *Science* 194: 491-497.
60. Chapman, V.J., *Seaweeds and Their Uses* (second edition), Methuen, London; Naylor, J., 1976, Production, trade and utilization of seaweeds and seaweed products, *FAO Fisheries Technical Paper* 159, Food and Agreiculture Organization, Rome.

Chapter 6   Disappearing Species: the Economics of Natural Resources

1. Dolzer, R., 1976, Property and environment: the social obligation inherent in ownership, *IUCN Environmental Policy and Law Paper* No. 12, International Union for Conservation of Nature and Natural Resources, Morges, Switzerland; Falk, R.A., 1971, *This Endangered Planet,* Random House, New York; Freeman, A.N., Haveman, R.G. and Kneese, A.V., 1973, *The Economics of Environmental Policy,* John Wiley, New York; Krutilla, J.V. and Fisher, A.C., 1975, *The Economics of Natural Environments,* Johns Hopkins University Press, Baltimore, Maryland; Sax, J.L., 1971, *Defending the Environment,* Knopf, New York.
2. Myers, N., 1976, The cheetah in Africa under threat, *Environmental Affairs* 5 (4): 617-647.
3. Gordon, H.S., 1954, The economic theory of a common property resource: the fishery, *Journal of Political economy* 62 (2): 124-142; Hardin, G., 1968, The tragedy of the commons, *Science* 162: 1243-1248; Hardin, G. and Baden, J. (editors), 1977, *Managing the Commons,* W.H. Freeman & Company, San Francisco.

4. Myers, N., 1973, The Masai: modernising the myth, *Association of Pacific Coast Geographers Yearbook* **35**: 147-164.
5. Hardin, G., 1968, The tragedy of the commons, *Science* **162**: 1243-1248.
6. Hardin, G. and Baden, J. (editors), 1977, *Managing the Commons,* W.H. Freeman & Company, San Francisco.
7. Schelling, T.C., 1971, On the ecology of micromotives, *Public Interest* **25**: 61-98.
8. Beddington, J.R., Watts, C.M. and Wright, W.D.C., 1975, Optimal cropping of self-reproductible natural resources, *Econometrica* **43**: 789-802; Clark, C.W., 1977, *Mathematical Bioeconomics: The Optimal Management of Renewable Resources,* John Wiley & Sons, New York; Koers, A.W., 1973, *International Regulation of Marine Fisheries,* Fishing News (Books) Ltd., London.
9. Gordon-Clark, J., King A. and Burton, J.A., 1975, Whales: time for a fresh start, *New Scientist* **65**: 206-209; Holt, S.J., 1974, *A Ten-year Moratorium on All Commercial Whaling: An Evaluation,* Report to International Union for Conservation of Nature and Natural Resources, International Ocean Institute, Msida, Malta; Japanese Whaling Association, 1974, *The Whaling Controversy: Japan's Position,* Japanese Whaling Association, Tokyo; Komatsu, R., 1974, *Whaling and Japan,* Japan Institute of International Affairs, Tokyo; Myers, N., 1975, The whaling controversy, *American Scientist* **63** (4): 448-455.
10. Schumacher, E.F., 1973, *Small is Beautiful: Economics as if People Mattered,* Harper & Row, New York; Ward, B., 1972, *What's Wrong with Economics,* Basic Books, New York.
11. Clark, C.W., 1977, *Mathematical Bioeconomics: The Optimal Management of Renewable Resources,* John Wiley & Sons, New York.
12. Laufs, R. and Steinke, H., 1975, Vaccination of non-human primates against malignant lymphoma, *Nature* **253**: 71-72.
13. Myers, N., 1978, Wildlife of savannah and grasslands: a common heritage of the global community, in: E. Schofield (editor), *Proceedings of Earthcare Conference* 385-409, Westview Press, Boulder, Colorado.
14. Brown, L.H., 1978, The worldwide loss of cropland, *Worldwatch Pamphlet* No. 24, Worldwatch Institute, Washington, D.C.; Pimentel, D. and eight others, 1976, Land degradation: effects on food and energy resources, *Science* **194**: 149-155.
15. Freeman, A.N., Haveman, R.H. and Kneese, A.V., 1973, *The Economics of Environmental Policy,* John Wiley, New York; Krutilla, J.V. and Fisher, A.C., 1975, *The Economics of Natural Environments,* Johns Hopkins University Press, Baltimore, Maryland; Mishan, E.J., 1972, *Cost-Benefit Analysis,* George Allen & Unwin, London; Schelling, T.C., 1971, On the ecology of micromotives, *Public Interest* **25**: 61-98.
16. Baumol, W.J. and Oates, W.E., 1975, *The Theory of Environmental Policy,* Prentice Hall, Englewood Cliffs, New Jersey; d'Arge, R.C., 1972, *On the Economics of Transnational Environmental Externalities,* Resources for the Future, Washington, D.C.; d'Arge, R.C. and Kneese, A.V., 1973, The economics of state responsibility and liability for environmental degradation, *Working Paper* No. 23, Program in Environmental Economics, University of California, Riverside; Leontief, W., 1970, Environmental repercussions and the economic structure: an input-output approach, *Review of Economics and Statistics* **52** (3): 262-271; Walter, I. (editor), 1976, *Studies in International Environmental Economics,* Wiley-Interscience, New York.

Chapter 7 Political and Legal Dimension of Species Conservation

1. Falk, R.A., 1971, *This Endangered Planet,* Random House, New York; Sax, J.L., 1971, *Defending the Environment,* Knopf, New York.
2. McDougall, M.S. and Schneider, J., 1977, The protection of the environment and world public order, in: B. Preger, H.D. Lasswell and J. McHale (editors), *World Priorities:* 81-114, Transaction Books, New Brunswick, New Jersey.

Chapter 8 The Special Case of Tropical Moist Forests

1. For well-documented accounts of tropical moist forests, from which this review is drawn, see Farnworth, F.G. and Golley, F.B. (editors), 1974, *Fragile Ecosystems,* Springer Verlag, New York; Golley, F.B. and Medina, E. (editors), 1975, *Tropical Ecological Systems,* Springer Verlag, New York; Gomez-Pompa, A., Vazquez-Waynes, C. and Guevara, S., 1972, The tropical rain forest: a non-renewable resource, *Science* 177: 762-765; Janzen, D.H., 1975, Ecology of plants in the tropics, *Institute of Biology's Studies in Biology* No. 58, Edward Arnold, London; Longman, K.A. and Jenic, J., 1974, *Tropical Forest and Its Environment,* Longman, London; Poore, D., 1976, *Ecological Guidelines for Development in Tropical Rain Forests,* International Union for Conservation of Nature and Natural Resources, Morges, Switzerland; Richards, P.W., 1977, Tropical forests and woodlands: an overview, *Agro-Ecosystems* 3 (3): 225-238; and 1973, The tropical rain forest, *Scientific American* 229 (6): 58-68; Sommer, A., 1976, An attempt at an assessment of the world's tropical moist forests, *Unasylva* 28 (112-113): 5-24; UNESCO, 1978, Tropical Forest Ecosystems, *Natural Resources Research* XIV, UNESCO, Paris; Whitmore, T.C., 1975, *Tropical Rain Forests of the Far East,* Clarendon Press, Oxford.
2. Gentry, A.H., 1977, Endangered plant species and habitats of Ecuador and Amazonian Peru, in: G.T. Prance and T.S. Elias (editors), *Extinction is Forever:* 136-149, New York Botanical Gardens, Bronx, New York.
3. Sommer, A., 1976, An attempt at an assessment of the world's tropical moist forests, *Unasylva* 28 (112-113): 5-24.
4. Sommer, A., 1976, An attempt at an assessment of the world's tropical moist forests, *Unasylva* 28 (112-113): 5-24.
5. Lieth, H. and Whittaker, R.H. (editors), 1975, *Primary Productivity of the Biosphere,* Springer Verlag, New York.
6. Prance, G.T., 1977, The phytogeographic subdivisions of Amazonia and their influence on the selection of biological reserves, in: G.T. Prance and T.S. Elias (editors), *Extinction is Forever:* 195-213, New York Botanical Gardens, Bronx, New York.
7. Medway, Lord, 1978, The tropical forests as a source of animal genetic resources, in: *Proceedings of Eighth World Forestry Congress,* FAO, Rome (in press).
8. Burley, J. and Styles, B.T. (editors), 1976, Tropical trees: variation, breeding and conservation, *Linnean Society Symposium Series* No. 2, Academic Press, London.
9. This is not invariably the case; in Central America, for example, seedlings of certain species respond vigorously to opening of the canopy; see Hartshorn, G.S. and Orians, G.H., 1978, *The Influence of Gaps in Tropical Forests on Tree Species' Richness,* Tropical Science Center, San Jose, Costa Rica.
10. Stern, K. and Roche, L., 1974, *Genetics of Forest Ecosystems,* Springer Verlag, New York.
11. Ramirez, B.W., 1970, Host specificity of fig wasps, *Evolution* 24: 680-691.

12. Sanchez, P.A., 1976, *Properties and Management of Soils in the Tropics,* John Wiley, New York.
13. Richards, P.W., 1977, Tropical forests and woodlands: an overview, *Agro-Ecosystems* 3 (3): 225-238.
14. Whittaker, R.H., 1975, *Communities and Ecosystems* (second edition), Macmillan, New York.
15. Brünig, E.F., 1977, The tropical rain forests — a wasted asset or an essential biospheric resource? *Ambio* 6 (4): 187-191.
16. Opler, P.A., Baker, H.G. and Frankie, G.W., 1977, Recovery of tropical lowland forest ecosystems, in: J. Cairns and K. Dickson (editors), *Recovery and Management of Damaged Ecosystems,* University of Virginia Press, Charlottesville, Virginia.
17. Persson, R., 1977, *Forest Resources of Africa,* Royal College of Forestry, Stockholm, Sweden.
18. Poore, D., 1976, *Ecological Guidelines for Development in Tropical Rain Forests,* International Union for Conservation of Nature and Natural Resources, Morges, Switzerland.
19. Myers, N., 1979, Conservation of forest animal and plant genetic resources in tropical rainforests, in: *Proceedings of Eighth World Forestry Congress,* FAO, Rome (in press).
20. National Academy of Sciences, 1975, *Underexploited Tropical Plants With Promising Economic Value,* National Academy of Sciences, Washington, D.C.
21. National Academy of Sciences, 1976, *Pest Control: An Assessment of Present and Alternative Technologies,* National Academy of Sciences, Washington D.C.; Van den Bosch, R., 1978, *The Pesticide Conspiracy,* Doubleday and Company, Garden City, New York.
22. Levin, D.A., 1976, Alkaloid-bearing plants: an ecogeographic perspective, *American Naturalist* 110: 261-284.
23. Lewis, W.H. and Elvin-Lewis, M.P.F., 1977, *Medical Botany,* John Wiley, New York.
24. Applezweig, N., 1977, Dioscorea — the pill crop, in: *Crop Resources* 149-163, Academic Press, New York.
25. Stout, G.H. and Schultes, R.E., 1973, Importance of plant chemicals in human affairs, in: L.P. Miller (editor), *Phytochemistry* Vol. III, 381-399, Van Nostrand Reinhold, New York.
26. Borzani, W., 1979, The ethanol-based economy — the Brazilian experiment, in: *Proceedings of World Conference on Future Sources of Organic Raw Materials,* Chemical Institute of Canada, Toronto, Pergamon Press, Oxford and New York.
27. Schultes, R.E., 1976, *Hallucinogenic Plants,* Golden Press, Racine, Wisconsin.
28. Baker, H.G., 1970, *Plants and Civilisation* (second edition), Wadsworth Publishing Company, Belmont, California.
29. Kunstadter, P., Chapman, E.C. and Sabhasari, S., 1978, *Farmers in the Forest,* University Press of Hawaii, Honolulu.
30. Davis, S.H., 1977, *Victims of the Miracle: Development and the Indians of Brazil,* Cambridge University Press, London; Tamson, R., 1974, Bibliography on medicinal plants and related subjects, *Technical paper* No. 171, South Pacific Commission, Naumea, New Calidonia.
31. Soejarto, D.D., 1977, Plants to control fertility, *World Health,* August-September: 16-19, UNESCO, Paris.

32. World Health Organization, 1977, *Special Program of Research, Development and Research Training in Human Reproduction, Sixth Annual Report,* WHO, Geneva, Switzerland.

33. Degens, E.T., 1979, *The Global Carbon Cycle,* John Wiley, New York; Molion, L.C.B., 1976, *A Climatonic Study of the Energy and Moisture Fluxes of the Amazonas Basin With Considerations of Deforestation Effects,* Instituto de Pesquisas Sao Paulo, Brazil; Stumm, W. (editor), 1977, *Global Chemical Cycles and Their Alterations by Man,* Abakon Verlag, Berlin; National Academy of Sciences, 1977, *Energy and Climate,* National Academy of Sciences, Washington, D.C.; Woodwell, G.M. and five others, 1978, The biota and the world carbon budget, *Science* 199: 141-146.

34. Bolin, B., 1977, Changes of land biota and their importance for the carbon cycle, *Science* 196: 613-615.

35. Bryson, R.A. and Murray, T.J., 1977, *Climates of Hunger,* University of Wisconsin Press, Madison.

Chapter 9 Regional Review

1. Hammond, A.L., 1977, Remote sensing: Brazil explores its Amazon wilderness, *Science* 196: 513-515.

2. Prance, G.T., 1977, Floristic inventory of the tropics: where do we stand?, *Annals of the Missouri Botanical Garden* 64: 659-684.

3. Prance, G.T., 1974, Phytogeographical support for the theory of Pleistocene forest refuges in the Amazon Basin, *Acta Amazonica* 3: 5-28; Van der Hammen, T., 1972, Changes in vegetation and climate in the Amazon Basin and surrounding areas during the Pleistocene, *Geologie en Mijnbouw* 51 (6): 641-643.

4. Hagerby, L., 1976, The forestry industry in the Amazon: capacity and production, *Research Report* No. 11, Brazilian Institute for Forestry Development, Brasilia, Brazil.

5. Anon., 1976, Peru reveals ambitious plan, *World Wood* April: 22.

6. Saleti, E. *et al.,* 1978, *Recycling of Water in the Amazon Basin: An Isotopic Study,* Division of Environmental Science, Center of Nuclear Energy and Agriculture, Piracicaba, Brazil.

7. Ashton, P.S., 1977, A contribution of rain forest research to evolutionary theory, *Annals of the Missouri Botanical Garden* 64 (4): 694-705.

8. Wells, D.R., 1971, Survival of the Malaysian bird fauna, *Malayan Nature Journal* 24: 248-256.

9. This economic summary is based on Chandrasekharan, C., 1977, Country Review, *Forest News for Asia and the Pacific* 1 (1): 6-36, and Resources Surveys of the FAO Regional Office, Bangkok, Thailand.

10. This review is based on Persson, R., 1977, *Forest Resources of Africa,* Royal College of Forestry, Stockholm, Sweden; Sommer, A., 1976, An attempt at an assessment of the world's tropical moist forests, *Unasylva* 28 (112-113): 5-24; Synnott, T.J., 1977, *Monitoring Tropical Forests: A Review with Special Reference to Africa,* International Council of Scientific Unions, Paris.

11. Hamilton, A., 1976, The significance of patterns of distribution shown by forest plants and animals in tropical Africa, for the reconstruction of Upper Pleistocene palaeoenvironments: a review, in: E.M. Van Zinderen Bakker (editor), *Palaeoecology of Africa, The Surrounding Islands and Antarctica:* 63-97, Balkema, Cape Town, South Africa; Kingdon, J., 1971, *East African Mammals: An Atlas*

of Evolution in Africa, Vol. I, Academic Press, London; Moreau, R.E., 1966, *The Bird Faunas of Africa and Its Islands,* Academic Press, London.
12. Synnott, T.K., 1977, *Monitoring Tropical Forests: A Review with Special Reference to Africa,* International Council of Scientific Unions, Paris.
13. Persson, R., 1977, *Forest Resources of Africa,* Royal College of Forestry, Stockholm, Sweden.

Chapter 10   Four Country Profiles
1. This short summary is based on extensive documentation to be found in Alvim, P. de T., 1977, The balance between conservation and utilization in the humid tropics, with special reference to Amazonian Brazil, in: G.T. Prance and T.S. Elias (editors), *Extinction is Forever:* 347-352, New York Botanical Gardens, Bronx, New York; Cox, V., 1977, Brazil: the Amazon gamble, *Development Digest* **15** (1): 82-86; Goodland, R.J.A. and Irwin, H.S., 1975, *Amazon Jungle: Green Hell to Red Desert?,* Elsevier Scientific Publishing Company, New York; Rosende, E., 1977, The Transamazon Highway, *Development Digest* **15** (1): 76-81; Smith, N., 1976, *The Transamazon Highway: A Cultural and Ecological Analysis of Settlement in the Humid Tropics,* doctoral dissertation, University of California, Berkeley.
2. Hammond, A.L., 1977, Remote sensing: Brazil explores its Amazon wilderness, *Science* **196**: 513-515.
3. Palmer, J.R., 1977, Forestry in Brazil — Amazonia, *Commonwealth Forestry Review* **56** (2): 115-130.
4. Cox, V., 1977, Brazil: the Amazon gamble, *Development Digest* **15** (1): 82-86.
5. Davis, S.H., 1977, *Victims of the Miracle: Development and the Indians of Brazil,* Cambridge University Press, London.
6. Irwin, H.S., 1977, Coming to terms with the rain forest, *Garden* **1** (2): 29-33.
7. Slud, P., 1960, The birds of Finca La Selva, Costa Rica, a tropical wet forest locality, *Bulletin of American Museum of Natural History* **121** (2): 49-148.
8. Dwoskin, P.B., 1975, Fast food franchises: market potential for agricultural products in foreign and domestic markets, *Economic Research Service* **596**, U.S. Department of Agriculture, Washington, D.C.
9. Parsons, J.J., 1976, Forest to pasture: forest development or destruction?, *Revista de Biologia Tropicale* **24**: 121-138.
10. Foreign Agricultural Service, 1976, *Costa Rica: Agricultural Situation,* United States Department of Agriculture, Washington, D.C.
11. Data from author's visit to Costa Rica, November 1976.
12. This account is based on the author's two extended visits to Indonesia in the last 3 years.
13. This section is based on the author's residence in Kenya for 17 of the past 21 years.
14. Turner, D.A., 1977, Status and distribution of the East African endemic species, *Scopus* **1** (1): 2-11.
15. Hamilton, A., 1976, The significance of patterns of distribution shown by forest plants and animals in tropical Africa, for the reconstruction of Upper Pleistocene palaeoenvironments: a review, in: E.M. Van Zinderen Bakker (editor), *Palaeoecology of Africa, The Surrounding Islands and Antarctica:* 63-97, Balkema, Cape Town, South Africa; Kingdon, J., 1973, Endemic mammals and birds of Western Uganda, *Uganda Journal* **37**: 1-7.

16. Lamprey, H.F., 1975, The distribution of protected areas in relation to the needs of biotic community conservation in Eastern Africa, *IUCN Occasional Paper* No. 16, International Union for Conservation of Nature and Natural Resources, Morges, Switzerland.

Chapter 11   Patterns of Exploitation

1. National Academy of Sciences, 1976, *Renewable Resources for Industrial Materials,* National Academy of Sciences, Washington, D.C.
2. Okita, S., 1974, Natural resource dependency and Japanese foreign policy, *Foreign Affairs* **52** (4): 714-724.
3. Food and Agricultural Organization, 1978, *1976 Yearbook of Forest Products,* Food and Agricultural Organization, Rome.
4. Pringle, S.L., 1977, The future availability of world pulp: a world picture, *Unasylva* **29**: 18-25.
5. Shimokawa, E., 1977, Japan's dependence upon wood chips pulp, *Unasylva* **29**: 26-27.
6. King, K.F.S., 1976, Wood: world-wide perspective, *American forests* **82** (4): 12-13 and 53-57.
7. Ewel, J. and Conde, L., 1976, *Potential Ecological Impact of Increased Intensity of Tropical Forest Utilisation,* Forest Products Laboratory, Madison, Wisconsin.
8. Hadi, S. and Suparto, R.S. (editors), 1977, *Proceedings of Symposium on the Long-term Effects of Logging in South-east Asia,* Regional Center for Tropical Biology, Bogor, Indonesia; Tinal, U. and Palenewen, J.L., 1974, *A Study of Mechanical Logging Damage After Selective Cutting in the Lowland Dipterocarp Forest of East Kalimantan,* Regional Center for Tropical Biology, Bogor, Indonesia; Suparto, R.S. and seven others (editors), 1978, *Proceedings of Symposium on the Long-term Effects of Logging in Southeast Asia,* Regional Center for Tropical Biology, Bogor, Indonesia; Whitmore, T.C., 1975, *Tropical Rain Forests of the Far East,* Clarendon Press, Oxford.
9. McNeely, J.A., Rabor, D.S. and Sumardja, E.A. (editors), 1979, *Wildlife Management in Southeast Asia,* Regional Center for Tropical Biology, Bogor, Indonesia (in press).
10. Wilson, W.L. and Wilson, C.C., 1975, The influence of selective logging on primates and some other animals in East Kalimantan, *Folia Primatologica* **23**: 245-274.
11. Struhsaker, T.T., 1972, Rainforest conservation in Africa, *Primates* **13**: 103-109.
12. Sommer, A., 1976, an attempt at an assessment of the world's tropical moist forests, *Unasylva* **28** (112-113): 5-24.
13. Clarke, W.C., 1976, Maintenance of agriculture and human habitats within the tropical forest ecosystem, *Human Ecology* **4** (3): 247-259; Greenland, D.J. and Herrera, R., 1977, Patterns of use of tropical forest ecosystems: shifting cultivation and other agricultural practices, *State of Knowledge Report,* UNESCO Paris.
14. Persson, R., 1977, *Forest Resources of Africa,* Royal College of Forestry, Stockholm, Sweden.
15. Denevan, W.M., 1976, The causes and consequences of tropical shifting cultivation, *Conference on Tropical Moist Forests,* FAO, Rome.
16. Arnold, J.E.M. and Jongma, J., 1978, Fuelwood and charcoal in developing countries, *Unasylva* **29** (118): 2-9.

17. Openshaw, K., 1978, Woodfuel — a time for re-assessment, *U.N. Natural Resources Forum,* October 1978.
18. Davis, S.H., 1977, *Victims of the Miracle: Development and the Indians of Brazil,* Cambridge University Press, London; Irwin, H.S., 1977, Coming to terms with the rain forest, *Garden* 1 (2): 29-33.
19. Potma, H.L., 1976, Brazil: A statistical digest of the forestry situation, *Research Report* No. 12, Brazilian Institute for Forestry Development, Brasilia, Brazil.
20. Osbourn, D.F., 1975, Beef production from improved pastures in the tropics, *World Review of Animal Production* 11 (4): 23-31; Parsons, J.J., 1976, Forest to pasture: development or destruction? *Revista de Biologia Tropicale* 24: 121-138.
21. During August 1978 - May 1979, the author is conducting a detailed survey of conservation rates in tropical moist forests; see forthcoming report for the National Academy of Sciences, Washington, D.C.

Chapter 12   Ways to Relieve Excessive Exploitation

1. Pringle, S.L., 1977, The future availability of world pulp: a world picture, *Unasylva* 29: 18-25.
2. Thomas, C., 1977, *The Paper Chain,* Earth Resources Research, London.
3. Lintu, L., 1978, Panels, paper and paperboard from agricultural residues, *Unasylva* 29 (118): 12-17.
4. Chow, P., 1976, The use of crop residues for board making, *Environmental Conservation* 3 (1): 59-62.
5. Palmer, E.R. and Tabb, C.B., 1974, Pulpwood production prospects, *Tropical Science* 16 (4): 207-236.
6. Tamolang, F.N., 1976, The utilisation of coconut trunk and other parts in the Philippines, *Technology Journal* (publication of the National Science Development Board of the Philippines) 1 (2): 36-48.
7. Johnson, N.E., 1976, Biological opportunities and risks associated with fast-growing plantations in the tropics, *Journal of Forestry* 74 (4): 206-211.
8. Palmer, E.R. and Tabb, C.B., 1974, Pulpwood production prospects, *Tropical Science* 16 (4): 207-236.
9. Hillis, W.E. and Brown, A.G. (editors), 1978, *Eucalypts for Wood Production,* Commonwealth Scientific and Industrial Research Organization, Melbourne, Australia.
10. Food and Agriculture Organization, 1978, *1976 Yearbook of Forest Products,* Food and Agriculture Organization, Rome.
11. Gregersen, H.N. and Contreras, A., 1975, *U.S. Investment in the Forest-based Sector in Latin America,* Johns Hopkins University Press, Baltimore, Maryland.
12. Potma, H.L., 1976, Brazil: a statistical digest of the forestry situation, *Research Report* No. 12, Brazilian Institute for Forestry Development, Brasilia, Brazil.
13. Clarke, W.C., 1976, Maintenance of agriculture and human habitats within the tropical ecosystem, *Human Ecology* 4 (3): 247-259; Greenland, D.J., 1975, Bringing the Green Revolution to the shifting cultivator, *Science* 190: 841-844; Greenland, D.J. and Herrera, R., 1977, Patterns of use of tropical forest ecosystems: shifting cultivation and other agricultural practices, *State of Knowledge Report,* UNESCO, Paris.
14. Pearson, C. and Pryor, A., 1978, *Environment North and South: An Economic Interpretation,* Wiley-Interscience, New York.

15. Nations, J.D. and Nigh, R.B., 1978, Cattle, cash, food and forest, *Culture and Agriculture* **6**: 1-5.
16. Bene, J.G., Deall, H.W. and Cote, A., 1977, *Trees, Food and People,* International Development Research Center, Ottawa, Canada; Douglas, J.S. and Hart, R.A. de J., 1976, *Forest Farming,* Watkins Publishers, London; King, K.F.S., 1968, *Agri-Silviculture,* University of Ibadan, Nigeria.
17. Van Nao, T., 1978, Agrisilviculture: joint production of food and wood, in: *Proceedings of Eighth World Forestry Congress,* FAO, Rome (in press).
18. Draper, S., 1975, Forestry in rural development, *Rural Development Working Paper* No. 2, Rural Development Division, The World Bank, Washington, D.C.
19. Keil, C., 1977, *Forestry Projects for Rural Community Development,* Rural Development Division, The World Bank, Washington, D.C.
20. Sanvictores, B.F., 1975, Moving away from log exports, *Unasylva* **27** (108): 10-14; Takeuchi, K., 1974, Tropical hardwood trade in the Asia-Pacific region, *World Bank Occasional Paper* No. 17, The World Bank, Washington, D.C.
21. King, K.F.S., 1976, Wood: world-wide perspective, *American Forests* **82** (4): 12-13 and 53-57; Zinkel, D.F., 1975, Chemicals from trees, *Chemtech* April 1975: 235-241.
22. Bente, P.F. (editor), 1978, *Bio-Energy Directive,* The Bio-Energy Council, Washington, D.C.; Calvin, M., 1976, Photosynthesis as a resource for energy and materials, *American Scientist* **64**: 270-278; Pollard, W.G., 1976, The long-range prospects for solar-derived fuels, *ibid:* 509-513.
23. Earl, D.E., 1975, *Forest Energy and Economic Development,* Clarendon Press, Oxford, England.
24. Chiang, T.I. *et al.,* 1976, *Pyrolytic Conversion of Agricultural and Forestry Wastes in Ghana: A Feasibility Study,* Georgia Institute of Technology, Atlanta, Georgia.
25. Tosi, J.A. and Voertman, R.F., 1975, Making the best use of the tropics, *Unasylva* **27** (110): 2-10.
26. Pirie, N.W. (editor), 1975, Food protein sources, *International Biological Program* No. 4, Cambridge University Press, London.

Chapter 13 The Role of Multinational Corporations

1. Connor, J.M., 1977, *The Market Power of Multinationals: A Quantitative Analysis of U.S. Corporations in Brazil and Mexico,* Praeger Publishers, New York; Strhasky, H. and Reisch, M. (editors), 1975, *The Transnational Corporations and the Third World: A Bibliography,* CODOC International Secretariat, Washington, D.C.
2. Tsurumi, Y., 1976, *The Japanese Are Coming: The Multinational Spread of Japanese Firms,* Ballinger Publishing Company, Cambridge, Massachusetts; Yoshino, M.Y., 1976, *The Japanese Multinational Enterprise: Strategy and Structure,* Harvard University Press, Cambridge, Massachusetts.
3. For some discussion of how multinational corporations can cause environmental degradation, see Walter, I. (editor), 1976, *Studies in International Environmental Economics,* Wiley-Interscience, New York.
4. Clark, C.W., 1977, *Mathematical Bioeconomics: The Optimal Management of Renewable Resources,* John Wiley & Sons, New York; Price, C., 1976, Blind alleys and open prospects in forest economics, *Forestry* **49** (2): 99-107.
5. This review derives from the author's consultations with Weyerhaeuser executives

in the United States and Indonesia, and from publications of the International Timber Corporation Indonesia, Jakarta.

6. Hadi, S. and Suparto, R.S. (editors), 1977, *Proceedings of Symposium on the Long-term Effects of Logging in South-East Asia,* Regional Center for Tropical Biology, Bogor, Indonesia.

7. Speech on *"Multinational issues; some observations and an example",* Weyer-haeuser Corporation, Tacoma, Washington.

8. United Nations Centre on Transnational Corporations, 1976, *Transnational Corporations: Issues Involved in the Formulation of a Code of Conduct,* United Nations Center on Transnational Corporations, New York.

9. Walter, I. (editor), 1976, *Studies in International Environmental Economics,* Wiley-Interscience, New York.

Chapter 14   The Role of International Aid Agencies

1. World Bank, 1978, *Forestry: Sector Policy Paper,* The World Bank, Washington, D.C.

2. Pearson, C. and Pryor, A., 1978, *Environment North and South: An Economic Interpretation,* Wiley-Interscience, New York.

3. International Institute for Environment and Development, 1978, *Banking on the Biosphere: Multilateral Aid and the Environment,* International Institute for Environment and Development, London.

Chapter 15   Zoos, Parks and other Protection Measures: How Many Make Enough?

1. Martin, R.D., 1975, *Breeding Endangered Species in Captivity,* Academic Press, New York; Olney, P.J.S., 1977, Breeding endangered species in captivity, *International Zoo Yearbook* Vol. 17, Zoological Society of London, London; Wemmer, C., 1977, Can wildlife be saved in zoos?, *New Scientist* **75** (1068): 585-587.

2. Frankel, O.H. and Hawkes, J.G. (editors), 1974, *Plant Genetic Resources for Today and Tomorrow,* Cambridge University Press, London; Thompson, P.A., 1976, Factors involved in the selection of plant resources for conservation as seed in gene banks, *Biological Conservation* **10**: 159-167.

3. Udvardy, M.D., 1975, A classification of the biogeographic provinces of the world, *IUCN Occasional Paper* No. 18, International Union for Conservation of Nature and Natural Resources, Morges, Switzerland.

4. The field of island biogeography is now characterized by an extensive literature: Diamond, J.M., 1975, The island dilemma: lessons of modern biogeographic studies for the design of natural preserves, *Biological Conservation* **7**: 129-146; McArthur, R.H. and Wilson, E.O., 1967, *The Theory of Island Biogeography,* Princeton University Press, Princeton, New Jersey; Simberloff, D.S. and Abele, L.G., 1976, Island biogeography theory and conservation practice, *Science* **191**: 285-286; Sullivan, A.L. and Shaffer, M.L., 1975, Biogeography of the megazoo, *Science* **189**: 13-17; Terborgh, J.W., 1974, Faunal equilibria and the design of wildlife preserves, in: F. Golley and E. Medina (editors), *Trends in Tropical Ecology,* Academic Press, New York.

5. Diamond, J.M., 1975, The island dilemma: lessons of modern biogeographic studies for the design of natural preserves, *Biological Conservation* **7**: 129-146.

6. Lack, D., 1976, Island biology, *Studies in Ecology* Vol. 3, Blackwell Scientific Publications, Oxford, England.

7. These calculations represent a preponderance of current opinion. But for some illuminating dissent, see Simberloff, D.S. and Abele, L.G., 1976, Island biogeography theory and conservation practice, *Science* **191**: 285-286.

8. Terborgh, J.W., 1974, Preservation of natural diversity: the problem of extinction-prone species, *BioScience* **24**: 715-722.

9. Whitmore, T.C., 1975, *Tropical rain forests of the Far East,* Clarendon Press, Oxford.

10. Medway, Lord and Wells, D.R., 1971, Diversity and density of birds and mammals at Kuala Lumpar, Pahang, *Malayan Nature Journal* **24**: 238-247.

11. Prance, G.T., 1977, The phytogeographic subdivisions of Amazonia and their influence on the selection of biological reserves, in: G.T. Prance and T.S. Elias (editors), *Extinction is Forever:* 195-213, New York Botanical Garden, Bronx, New York.

12. Wetterberg, G.B. *et al.,* 1976, An analysis of nature conservation priorities in the Amazon, *Technical Series* No. 8, Brazilian Institute for Forestry Development, Brasilia, Brazil.

Chapter 16   Economic Factors: Problems and Opportunities

1. For further discussion on the principle of community action to meet collective needs, see Haefele, E.T. (editor), 1974, *The Governance of Common Property Resources,* Johns Hopkins Press, Baltimore, Maryland.

2. Clark, C.W., 1977, *Mathematical Bioeconomics: The Optimal Management of Renewable Resources,* John Wiley & Sons, New York; Krutilla, J.V. and Fisher, A.C., 1975, *The Economics of Natural Environments,* Johns Hopkins University Press, Baltimore, Maryland; Myers, N., 1977, Discounting and depletion: the case of tropical moist forests, *Futures* **9** (6): 502-509; Pearce, D., 1976, The limits of cost-benefit analysis as a guide to environmental policy, *Kyklos* **29**: 97-112; Price, C., 1973, To the future: with indifference or concern? The social discount rate and its implications in landuse, *Journal of Agricultural Economics* **24**: 393-397.

3. Lessey, J., 1976, Taxes for conservation, *New Scientist,* 7th October, 30; Myers, N., 1977, Discounting and depletion: the case of tropical moist forests, *Futures* **9** (6): 502-509.

4. Baumol, W.J. and Oates, W.E., 1975, *The Theory of Environmental Policy,* Prentice Hall, Englewood Cliffs, New Jersey; Freeman, A.N., Haveman, R.H. and Kneese, A.V., 1973, *The Economics of Environmental Policy,* John Wiley, New York.

5. Bishop, R.C., 1978, Endangered species and uncertainty: economics of a safe minimum standard, *American Journal of Agricultural Economics* **61**: 10-18.

Chapter 17   Some Legal and Political Options

1. Falk, R.A., 1971, *This Endangered Planet,* Random House, New York; Sax, J.L., 1971, *Defending the Environment,* Knopf, New York.

2. Kiss, A.C., 1976, Survey of current development in international environmental law, *IUCN Environmental Policy and Law Paper* No. 10, International Union for Conservation of Nature and Natural Resources, Morges, Switzerland.

3. Levin, A.L., 1977, *Protecting the Human Environment: Procedures and Principles for Preventing and Resolving International Controversies,* United Nations Institute for Training and Research, New York.

Chapter 18   What Developing Countries can do for the Global Heritage
1. Gregersen, H.M. and Brooks, K., 1978, *Economic Analysis of Watershed Projects,* FAO, Rome.
2. Myers, N., 1978, Forests for people, *New Scientist* **80** (1134): 951-953.
3. Pollisco, F.S., 1975, Forest resources: a vital cog in Philippine economic development, *Canopy* **1** (7): 6.
4. Curzon, V.I. and Sokolov, A.A., 1978, The impending water famine, *Courier* (UNESCO Monthly) February 1978: 5-9.

Chapter 19   What Developed Countries can do for the Global Heritage
1. Myers, N., 1978, Whose hand on the axe?, *Mazingira* (quarterly publication of the United Nations Environment Program), 6: 66-73.
2. For a review of the need for compensatory measures at international level, see Boulding, K.E., 1974, *The Economics of Love and Fear: A Preface to Grants Economics,* Wadsworth Publisher, Belmont, California; Laszlo, E., 1977, *Goals for Mankind,* E.P. Dutton, New York; Oldfield, M.L., 1979, *The Value of the Conservation of Genetic Resources,* Department of Agriculture, University of Texas, Austin, Texas; Pearson, C. and Pryor, A., 1978, *Environment North and South: An Economic Interpretation,* Wiley-Interscience, New York; Peccei, A., 1977, *The Human Quality:* Pergamon Press, Oxford.
3. McLeod, S., 1974, Financing environmental measures in developing countries: the principle of additionality, *IUCN Environmental Policy and Law Paper* No. 6, International Union for Conservation of Nature and Natural Resources, Morges, Switzerland; Schneider-Sawaris, S., 1973, The concept of compensation in the field of trade and environment, *IUCN Environmental Policy and Law* Paper No. 4, International Union for Conservation of Nature and Natural Resources, Morges, Switzerland.
4. Steinberg, E.B. and Yager, J.A., 1978, *New Means of Financing International Needs,* Brookings Institution, Washington, D.C.
5. Steinberg, E.B. and Yager. J.A.. 1978, *New Means of Financing International Needs,* Brookings Institution, Washington, D.C.
6. Tinbergen, J., 1976, *Reshaping the International Order,* E.P. Dutton, New York.
7. Comptroller General of the United States, 1977, *Food Waste: An Opportunity to Improve Resource Use,* United States General Accounting Office, Washington, D.C.
8. Jolly, R. (editor), 1978, *Disarmament and World Development,* Pergamon Press, Oxford, England; Sivard, R.L., 1978, *World Military and Social Expenditures 1978,* World Military and Social Expenditure Publications, Leesburg, Virginia.
9. Brown, L.R., 1978, *The Twenty-ninth Day,* W.W. Norton, New York.

Chapter 20   Conservation of Species and the New World Order
1. Erb, G.F. and Kallab, G. (editors), 1975, *Beyond Dependency,* Overseas Development Council, Washington, D.C.
2. World Bank, 1978, *World Development Report 1978,* The World Bank, Washington, D.C.

Index

303